Michaela Koch
Discursive Intersexions

Practices of Subjectivation | Volume 9

Editorial

Post-structuralism and practice theories have shaken the Cartesian universal notion of the self-reflecting subject to its core. No longer is the subject viewed as the autonomous point of origin for initiative, but rather is analysed in the context of its respective social identity constructed by discourse and produced by social practices. This perspective has proven itself to be of exceptional utility for cultural and social analysis. The analytical value of the ensuing concept of subjectivation is the potential of supplementing related terms such as individualisation, disciplinary power, or habitualization by bringing new aspects of self-making to the fore. In this context, the analyses of the DFG Research Training Group "Self-Making. Practices of Subjectivation in Historical and Interdisciplinary Perspective" aim to contribute to the development of a revised understanding of the subject. They still take the fundamental dimensions of subjectivity such as agency and reflexivity into account, but do not overlook or lose sight of the historicity and sociality of the subject. Thus, the ultimate aim is to reach a deeper understanding of the interplay of *doing subject* and *doing culture* in various spaces of (and in) time.

Editors of this series are

Professor Thomas Alkemeyer, Institute of Sport Science at Carl von Ossietzky University Oldenburg, field of expertise: Sociology and Sport Sociology

Professor Thomas Etzemüller, Institute of History at Carl von Ossietzky University Oldenburg, field of expertise: Modern and Recent History

Professor Dagmar Freist, Institute of History at Carl von Ossietzky University Oldenburg, field of expertise: Early Modern History

Professor Gunilla Budde, Institute of History at Carl von Ossietzky University Oldenburg, field of expertise: German and European History of the 19th and 20th Century

Professor Rudolf Holbach, Institute of History at Carl von Ossietzky University Oldenburg, field of expertise: Medieval History

Professor Johann Kreuzer, Institute of Philosophy at Carl von Ossietzky University Oldenburg, field of expertise: History of Philosophy

Professor Sabine Kyora, Institute of German Studies at Carl von Ossietzky University Oldenburg, field of expertise: Modern German Literature

Professor Gesa Lindemann, Institute of Social Sciences at Carl von Ossietzky University Oldenburg, field of expertise: Sociology

Professor Ulrike Link-Wieczorek, Institute of Protestant Theology at Carl von Ossietzky University Oldenburg, field of expertise: Systematic Theology and Religious Education

Professor Norbert Ricken, Institute of Educational Science at Ruhr-University Bochum, field of expertise: Theories of Education and Educational Science

Professor Reinhard Schulz, Institute of Philosophy at Carl von Ossietzky University Oldenburg, field of expertise: Philosophy

Professor Silke Wenk, Cultural Studies Institute at Carl von Ossietzky University Oldenburg, field of expertise: Aesthetics and Art History

Michaela Koch (PhD) teaches Anglophone Literary and Cultural Studies at the University of Oldenburg. Her research interests include queer studies, animal studies, and literary discourse analysis.

Michaela Koch
Discursive Intersexions
Daring Bodies between Myth, Medicine, and Memoir

[transcript]

Originally submitted as a dissertation at the University of Oldenburg, 2016.

Printed with the generous support of the German Research Foundation (DFG).

Bibliographic information published by the Deutsche Nationalbibliothek
The Deutsche Nationalbibliothek lists this publication in the Deutsche Nationalbibliografie; detailed bibliographic data are available in the Internet at http://dnb.d-nb.de

© 2017 transcript Verlag, Bielefeld

All rights reserved. No part of this book may be reprinted or reproduced or utilized in any form or by any electronic, mechanical, or other means, now known or hereafter invented, including photocopying and recording, or in any information storage or retrieval system, without permission in writing from the publisher.

Cover concept: Kordula Röckenhaus, Bielefeld
Cover illustration: Ronja Korfe
Printed by Majuskel Medienproduktion GmbH, Wetzlar
Print-ISBN 978-3-8376-3705-2
PDF-ISBN 978-3-8394-3705-6

Table of Contents

Acknowledgments | 9

Introduction: Facing the Octopus | 11

PART I: HERMAPHRODITE NARRATIVES

At a Glance I: Hermaphrodite History | 27
Myth, Monster, and Marvel | 29
Sciences of the Sexes | 38

Truth or Dare: The Memoirs of Herculine Barbin | 45
'At the Bottom of Sex, There Is Truth': Locating the Text | 45
'That Vast Desire for the Unknown': Questioning the Text | 49
'What Strange Blindness Made Me Hold on Until the End?' Closing the Text | 73

N.O. Body and the Making of a True Man | 75
What Makes a Man? | 75
Narration and Focalization | 85
Sexology | 102
Manning the Binary | 109

PART II: INTERSEX NARRATIVES

At a Glance II: Intersex History | 113
Naming the Parts: *Hermaphroditism* and *Intersex* (1900-1940s) | 114
Baltimore Protocols (1940s-1980s) | 118
Early Intersex Activism and Politics (1980s-2005) | 125
Naming Other Parts: *Intersex* and *DSD* (2005 and counting) | 136

Facts and Figures of Speech in Science and Activism | 141
Look Who's Talking: David Reimer's Story | 141
The Doctor Knows Best: The Case of John Money | 148
More Than the Truth: ISNA's Testimonies | 158
Nothing but the Truth | 177

Hermaphroditus ♥ *Middlesex*
Novel Interpretations of Old Myth | 179
Lo(o)sing Plenty: Intersex in Fiction and Myth | 179
Pooling with Hermaphroditus: *Middlesex* and the *Metamorphoses* | 195
The Metamorphosis of *Middlesex* | 214

Intersex in Pieces
Thea Hillman Refuses to Know Better | 217
Intersex at the End of Grand Narratives | 217
To Be or Not to Be Intersex: The Matter of Representation | 220
Does Doctor Know Best? Paternalism Revisited | 224
Words Don't Come Easy: Intersex by Negotiation | 227
Performing Intersex Bodies: Essentialism Revisited | 232
A Shamed Subject: How Intersex Bodies Come to Matter | 240

Conclusion: Teaching the Octopus | 243

Appendix:
Bodies beyond the Binary in Books and Movies:
An Anglophone Chronology | 255

Bibliography | 261

Acknowledgments

I would like to express my sincere gratitude to my advisor Prof. Dr. Anton Kirchhofer, who supported this project from its earliest stages to the final manuscript and who offered perspective and orientation whenever I was lost. Besides my advisor, I would like to thank my thesis readers: Prof. Dr. Eveline Kilian and Prof. Dr. Barbara Paul for their insightful comments, probing questions, and last minute availability. My sincere thanks also goes to Prof. Dr. Silke Wenk who generously shared her expertise and time, and who was never satisfied with reduced complexity.

This thesis benefitted tremendously from the inspiring discussions with fellow Ph.D. students, post-doctoral researchers, and professors from the DFG research training group "Self-Making: Practices of Subjectivation in Historical and Interdisciplinary Perspective." Moreover, I would like to thank the professors – especially Prof. Dr. Martin Butler – and Ph.D. students from the weekly colloquium in literary studies that helped me to arrange my thoughts and to turn ideas into a coherent research project.

My highly esteemed colleagues Dr. Christian Lassen and PD Dr. Michaela Keck deserve not only a capitalized THANK YOU for reading and commenting on various drafts of this study, but also for their unceasing encouragement, chocolate cookies in times of need, and for setting examples in excellent and cooperative research.

I am also extremely grateful to Dr. Rachel Ramsay who proofread the final version of this manuscript with patience and precision, and still let me believe that I was good with English pronouns. Moreover, I am very thankful to the proofreaders of earlier drafts: Dr. Anna Auguscik and Daniel Síp, Alice Detjen, Sören Koopmann, Dr. Sabine Pfaudler, Dr. Irina Schmitt and Dr. J. Seipel.

A loving thank you also goes to my mother and my sister, who believed in my abilities and accepted my decision to spend years poring over books rather than finding a job in the "real" world.

Finally, an extra bold **thank you** is reserved for Dr. Smilla Ebeling, my partner in life, who nurtured this project through listening during spring walks alongside various rivers, who helped to shape it on warm summer nights that we spent sketching ideas on restaurant napkins, who challenged my too bold presumptions during windy escapes to the sea, and with whom I share all the books that I love over hot cups of tea in winter.

Introduction: Facing the Octopus

SUBJECT MATTERS

In a 2009 special issue of the Journal of Lesbian and Gay Studies (GLQ) on intersex, guest editor, intersex scholar and activist Iain Morland describes the current medical model of intersex as "octopus-like" ("Lessons" 195). The metaphor of the agile and limber octopus with tentacles in every direction stands for a model of intersex developed and solidified in different strands of Western medicine, psychology, biology and others since the second half of the twentieth century. Within this model, intersex is understood as a deviation from a binary sexual norm and normalizing interventions such as hormone treatment and genital surgery, preferably at a young age, is promoted. These interventions have been targeted by activists since the early 1990s as extremely painful, poor in their long term outcomes, and highly damaging for the intersex person's sense of physical integrity and psychological well-being. In 2014, a group of international organizations such as UNICEF, the World Health Organization (WHO), UN Women, the Office of the High Commissioner for Human Rights (OHCHR) and four others issued a joint statement that demands the stopping of this practice and the postponing of "irreversible invasive medical interventions […] until a child is sufficiently mature to make an informed decision, so that they can participate in decision-making and give full, free and informed consent" (WHO et al. "Eliminating" 7).

This statement follows a line of similar declarations by the Special Rapporteur on torture for the UN Human Rights Council from 2013[1] and the German Ethic Council in 2012.[2] Already in 2008, a German intersex person won a lawsuit against the surgeon who castrated her without obtaining her informed consent and she was awarded 100,000 € in damages.[3] Another lawsuit against non-consensual surgery on a child is currently being held in the US in both state and federal courts.[4] These and other events during the last couple of years document some changes and developments in political and legal discourses. Yet the effectiveness of some of the legal developments is disputed.[5] Moreover, the guidelines for

---

1 UN-Special Rapporteur Juan Méndez recommends to "repeal any law allowing intrusive and irreversible treatments, including forced genital-normalizing surgery, involuntary sterilization, unethical experimentation, medical display, […], when enforced or administered without the free and informed consent of the person concerned. He also calls upon them to outlaw forced or coerced sterilization in all circumstances and provide special protection to individuals belonging to marginalized groups" ("Report" 23).

2 The Ethic Council finds: "Irreversible medizinische Maßnahmen zur Geschlechtszuordnung bei DSD-Betroffenen [sic], deren Geschlechtszugehörigkeit nicht eindeutig [sic] ist, stellen einen Eingriff in das Recht auf körperliche Unversehrtheit, Wahrung der geschlechtlichen und sexuellen Identität und das Recht auf eine offene Zukunft und oft auch in das Recht auf Fortpflanzungsfreiheit dar. Die Entscheidung über solche Eingriffe ist höchstpersönlich und sollte daher grundsätzlich von den entscheidungsfähigen Betroffenen selbst getroffen werden" (Dt. Ethikrat "Stellungnahme" 174).

3 The trial is documented in Christiane Völling's autobiography *Ich war Mann und Frau* (2010).

4 For updates on the lawsuit "M.C. v. Aaronson" see the website of *Advocates for Informed Choice* (www.aiclegal.org).

5 Following the recommendations of the German Ethic Council, the government revised the regulations of the civil status in 2013. The revised regulation was misleadingly called the "third gender option" in media discourses (cf. Paramaguru *Time Magazine*, Nandi *The Guardian*), but criticized by intersex activists due to its lack of choice. See reactions by intersex advocacy organizations such as *Internationale Vereinigung Intergeschlechtlicher Menschen (IVIM)*, *TransInterQueer (TrIQ)* and *Zwischengeschlecht*.

the medical treatment of intersex people seem not to have changed much to date.[6]

With Morland's octopus metaphor, the resilience or hardiness of the 1950s intersex model may be attributed to the model's multidisciplinary character. Its various tentacles make the octopus seemingly invincible. Yet Morland points out that this strength may also be the model's weakness and asks for similarly multidisciplinary criticism to challenge each tentacle of the octopus. The *GLQ* issue, titled *Intersex and After*, brings together contributions from various fields of research: Alice Dreger (historian of science) and April Herndon (gender studies scholar) – both are former directors of the Intersex Society of North America (ISNA), an influential advocacy organization – report on the history of intersex activism in the U.S. and its relation to academic feminism; philosopher Ellen K. Feder reflects on the latest shift in medical terminology from *intersex* to *DSD* and the consequences for intersex politics; Sarah Creighton (gynecologist) Julie Greenberg (legal scholar), Del LaGrace Volcano (visual artist), and Katrina Roen (social scientist) discuss political strategies to change the situation of intersex people; "The Herm Portfolio" by Volcano challenges visual boundaries of sex and gender and explores sexual norms; medical psychiatrist Vernon Rosario reviews current genetic studies of sex determination and explains that biological sex is more complex and diverse than suggested in popular science; and Morland explores the potential of queer theory for intersex. This collection of authors and texts is by far not the only edited volume or monograph on intersex published in the 21st century. What it has in common with other critical works like Dreger's *Intersex in the Age of Ethics* (1999), Sharon Preves' *Intersex and Identity* (2003), Erik Parens' *Surgically Shaping Children* (2006), Sharon Sytsma's *Ethics and Intersex* (2006), Catherine Harper's *Intersex* (2007), or Katrina Karkazis' *Fixing Sex* (2008) is that critical analyses of literary and cultural

---

6   In Germany, the medical guidelines have been revised in 2016 by the German Network of Scientific Medical Societies, AWMF. See "Varianten der Geschlechtsentwicklung (174-001)" (www.awmf.org). Despite suggestions against invasive diagnostic methods and surgical intervention on children, an empirical study by Ulrike Klöppel revealed that the numbers of surgical interventions on children have not decreased ("Zur Aktualität kosmetischer Operationen").

representations of intersex are missing. The present study takes this absence as a starting point and aims at participating in the multidisciplinary analysis of intersex from the perspective of literary and cultural studies.[7] Autobiographical and fictional narratives on hermaphroditism and intersex, I contend, not only transport, but also produce knowledge and meaning on these issues. A study of these narratives may then tie in with and contribute to the multidisciplinary critical work on the conservative model and participate in the analysis of the workings of the octopus.

I pursue the following study from a position quite removed from most of the texts and materials I work with. "Removed" in time and place – I am located at a German university, this study serves as my doctoral dissertation, and I conducted my research between 2009 and 2015 – and "removed" from the texts in experience, because I speak as a non-intersex scholar with an academic background in Anglophone literary and cultural studies. However, "being removed" does not mean that I look at the texts from a detached, abstract, or outside position. Rather, I am entangled with these texts in different ways: As an intersex ally who values the voices of intersex people for political reasons; as a genderqueer person whose experiences in a heteronormative society shape my awareness of the violence of sex and gender norms, and not least as an avid reader of texts that critically negotiate the gender binary. Speaking with Donna Haraway my position is therefore necessarily partial and situated.[8] Therefore, I understand this study as one more contribution to the critical alliance against the octopus model and as a contribution to an ongoing debate and struggle.

Most of the texts analyzed in this study were produced by people who consider themselves or were considered by others intersex or hermaphrodite authors. By (re-)introducing these texts to academic discourse, I aim to emphasize their position as meaningful for the understanding of hermaphroditism/intersex at a given time and place – a position that has been denied all too often in the past. At the same time, however, I am aware that I am making these texts the object of my analysis and am caught up in

---

7   Viola Amato's recently published *Intersex Narratives* starts with a similar observation (cf. Amato 14). I refer readers interested in another reading of contemporary cultural texts on intersex to this publication.

8   See Haraway "Situated Knowledges."

a patriarchal trap: the non-intersex scholar analyzes and produces unsolicited meaning about hermaphroditism and intersex. Thus, I am continuously working on the dilemma of participation and representation at the juncture of academia and activism in my papers, at conferences, and in the German network *Inter_Trans_Wissenschaft* and I hope that the present study will encourage debate and pluralize notions rather than reproduce a normative understanding of intersex or hermaphroditism.[9]

COMING TO TERMS

The short term *intersex* has become the most common signifier to describe a body that is perceived as challenging the norms of what is considered standard male and standard female anatomy. The term shares a history with its longer form *intersexuality*. Both were first used by German biologist Richard Goldschmidt in 1916 and were then adopted in medical discourse to replace the much older term *hermaphroditism*.[10] While the second part of the compound inter*sexuality* places the concept in the vicinity of the terms hetero*sexuality* and homo*sexuality*, two terms rooted in 19th century medical and psychological discourse that have come to signify a specific form of sexual desire (cf. Katz *Invention*), the shorter form *intersex* emphasizes anatomy, *sex*, rather than desire, *sexuality*, and seems the most commonly used term at the moment. Variations like *inter** and – in German-speaking contexts – *intergeschlechtlich* are also currently in use among activists.[11] These variations further remove the distance to the biomedical term *intersexuality*, express an awareness of the diversity of intersex experiences and identities, and show the ongoing productivity of

---

9   See Hoenes/Koch (eds.): Trans*fer und* Inter*aktion*; esp. "Introduction" and my article "Niemand will's gewesen sein."
10 On Goldschmidt's understanding of the terms intersex and intersexuality see Voß *Making Sex Revisited* (212ff).
11 See, for example, the brochure "Inter* & Sprache" 2016 by TransInterQueerProjekt and the websites of the *Organisation Intersex International OII*, its German branch *Internationale Vereinigung Intergeschlechtlicher Menschen* (IVIM), and the Austrian human rights group *Zwischengeschlecht*.

the Latin root of the term. Although *intersex* and its variations seem to have been the preferred terms since the second half of the 20th century, the term *hermaphroditism* and attached qualifications like *pseudo* or *true* or variations such as *hermaphrodism* have anything but disappeared. Early usage of the term dates back to Greek mythology and stories about the son of Hermes and Aphrodite and the term has been widespread throughout and since the Middle Ages.[12] With the rise of *intersex* throughout the 20th century, the older term was used less frequently, but never disappeared as the report from a 2005 conference in Chicago demonstrates: Medical professionals from all over the world and two representatives of intersex organizations saw the need to adopt a new official term, *Disorders of Sex Development* (DSD), because terms "such as 'intersex,' 'pseudohermaphroditism,' 'hermaphroditism' [...] are particularly controversial. These terms are perceived as potentially pejorative by patients and can be confusing to practitioners and parents alike" (Lee et al. "Consensus" 488). Since its introduction, the term *DSD* has been criticized for its pathologizing character and has been rejected by numerous advocacy organizations and political institutions.[13] It remains in use in clinical contexts, but rarely occurs outside of these.

The present study is not limited to contemporary representations of intersex, but favors a diachronic approach including material dating back to the 19th and early 20th century. I use the coinage of the term *intersex* in 1916 as a historical marker to distinguish between the two parts of the study. The first part is called "Hermaphrodite Narratives" and addresses material prior to the coinage of the term intersex. The second part, "Intersex Narratives," centers on material from the mid-20th to the early 21st century. The terminology I apply is specific to each chapter and historical period. Moreover, I try to use pronouns that reflect and respect the characters' gender identification, sometimes resulting in a switch of gendered pronouns from feminine to masculine or vice versa or in alternative pronouns such as *hir* (read: /hɪər/) and *ze* (read: /ziː/).

---

12 In German contexts the term *Zwitter* was also common. See chapter "At a Glance I: Hermaphrodite History" for further details.

13 See chapter "At a Glance II: Intersex History" for an overview of the debate and further references on the topic.

DOING THE TRICK BY THE BOOK

The intersex and hermaphrodite narratives examined in this study are diverse and do not form a coherent or enclosed corpus. One of the stories under scrutiny is labeled fiction; another is called a medical case study; one is referred to as myth; and the majority of texts may be categorized as life narratives, e.g. as autobiography, memoir, or testimony.[14] In line with French philosopher Michel Foucault, I understand each of these publications as a *discursive event* and an *ensemble of discursive events* as *discourse* (cf. "Discourse on Language" 233). Discourse, Foucault supposes, is "at once controlled, selected, organised and redistributed according to a certain number of procedures" (216) and an analysis of the literary discourse on intersex and hermaphroditism requires studying "its conditions, its activity and its effects" (229). Foucault's understanding of discourse as a series of structured (and not 'arbitrary' or 'free') practices allows for a systematic study of discursive events and he describes four methodological principles that may govern an analysis in this mode: firstly, the critical principle of *reversal* contains a focus away from what is taken for granted in a given discourse and towards the reversal of that notion, e.g. the *author* should no longer be understood as original or creative, but as a function that cuts out and rarefies a possibly endless discursive flow (cf. 229).[15] With respect to the present study, I suggest reversing the notion of *intersex* and *hermaphroditism* as 'naturally given' or as 'essential

---

14 Following Smith and Watson, I use the term *life narrative* as an inclusive umbrella term that designates "not a single unitary genre or form, 'autobiography.' Rather, historically situated practices of self-presentation may take many guises as narrators selectively engage their lived experiences and situate their social identities through personal narratives" (Smith and Watson *Reading* 18).

15 On the author function see Foucault "What is an Author?" Anton Kirchhofer summarizes further examples of Foucault's principle of reversal: "the re-evaluation of the 'soft' and humane psychiatry [...] as the substitution of mental for physical confinement, [...] the contention that 'man' is the effect and product of the humanities rather than their object, [...] the assertion that 'the soul is the prison of the body' [...], or that sexuality is not repressed but produced by power" ("Foucault Complex" 281).

characteristics'. With Foucault, both may be understood as effects – as very real and material effects, I want to emphasize – of specific, historically contingent discursive practices. A number of these practices are described in studies on the history of intersex and hermaphroditism that have been published since the early 1990s[16] and the notions of *hermaphroditism* and *intersex* that emerge from these different studies describe them as complex and contested. Time, place, politics and – quite literally – the tools available, shape, classify and sort diverse human bodies into seemingly neatly separated sexed categories.

As mentioned above, the present study is chronologically structured and roughly divided into a first part on *hermaphroditism* and a second part on *intersex*. Both parts are headed by chapters on the respective historical context that sketch the contemporary usage of each term. But just as little as this introduction do these chapters provide elaborate definitions of each term. Rather, they outline some of the major developments in the usage of the terms and point to contemporary centers of debate and negotiation. In addition to the principle of *reversal*, Foucault suggests three more principles for writing a genealogy of any given discourse, namely the principles of *specificity*, *discontinuity*, and *exteriority*. The principle of *specificity* holds that "a particular discourse cannot be resolved by a prior system of significations" and that one should "conceive discourse as a violence we do to things, […] as a practice we impose upon them" (229). In other words, terms and concepts do not have an inherent – or inherited – meaning but each discursive event, i.e. the occurrence of a term, is to be analyzed as a *specific* event. Moreover, according to the principle of *discontinuity*, discourse "must be treated as a discontinuous activity, its different manifestations sometimes coming together, but just as easily unaware of, or excluding each other" (229). Each occurrence of a term is then not only to be treated as a specific occurrence, but equally repeated occurrences of the same term cannot be assumed to be invested with the same meaning. With the principle of *exteriority*, Foucault advises that we do not look for "the hidden core of discourse" (its 'inner meaning'), but to focus on "the discourse itself, its appearance and its regularity, […] its

---

16 I rely on and introduce studies on the medical, biological, and legal construction of intersex and hermaphroditism in the chapters "Hermaphrodite History" and "Intersex History" respectively.

external conditions of existence" (229). One way of doing discourse analysis according to Foucault, as literary scholar Anton Kirchhofer summarizes, would then mean describing "the conditions by which the appearance of discontinuous and specific discursive events is made possible" ("Foucault Complex" 280).

In line with Foucault's suggestions, the first step of this study was to identify the various publications on intersex and hermaphroditism, to order them chronologically and geographically, and to sort them according to their external conditions of production. The appendix "Bodies beyond the Binary in Books and Movies" summarizes the results of this first step. Yet this study does not aim at writing a 'complete' genealogy of *hermaphroditism* or *intersex*, but focuses on five distinct 'moments' in the discursive histories of these phenomena. Each 'moment' corresponds to an analysis of a publication of one literary text or a group of texts that provoked responses in other parts of the discursive ensemble on *intersex* and *hermaphroditism* or that was published in response to aspects negotiated within the extra-literary discourse on *intersex* and *hermaphroditism*. The five distinct moments of analyses – representing the analytical chapters of the study – provide snapshots of the discursive field at a given time but refrain from constructing a continuous and unified history of a discourse (principle of *discontinuity*). Paying special attention to the use of terminology, a specific discursive context with a focus on gaps, overlaps, ruptures and dissonances is then re-constructed for each moment and the text's position within this discourse described (principle of *specificity*). Moreover, the respective conditions of production for each text and its echoes in public debate are traced including publishing, marketing, reviews, and prizes (principle of *exteriority*).

These principles of discourse analysis, I would like to point out, do not lead to a standardized method or a uniformed analytical practice. Rather, the principles facilitate a variety of analyses and approaches to texts and are especially productive in addressing interdisciplinary research questions. Therefore, discourse analysis ties in easily with Mieke Bal's call for a focus on *concepts* and their specific usages rather than *methods* in interdisciplinary research in the humanities. "But concepts," Bal warns, "are not fixed. They travel – between disciplines, between individual scholars, between historical periods and between geographically dispersed academic communities" ("Working with Concepts" 20). Bal's elaboration of the conception of concepts and its relation to method is useful for my study because she emphasizes that concepts need to be "kept under scrutiny through confrontation with, not application to, the cultural objects being examined" (19). As Bal suggests, literary and cultural analyses should not end with analyses of 'contexts' or 'concepts' but merely begin with such questions. The necessary and crucial next step (or the first and constantly recurring step?) in analysis should contain a "practice of close reading" (16). Close reading is necessary to grant "the object [its status of a participant] in the production of meaning that 'analysis' constitutes" (16) and to account for the relationship between the subject and object of analysis that she characterizes as "interaction" (20). This study takes up Bal's suggestion and combines a Foucauldian discourse-oriented analysis with close readings of primary texts. Chapter-specific research problems emerged from the observation of the interaction between primary text and discursive context and each analysis is complemented by the respective theoretical and methodological background for the analysis. The theoretical tool-kit of the study addresses various practices of subjectivation ranging from *confession* to *performativity*, and from *trauma* to *adaptation*, and to *shame*.

Each of the texts I analyze negotiates the position of a character or characters that either claim or reject an intersex or hermaphrodite subject position upon very different grounds. These reasons for rejection, appropriation or something in between are diverse and so are the specific notions of what intersex and hermaphroditism signify. Each notion of hermaphroditism and intersex is embedded within historically specific extra-literary discursive events such as publications and other events in medicine, psychology and many other disciplines and fields of interest such as human rights activism. These diverse discursive events intersect, fold into each other and together form a process of negotiation around the meanings of intersex or hermaphroditism. The literary text may act as a juncture where the different strands of the discursive ensemble are brought together, intertwined, and a process of negotiation is acted out. Rendering these processes of negotiation visible is one aspect of this study and I aim at contributing to an understanding of hermaphroditism and intersex as historically and locally specific, socially produced corporeal phenomena. However, a literary text is more than a mere representation of a discursive ensemble at a given time. Understood as a discursive event in itself, this event contributes to the discourse and engages with other discursive events. Moreover, the literary text as a discursive event is controlled, selected and organized by specific discursive procedures such as genre conventions, literary traditions, publication policies or distribution strategies by publishing houses. Far more than rendering an extra-literary discourse visible through representation, literary texts – governed by specific practices – provide their own unique contribution to the discursive ensemble. They may represent medical or psychological contributions to the discourse more or less truthfully and they may enforce or reject any of the claims. Moreover, some extra-literary contributions to the discourse may be ignored, others highlighted. The positions and authority of these contributions may be undermined, criticized and challenged, explored, illustrated or supported. The position as a literary text offers a wide (but not endless) range of possible statements on hermaphroditism and intersex.

This study, then, aims to reconstruct the specific position of the literary text within the discursive ensemble and to examine its potential for or significance within discourse. Literature, I suggest, serves its own needs and obligations, follows its own rules and a discourse analytical study of literary texts like the present one evaluates the literary texts against their reverberations within a larger discursive context. What positions are advertised in the various narratives that form the core of the present study? Do the narratives construct notions of intersex and hermaphroditism that agree or disagree with medical, biological, juridical, religious or political notions of the concepts? What alternative models do they offer? And how are the texts received by intersex people, by doctors, psychologists, and geneticists? What are their workings within and their significance for the intersex discourse? By focusing on these questions, a discourse analytical study of literary texts will not only produce knowledge about a specific notion of hermaphroditism or intersex within a text, but will also provide unique insights into the way discursive ensembles are entangled and how these ensembles interact. Moreover, literary texts will be shown to be heavily involved in the negotiations about the meaning of intersex or hermaphroditism, and their potential to challenge the octopus will be explored.

THE BODY OF THE BOOK

The first part of the study, "Hermaphrodite Narratives," consists of a sketch of the historiography on hermaphroditism from Antiquity to the 20th century ("At a Glance I: Hermaphrodite History") and close readings of two autobiographical texts. The memoirs of Herculine Barbin, who took hir own life in 1868, were published posthumously in the second half of the 19th century in a medical textbook. Roughly a century later, the text was rediscovered by Foucault and published in French, English and later German. While the memoirs had been declared merely an illustration of the medical case study in the 19th century, Foucault made the memoirs the main attraction of his 20th century edition. Yet he kept the medical reports and even added further original documents to the publication. The text and the documents show that 19th century doctors were intrigued by the issue of 'true' sex and aimed to straighten up Barbin's body (and to straighten out hir relationships to hir lovers) in various ways. Late 20th century criticism and intersex activism celebrated the text as the earliest 'true' hermaphrodite voice. My analysis shows how both readings, contemporary and current, are embedded in their historical perspectives, and emphasizes the text's potential to resist both 19th and 20th century attempts to usurp and fix Barbin's sex. "Truth or Dare: The Memoirs of Herculine Barbin" scrutinizes the text's strategy to evoke and ultimately reject the medical discourse about 'true' sex. Moreover, I suggest, the text radically challenges the discourse on 'truth' as such and unmasks the confession as a normative practice of identity production.

N.O. Body's *Aus eines Mannes Mädchenjahren* ('*Memoirs of a Man's Maiden Years*'), first published in Germany in 1907, tells the story of a young man who was mistaken for a girl at birth. Pioneering gay rights activist and sexologist Magnus Hirschfeld provided a medical report for N.O. Body's legal transition from female to male and wrote an epilogue for the memoir. In 1993, German historian Hermann Simon re-published the memoir and identified N.O. Body as the pseudonym of Jewish functionary Karl M. Baer. The text was translated into English in 2006 and the new edition was expanded with an introductory essay by literary scholar Sander L. Gilman. "N.O. Body and the Making of a True Man" does not attempt to answer the question of N.O. Body's 'true' sex, but wonders why the question has never been asked. After all, Body admitted that there had been doubts about his sex after birth and that he lived as a girl and woman for the first twenty years of his life. The answer to his unequivocal maleness, I argue, lies in the text's (not in Body's body's) paradoxical ambiguity between the simultaneous reproduction and transgression of the binary sexual order.

The second part of the study, "Intersex Narratives," is introduced by a historical sketch of the development of intersex discourses in the 20th century ("At a Glance II: Intersex History") and followed by three analyses. The first one, "Facts and Figures of Speech in Science and Activism," focuses on writings from the 1950s to the 1990s by medical doctors and intersex activists. Doctors and psychologists such as John Money claim expert knowledge about intersex and legitimate their claims by presenting their knowledge as evidence-based and supra-individual. The effect of 'scientific objectivity' is produced by writing in a scholarly or medico-scientific mode. Intersex activists around Cheryl Chase reject the legitimacy of 'scientific objectivity' and counter it with individual, subjective experiences as a source of knowledge about intersex. In the testimonial mode, activists write as experts of their own experience, challenging the medico-scientific claims to 'true' knowledge about intersex and presenting their own experiences as 'true.'

In contrast to medico-scientific and testimonial writings, fictional representations explicitly refrain from 'truth' claims. Rather, the historical sketch of fictional representations from 1960s feminist science fiction to 2010s bizarro fiction shows the representations to be governed by classic myth and metaphor. Intersex and hermaphrodite figures predominantly oscillate between the poles of deficit and loss, or excess and plenitude. Moreover, "Hermaphroditus ♥ *Middlesex*: Novel Interpretations of Old Myth" explores Jeffrey Eugenides' *Middlesex* (2002) and its investment in Ovid's *Metamorphoses*. The Pulitzer Prize awarded novel employs an unreliable narrator who renders the account of his_her own life a myth, but succeeds – accidentally – in establishing this life as the quintessential intersex narrative of the early 21st century.

In 2008, spoken word artist and intersex activist Thea Hillman published her memoir *Intersex (for Lack of a Better Word)*. The text contains 47 pieces, or chapters, that present the intersex self as torn *and* whole, as caught between colonizing discourses such as medical, activist, and fictional *and* as autonomous and complete. "Intersex in Pieces: Thea

Hillman Refuses to Know Better" argues that *Better Word* rejects the notion of a 'true' intersex identity, but embraces localized and temporary narratives. In place of certainties and answers, the collection provokes questions, embraces doubt, and invites plurality. Moreover, *Better Word* presents intersex as both rooted and manifested in the body *and* as an effect of performative practices. Ultimately, Hillman's intersex experience goes beyond either constructivist or essentialist approaches to identity and shows intersex individuals as whole human beings.

The conclusion "Teaching the Octopus" connects and reviews the findings of the analytical chapters and comes full circle when it returns to Morland's octopus metaphor and summarizes the studies' contribution to the analysis of the octopus. Finally, the appendix "Bodies beyond the Binary in Books & Movies: An Anglophone Chronology" completes the detailed analyses of specific publications as singular discursive events and positions these events within a larger discursive frame. Limited to English-language publications, the comprehensive bibliography lists fictional and autobiographical representations of intersex and hermaphroditism in print and on screen from the 1960s to 2013. It provides an overview of the possible material for future analyses and rounds off the findings of the present study.

PART I: Hermaphrodite Narratives

At a Glance I: Hermaphrodite History

The figure of the hermaphrodite subject that emerges from historiographic studies on hermaphroditism is neither clear-cut nor one-dimensional. Rather, the hermaphrodite evolves as a shifting and highly controversial subject position that was constructed and experienced as a liminal position within any given social order. Studies that focus on the history of the legal status of hermaphrodites, the medical treatment, the social management or religious implications of the hermaphrodite share one feature – despite their different approaches, foci and conclusions: they show the hermaphrodite as a subject position embedded in, bound by, and produced by normative discourses. Rather than taking the existence of the hermaphrodite subject *as such* for granted and assuming a natural, universal and fixed meaning of *hermaphroditism*, it seems more promising to assume a constructivist position and to analyze hermaphroditism as an effect of historically contingent discursive practices. Using a constructivist lens for the analysis does not mean that hermaphroditism is less corpo-*real* or less *natural* than an essentialist lens may suggest. Yet within a constructivist paradigm, variations in meaning may be more easily accommodated as the hermaphrodite subject is described as socially and historically positioned. In my opinion, a constructivist approach strengthens rather than weakens the corpo*reality* of hermaphroditism as it emphasizes the specificity of the experience and is open to different, even contradictory meanings and experiences.

Historical studies provide rich evidence for the various meanings the sciences, medical, political, religious, and legal discourses have ascribed to bodies (and behavior) that have challenged the dominant norms of male and female. Put simply, whether a body was called hermaphroditic or not, at times, seemed to depend less on the body that was studied and more on the person who studied the body. But why was the hermaphroditic body such a hotly debated issue at all? Why did the hermaphrodite become a subject of interest in so many discourses over such a long time? The reason, I suggest, is the hermaphrodite's significance for the order of the sexes, or, more accurately, its position as a possible threat to a binary sexual order. To study the hermaphrodite always means to study *man* as well. And with Foucault, studying *man* means investigating the power relations that the subject is placed in (cf. "Subject" 209). The question of the hermaphrodite, then, is intricately linked to the question, what makes *man*? And, what should genitals look like and what do they mean? In the light of the history of hermaphroditism these questions are neither trivial nor dubious. They rather point to contested areas of knowledge and power: religion (who is allowed to marry whom?), law (who is allowed to inherit? Who is allowed to bear witness before court?), politics (who is allowed to vote?), philosophy and ethics (what is the appropriate relationship between the sexes and who is allowed to have sex with whom?), and the different strands of medicine and biology (what makes a man? What makes a woman? And, what happens if the question cannot be easily answered?).

"At a Glance I: Hermaphrodite History" sketches the development of the various answers given to the overall question: what makes someone a hermaphrodite? The following analyses of the writings on and by Herculine Barbin and N.O. Body examine the constructions of the supposedly hermaphrodite subjects in their respective discursive contexts in detail and scrutinize the web of power relations the hermaphrodite is embedded in.

In this chapter, I rely on studies on the history of hermaphroditism and the sexual order and, therefore, study the historiography of hermaphroditism rather than 'real,' i.e. empirical, historical events. Maybe as a result of Thomas Laqueur's 1990 study, *Making Sex: Body and Gender from the Greeks to Freud*, interest in the history of the binary sexual order and the limits of the binary gained momentum in the 1990s. While Joan Cadden (1993) and Maximilian Schochow (2009a and 2009b) focus on sex differences in Europe in the Middle Ages, Lorraine Daston and Katharina Park (1995) scrutinize Early Modern France, Ruth Gilbert (2002) focuses on Early Modern England and Fabian Krämer (2005) looks at Early Modern Germany. In a huge undertaking Julia Epstein (1995) and Anne Fausto-Sterling (*Sexing* 2000) present a rather broad overview from

Antiquity until the present. However, the majority of studies have their focus on the 19th and early 20th century (Alice Dreger 1998, Ulrike Klöppel 2010, Geertje Mak 2005, Florian Mildenberger 2005, Heinz-Jürgen Voß 2010). While Elisabeth Reis (2009) and Alison Redick (2005) write the history of intersex and hermaphroditism in the US, the other studies almost exclusively analyze German, French and English discourses. Fausto-Sterling explains why the U.S. do not play a significant role in the history of hermaphroditism and also gives a reason for the interest in the history of ambiguous sexes: "In tracking the history of medical analyses of intersexuality, one learns more generally how the social history of gender itself has varied, first in Europe and later in America, which inherited European medical traditions" (*Sexing* 33).[1] Actually, the impact of the U.S. in the history of intersexuality should not be underestimated – but this history does not start before the 20th century. Hence, I will focus in this chapter on (mostly western) European discourses on hermaphroditism from Antiquity until the early 20th century.

MYTH, MONSTER, AND MARVEL

The term *hermaphrodite* is a compound of the two gods' names Hermes and Aphrodite. According to a Greek myth canonized by the retelling of Ovid (around 8 A.D.), the nymph Salmacis fell desperately in love with the beautiful son of the two gods. Overwhelmed by desire for Hermaphroditus, she asks the gods to unite the two. They grant her wish, but instead of a marriage they merge the bodies of the female Salmacis and the male Hermaphroditus into an androgynous[2] figure. The myth is presented by

---

1   Reis' study basically confirms Fausto-Sterling's argument: in her chapter on hermaphroditism in Early America, she explains that American developments largely reflect "a European intellectual tradition going back centuries" (*Bodies* 2).

2   Groneberg shows that *androgyny* was a common term to denote mythical figures as well as individuals with non-standard sex characteristics during Antiquity. In 77 A.D., Pliny writes that *androgyny* was an earlier term for *hermaphroditism*, and that both terms could be used interchangeably (cf. Groneberg 102). *Androgyny* at least refers back to Plato's *Symposium* (around

Ovid in the fourth book of his *Metamorphoses,* which was read and published widely in his own times, right through the Middle Ages and still serves as a popular source for Greek mythology. The androgynous mythical figure served as the eponym for individuals with non-standard sexual characteristics until the 20th century. While the hermaphrodite in Ovid is described as a double-being, both male and female, Galen (129 – 199/217 A.D.) perceived of the hermaphrodite as an intermediate sex between male and female and felt that the idea of the continuum of the sexes was supported by hermaphroditic bodies.[3] For Galen, hermaphroditic individuals did not question the natural order of the sexes at all, rather they proved it: within a continuum of sexes there is naturally room for individuals that show some form of intermediary state. Nevertheless, the hermaphrodite newborn was subject to severe legal restrictions in Greece and early Rome, e.g. Romulus passed a law to kill malformed individuals in 800 B.C. as they were understood as portents or monsters. This notion changed and in 100 A.D., Pliny states that androgynes had been understood as portentous, but were now considered to be entertaining (cf. Groneberg 109). The

---

385 B.C.) and Aristophanes' speech about the origin of love: Originally, earth was populated by three groups of spherical creatures with two heads, four limbs and a double set of sexual characteristics. Each creature was either of the male-male sex, female-female sex or the male-female, i.e. the androgynous sex. The spherical creatures angered the gods and Zeus decided to split them in half to teach them respect. Since that day, humans have been looking for their other half and that is the origin of love. The story was popularized in the 1998 musical *Hedwig and the Angry Inch* by John Cameron Mitchell. A movie of the same title was produced in 2001. The 2014 Broadway production of the musical won four Tony Awards.

3   See Laqueur on the continuum of the sexes and the one-sex model that, according to Laqueur, dominated medical thinking from Antiquity until the late 18th century when political and social developments furthered the need for two distinct sexes. Laqueur's argument is based, e.g. on Vesalius *De humani corporis fabrica* (1543), which marks the beginning of modern anatomy and clearly depicts the homology of the male and female sexual organs (cf. Laqueur 25-62). Voß summarizes the critique on Laqueur's assumed rigid shift from a one-sex to a two-sex model and argues instead for a co-existence of competing models.

development was finally mirrored in legislation in the 6th century A.D. when Roman emperor Justinian took up earlier suggestions and decreed that a newborn was to be assigned the predominant sex in the *Corpus Juris Civilis*. In her study on sex differences in the Middle Ages, historian Joan Cadden refines the anaysis of Thomas Laqueur and draws a more detailed picture of the order of the sexes and describes the various treatments of hermaphrodites.[4] Another study by Daston and Park ("Orders") argues that, in Early Modern France, the hermaphrodite was seen less as a threat or a monster than as a *wonder*. Daston and Park report on the taxonomy of hermaphrodites proposed by French surgeon Ambroise Paré in 1573 as one of the earliest classification systems. In his work *On Monsters and Marvels*, Paré identifies four types of hermaphrodites: the male hermaphrodite, who produces sperm and is capable of impregnating women; the female hermaphrodite, who experiences menses; hermaphrodites who are neither male nor female as they have no 'functional' sexual organs, i.e. organs that can be used in reproduction, and hermaphrodites who are both male and female at the same time, i.e. hermaphrodites who have two sets of 'functional' sexual organs (cf. Paré 26ff). Paré's taxonomy was among the first but by no means the last taxonomy of hermaphrodites: about a century later, French surgeon Nicolai Venette published *La Génération de l'Homme ou Tableau de l'Amour Conjugal* in 1687; publications in English (*Conjugal Love, or The Pleasure of the Marriage Bed*, n.d.) and German (*Von Erzeugung der Menschen*, 1698) followed shortly after and altogether more than 130 editions have been counted. The very popular tract contained a description of as many as five types of hermaphrodites (cf. Schochow "Bürger" 90f).

An anecdote from the American colonies shows that hermaphroditism or the question of ambiguous sex was a serious business not only for the medical profession but also for the jurisdiction of the time: A court in Virginia in 1629 declared Thomas/ine Hall to be both a man *and* a woman and ordered hir to wear men's *and* women's clothes publicly at all times to demonstrate hir double sex.[5] Hall had lived as a woman and as a man and declared hirself to be both male and female. Ze was physically examined by

---

4   See Rolker 2013 for a critique on Laqueur and Cadden.
5   See Katz (*Gay/Lesbian*) for a discussion of the case. Also: Reis *Bodies* 10-14. Reis lists further references on Thomas/ine Hall, footnote 26, p.167.

legal and medical practitioners and by groups of men and women who simply felt the need to know the 'truth' and forced examinations on Hall. The examinations led to opposing results and the court decision left the public disconcerted and unsatisfied. Probably, the main objective of the court was not to determine one (either 'true' or 'predominant') sex for Hall. The real problem was rather to eliminate the possibility of sexual transgression. Had Hall been ruled to be male, *he* would have been allowed to have intercourse with women. Had Hall been ruled to be female, *she* would have been allowed to have intercourse with men. But, what if the court's decision was wrong and, although ze had been ruled male, Hall was *in fact* female and had had intercourse with women? Obviously, the criteria for the assignment of a sex were unclear, but the possible consequences of such a ruling were already too delicate for the court and so they decided to follow Hall's self-description and declare hir male *and* female. Hall's 'case' shows how the question of sex is intricately and, for the time inextricably, linked to the question of sexuality.

In 1718, British legal writer Jacob Giles explains the regulations of the English Civil Law for hermaphrodites and thereby elucidates the criteria for the assignment of a sex:

But the Civil Law does not regard Hermaphrodites as Monsters, it permits them to make a Choice of either of the two Sexes for the Business of Copulation, either in the Capacity of Men or Women; but if the Hermaphrodite does not perform his Part agreeable to Nature, the same Law inflicts the Punishment due to Sodomy, because he has abus'd one Part, contrary to Natures Laws. This must be determin'd by the Predominancy of the Parts, for there are some Hermaphrodites so very vigorous as to embrace Women, and others whose Parts are so dispos'd as to receive with pleasure the Caresses of Men; and where there is nothing to hinder the amorous Action, but that they are capable of enjoying mutual Pleasure, it would be a piece of injustice to prohibit their Nuptials. (4f)

Giles' interpretation of the English law points to the major aspects of the regulation: The hermaphrodite was offered a choice between man and woman, but it was expected that this choice was in accordance with the sex that was understood to prevail in his or her body. If the hermaphrodite chose between one of the two sexes, he or she was given full citizen's rights. The law is also clear about the strictly required non-ambiguity of the hermaphrodite: sodomy (or tribadism, depending on the choice of the hermaphrodite) was to be avoided under all circumstances – and to be punished in case of transgression. Similar to the case of Thomas/ine Hall, protection of the institution of heterosexuality is at the center of the law.[6]

With respect to the 19th century, historian Alice Dreger introduces the "one-body-one-sex rule" (*Hermaphrodites* 30). However, in my view the strict regulations for the hermaphrodite to choose one and only one sex is already an early expression of this rule: While during Antiquity and the Middles Ages the hermaphrodite was sometimes believed to be double-sexed, i.e. to simply *have* or *be* two sexes, the Early Modern hermaphrodite was required to limit hirself to one of two sexes – although at the time it was still possible that the hermaphrodite *was* not this *one* sex. Rather, it was more or less agreed that the hermaphrodite carried aspects of both sexes to varying degrees. But, to protect the moral order, one of the two socially accepted subject positions had to be chosen.[7]

In 1735 the Swedish botanist and zoologist Carl Linné published the first volume of his *Systema naturæ* and thereby advanced the professional craze for the systematic ordering and categorization of the world. Although the first taxonomies of different types of hermaphrodites were circulated long before the 18th century, the categorization was still far from being completed. Rather, the systematization gained in pace and while Italian surgeon Fabrici Aquapendente promoted four types of hermaphrodites (cf. Schochow "Bürger" 97) in 1716, the debate was fueled by considerations that shifted from the *de*scription of hermaphroditic types to their *pre*scription: Aquapendente and, in a similar manner, German surgeon

---

6 I quote the English law here as a representative example for the legislation on hermaphrodites in Europe in the 17th and 18th century. Similar regulations that rest on Justinian law from the 6th century A.D. were codified in the *Römisches Recht* or the *Sachsenrecht* and reported in encyclopedias (cf. Klöppel *XXOXY* 203ff).

7 Epstein refers to British doctor James Parsons, who pondered on the one-body-one-sex rule in his 1741 treatise *A Mechanical and Critical Enquiry into the Nature of Hermaphrodites*: "If there was not so absolute a law with respect to the being of only one sex in one body we might then indeed expect to find every day many preposterous digressions from our present standard" (qtd. in Epstein *Altered* 115).

Peter Dionis discuss the surgical reduction of the ambiguously-sexed hermaphrodites to one clear sex in 1712. Both deem amputations of excess material, i.e. genital material that renders the body sexually 'ambiguous', possible, but unisono advise surgeons to refrain from such procedures as they were highly dangerous for the life of the patient and tremendously painful. Aquapendente and Dionis also agree that every hermaphrodite could be assigned a 'true' sex. Therefore, both their systems lack a category for 'true hermaphrodite,' i.e. a person who 'really' *was* two-sexed (cf. Schochow "Bürger" 97ff).

Despite the careful warnings of Aquapendente and Dionis, the first recorded genital surgery took place merely forty years later: In 1750, French surgeon Georges Arnaud de Ronsil performed a surgery on a hermaphroditic woman who had asked him to make her more female. The procedure was described and evaluated in detail in a Supplement to Arnaud's and Diderot's *Encyclopedia* and published in 1777.[8] Diderot who, according to Schochow, understood hermaphrodites as deviant forms of nature that needed to be corrected and normalized by surgeons, praised Arnaud's operation as a success and with his discussion of the case, surgery as a method to treat hermaphrodites was canonized and became part of the knowledge of the time (cf. "Bürger" 100ff). Schochow's study shows that surgical interventions on hermaphroditic bodies had become a regular practice by the end of the 18th century (cf. 102f): Beginning with amputations of so-called excess genital material in female hermaphrodites, the early 19th century also saw a rise in surgical intervention in male hermaphrodites (cf. 103).

Klöppel describes the treatment of hermaphrodites in the 18th century as a double process of naturalization and medicalization and also links this development to the rise of obstetrics as a medical discipline distinct from midwifery. The first professorship for obstetrics in Germany was established in Göttingen in 1751 and, according to Klöppel, members of the

---

8   Klöppel discusses the entry on hermaphroditism in the French Encyclopedia and compares it to entries in German contemporary encyclopedias and medical journals. Her analysis points to inconsistencies and contradictions between the different texts but also within single entries. At the time, doctors were still divided upon the question whether hermaphrodites were really one or two sexes (cf. Klöppel *XXOXY* 165-178).

young discipline worked hard for its institutionalization. On the one hand, this was done by abating or depreciating midwives. On the other hand, the problems and dangers encountered in birthing were presented as complex, meaningful and of high importance. The much debated question of the true sex of hermaphrodites was therefore welcomed by the profession to prove its value and necessity (cf. *XXOXY* 209f). Klöppel's argument supports Schochow's thesis that the medicalization of hermaphrodites had already started in the second half of the 18th century.

Dreger had postulated that medicalization started in the second half of the 19th century and referred to the time from 1870 to 1915 as the "age of gonads" (cf. *Hermaphrodites* 139-66). Her analysis of classification systems of hermaphroditism shows an increasing emphasis on gonadal tissue as decisive for the determination of the sex of an individual before that time: a taxonomy introduced in the 1830s by French teratologist Isidore Geoffroy Saint-Hilaire divided the human body into six "segments" and any combination of male and female "segments" in one body would invariably lead to one form of hermaphroditism (cf. Dreger 140-2). Also in the 1830s, British obstetrician Sir James Young Simpson separated "spurious hermaphroditism" from "true hermaphroditism," but counted any "actual mixture or blending together, upon the same individual, of more or fewer of both the male and female organs" as "true hermaphroditism" (qtd. in Dreger 143). Only in 1876, when German pathological anatomist Theodor Albrecht Edwin Klebs popularized his taxonomy of hermaphroditism, did the gonads become the one and only decisive factor in sex determination. Dreger argues that Klebs was the first one to divide hermaphroditism into "true hermaphroditism," i.e. the presence of both ovarian and testicular tissue in one body, and "pseudohermaphroditism," i.e. either ovarian or testicular tissue in one body that otherwise showed any mixture of sexual characteristics. Individuals labeled "true hermaphrodites" in Simpson's taxonomy were usually rendered male or female "pseudohermaphrodites" in Klebs' system as they did display a blend of anatomical features considered male and female, but did not have testicular *and* ovarian tissue. Under the aegis of the gonads, the idea of one 'true' sex for each individual gained momentum and doctors took it upon themselves to identify the 'true' sex of any person who would have been called hermaphroditic and, therefore, a blend of two sexes before that time. Previously "true hermaphrodites" were often reclassified as truly male or female "pseudohermaphrodites," while the mere existence of "true hermaphroditism" in humans was doubted by a number of experts (cf. 145-50). As a reason for the rise and dominance of the gonad, Dreger suggests the focus on reproductive abilities as the major difference between men and women by the end of the century (cf. 150-54). Klöppel and Schochow do not oppose Dreger's argument emphasizing the significance of the gonads, but they challenge the time period that Dreger suggests. According to Klöppel, gonads had already been identified as significant for sex determination at the beginning of the 19th century. She further argues that the emergence of endocrinology and genetics towards the last third of the 19th century brought about a decrease in the significance of the gonads and postulates that the age of gonads runs from approximately 1800 to 1850 (cf. Klöppel 258).[9]

While there was a heated debate over hermaphroditism in medical circles during the 19th century, the legal debate calmed down or ceased completely. Implemented in 1804, the French *Code Civil* does not mention hermaphrodites at all. Apparently, in France the question of ambiguous sex was not perceived to be a legal matter anymore. Diderot and his contemporaries trusted the techniques of the surgeons to 'repair' natural variations. Therefore, the legal subject *hermaphrodite* that was constituted around 800 B.C., which was the object of ever-changing legislative practices for centuries, ceased to exist with the turn to the modern legislative system. Only in Prussian law was the legal hermaphrodite allowed to exist for another century. Yet the increasing influence of the medical profession and its advancing institutionalization is reflected in the

---

[9] Findings by Voß (2010: 188-218) and Mak (2005) support Klöppel's critique on the periodization. Voß and Mak also stress that, despite a theoretical approach that centered on the primacy of gonadal tissue, doctors frequently did not act upon this theory or their findings, or, as Mak explains in one of her medical case studies, "while paying lip service to the dominant medical theory on 'true' gonadal sex, Goffe [a doctor, M.K.] proves much more concerned with hiding visible sexual ambiguity through medical surgery" (75). In fact, they argue, the gonads did not have the impact that Dreger suggests. Doctors often assigned a sex based on various characteristics, anatomical and social, and performed surgeries to match the external anatomy as much as possible to the assigned sex – in these cases gonads were only theoretically decisive.

Allgemeines Landrecht für die Preußischen Staaten (ALR, 'Prussian Civil Code') as well. Introduced in 1794, the ALR basically confirmed the hermaphrodite's right to choose one of the two sexes, but it refined the regulations and introduced a new actor into the management of hermaphroditism:

> §19 If children are born hermaphroditic, the parents decide which sex they shall be raised as. §20 However, at the age of eighteen such a person is free to choose to which sex he wants to belong. §21 This choice determines his future rights. §22 However, if the rights of a third party are dependent on the sex of a putative hermaphrodite, that party may petition to have this person examined by experts. §23 The findings of the experts supersede the choice of the hermaphrodite and his parents.[10]

An examination through an expert was not mandatory, but could be requested if a third person's rights depended on the sex of the individual, e.g. in the case of marriage (cf. Klöppel 203ff; 587f; Wacke "Rechtsgeschichte"). Whereas the ALR does not specify the nature of the "expert," Schochow's analysis of contemporary legal interpretations shows that the opinion of the expert in question was indeed the opinion of a "Physici" or a "Medici" (93). The priest, he points out, had the power to marry a hermaphrodite, but only after the judge had approved the choice of sex of the person. The judge should base his ruling on the learned opinion of a doctor or medical practitioner. Although the hermaphrodite was still an object of legal discourse by the end of the 18th century, the influence of so-called medical experts had increased significantly over the century.

---

10 Allgemeines Landrecht für die Preußischen Staaten von 1794: Erster Theil. Von Personen und deren Rechten überhaupt. [Rechte] der Zwitter. §19. Wenn Zwitter geboren werden, so bestimmen die Aeltern, zu welchem Geschlechte sie erzogen werden sollen. §20. Jedoch steht einem solchen Menschen, nach zurückgelegtem achtzehnten Jahre, die Wahl frey, zu welchem Geschlecht er sich halten wolle. § 21. Nach dieser Wahl werden seine Rechte künftig beurtheilt. § 22. Sind aber Rechte eines Dritten von dem Geschlecht eines vermeintlichen Zwitters abhängig, so kann ersterer auf Untersuchung durch Sachverständige antragen. § 23. Der Befund der Sachverständigen entscheidet, auch gegen die Wahl des Zwitters, und seiner Aeltern. (ALR 55)

Nevertheless, until 1900, when the *Bürgerliches Gesetzbuch* (BGB 'German Civil Code') replaced the ALR, the hermaphrodite had been admitted an, albeit limited, but nonetheless codified right to exist as hermaphrodite – including the right and the obligation to choose exactly one of two strictly delineated sexes.

SCIENCES OF THE SEXES

A sign for the decline of the term *hermaphrodite* as a distinct legal category was its usage by gay rights pioneer Karl Heinrich Ulrichs[11] (1825 Aurich – 1895 L'Aquila). Ulrichs revived the category *hermaphrodite* in his writings on men who desire men and thereby changed the context of the term. Between 1864 and 1879, Ulrichs, a lawyer, published numerous works and argued for the legalization of what is today called *homosexuality*.[12] He understood sexual desire to be innate, therefore natural, and distinct from biological sex. In his opinion, a physiological male could either desire a female or another male. If a male desires a female, Ulrichs called them *dioning*. If a male desires a male, he referred to them as *urning*. In his sense, an *urning* was not a 'full' man, but a man with a female soul, which he summarized in the Latin phrase *anima muliebris virili corpore inclusa* ('a female psyche confined in a male body'). Ulrichs compared the urning to a hermaphrodite and explained that, while a male hermaphrodite displayed some female physiological characteristics, a male urning

---

11 Ulrichs published his first articles under the pseudonym Numa Numantius, but began to speak and publish under his full name in 1867 (cf. Sigusch *Geschichte*; Hubert Kennedy *Life*). On Ulrichs' theories of sexual differentiation see Mehlmann 133-50. Mehlmann elaborates the discursive history of the concept of *sex* with respect to *hermaphroditism* and *homosexuality* in the 19th and early 20th century and describes the entanglements between the theories of Darwin, Ulrichs, Krafft-Ebing, Hirschfeld, Weiniger, Freud and others.

12 The term *homosexuality* was coined by Karl Maria Kertbeny in 1869. The analogous *heterosexuality* was first used by Kertbeny in a private letter in 1868. The terminology was appropriated by Richard von Krafft-Ebing who borrowed the terminology from an 1880-publication by Gustav Jäger, *Entdeckung der Seele* (cf. Sigusch *Geschichte* 146, Katz *Invention*).

displayed some female psychological characteristics. He developed the idea in analogy to contemporary concepts of embryology that had shown that male and female gonads developed from the same, sexually undifferentiated tissue. Each embryo therefore had the potential to develop either male or female sexual characteristics. Ulrichs argued that each individual had not only a somatic sex that could develop either way, but also a psychological sex that could develop either way. Ulrichs had realized that the gonads as single markers for 'true' sex in an individual were contested at the time and challenged the idea that sexual desire was situated either in testicles or ovaries. He suggested, though, that desire might be situated in the brain.[13] Thus, Ulrichs coined the terms *Leib-Seele-Zwitter* or *körperlich-seelischer Hermaphrodit* and the figure of the psychological hermaphrodite as an individual with a female soul in a male body spread (cf. *Memnon Teil I, Memnon Teil II, Vindex, Inclusa*).

While Ulrichs started to lead his public struggle against the criminalization of men who desire men mostly alone, his cause soon became the center of attention of a whole group of professionals: Psychiatrist Carl Westphal (1833 Berlin – 1890 Konstanz) 'discovered' the 'contrary sexual feeling' (*Conträre Sexualempfindung*) in 1870 and describes it as a psychiatric disorder. Richard Freiherr von Krafft-Ebing (1840 Mannheim – 1902 Graz) developed Westphal's model and established a classification system of sexual deviations and disorders.[14] His *Psychopathia Sexualis* (first published in 1886) is often referred to as the seminal work on the psychiatrist's perspective on sexual pathologies. Krafft-Ebing understood homosexuality as a biological anomaly that provoked a sexual inversion of the brain. This reasoning led Krafft-Ebing and other psychiatrists to argue for the de-criminalization of homosexual-

---

13 Es ist "irrig [...] anzunehmen: 'neben Testikeln sei stets männliche Geschlechtsliebe von Natur vorhanden, sie stecke gleichsam in den Testikeln', oder: weibliche Geschlechtsliebe sei nur da von Natur vorhanden wo Eierstöcke vorhanden sind.' Der Sitz der Geschlechtsliebe dürfte vielleicht überhaupt ganz anderswo zu suchen sein, als in den Testikeln oder in den Eierstöcken, oder auch als in den übrigen geschlechtlichen Körpertheilen, nämlich im Gehirn" (Ulrichs qtd. in Mehlmann 140).

14 On the concepts of 'contrary sexual feeling' and 'inversion' by Westphal and Krafft-Ebing cf. Mehlmann 150-80.

ity.[15] However, this argument was uttered only on the grounds that the former crime was turned into a mental disorder in need of psychiatric treatment. Krafft-Ebing revised his classificatory systems with each new edition of the *Psychopathia Sexualis* and Mehlman points out that he expanded his system for the fourth edition, 1889, and introduced the category "psychische Hermaphrodisie" (Mehlmann 175). According to Mehlmann, it denoted an individual who displays mostly homosexual desire, but values heterosexual desire to a certain extent as well.[16] This category is distinct from Ulrichs 'psychological hermaphrodite,' and it shows that homosexuality and hermaphroditism were very blurry concepts at the time.

Magnus Hirschfeld (1868 Kolberg – 1935 Nizza)[17] entered the debate in 1896 with his first emancipist writing called *Sappho und Sokrates*. Similar to Ulrichs, he also chose a pseudonym for his first publication: Th. Ramien. One year later, he founded the *Wissenschaftlich-humanitäre Komitee* (WhK 'Scientific-Humanitarian Committee'), the world's first gay rights organization, and worked towards a repeal of section 175 (§175) that criminalized male homosexual acts in Germany.[18] Today, Hirschfeld is little-known as a researcher or doctor, but famous for his political activism.

---

15 Krafft-Ebing was one of the first supporters of Hirschfeld's initiative to repeal section 175. He signed the petition in 1897. Colleagues such as Albert Moll followed his example (cf. Sigusch 179f).

16 Krafft-Ebing's category is part of a taxonomy that described innate inversion in four steps. Mehlmann writes: "Als neue erste Stufe führt Krafft-Ebing die sog. 'psychische Hermaphrodisie' ein, bei der neben homosexuellen Empfindungen und Neigungen noch heterosexuelle Restempfindungen vorhanden sein. Die zweite Stufe, die 'einfache Homosexualität' (ausschließliche sexuelle Neigung zum eigenen Geschlecht), geht in die 'Effeminatio bzw. Viraginität' (der biologische Mann fühlt sich weiblich und passiv, die biologische Frau männlich und aktiv) über. Am Ende steht die 'Androgynie bzw. Gynandrie', bei der sich der Körperbau demjenigen Geschlecht annähere, zu welchem sich das Individuum zugehörig fühlt" (175).

17 For extensive information on life and work of Magnus Hirschfeld cf. Sigusch; Dobler; Keilson-Lauritz; Herrn; Steakley *Homosexual*; Herzer.

18 Section 175 was introduced in 1871 and revised several times until its final abolishment in 1994 (cf. Schulz *Paragraph 175*).

His family was Jewish, but his religion was science and he chose the motto *per scientiam ad iustitiam* ('justice through science') for his struggle. To reach his goal, the de-pathologization and de-criminalization of homosexual acts, he strongly promoted the sciences of the sexes and worked tirelessly towards an institutionalization of sexology as an academic discipline. He published the interdisciplinary *Jahrbuch für sexuelle Zwischenstufen unter besonderer Berücksichtigung der Homosexualität* ('Yearbook of Sexual Intermediaries with Special Consideration of Homosexuality') from 1899 to 1923, the *Zeitschrift für Sexualwissenschaft* in 1908, founded the *Ärztliche Gesellschaft für Sexualwissenschaft und Eugenik* in 1913 with colleagues Iwan Bloch and Albert Eulenburg, organized the first international congress on sexology in Berlin in 1921, and was a founding member of the *Weltliga für Sexualreform* (1928). Since 1919, his work was based in the *Institut für Sexualwissenschaften,* which he had founded with neurologist Arthur Kronefeld and dermatologist Friedrich Wertheim in Berlin. Hirschfeld was an organizer and public reformer who was convinced that science would prove homosexuality to be 'natural' and therefore 'normal'. On top of the medico-scientific discourse that he fueled with his constant publications, journals and institutions, he participated in more public discourses as well: he held weekly lectures at his institute, wrote for newspapers and journals, participated in or supported movies,[19] worked as an expert witness in numerous, sometimes spectacular legal trials,[20] and saw patients in his clinic.

Hirschfeld understood homosexuality as one aspect in the field of sexuality and in his clinic and journals he did not focus on homosexuality alone, but addressed numerous variations of sexuality, sex and gender. On the one hand, this gave him a more open perspective on female homosexuality, and female sexual activity in general. Earlier scholars such as Krafft-Ebing and Ulrichs had more or less ignored female desire and

---

19 *Anders als die Anderen* (1919) Prod. Richard Oswald. *Steinachs Forschungen/Der Steinach-Film* (1922/23) Prod. Nicholas Kaufmann (cf. Peters 158, footnote 17).

20 See for example Hirschfeld's role in the "Eulenburg affair," a series of legal trials (1906-1908) on the supposed homosexuality of prominent members of Wilhelm II's cabinet and the military. The trials are deemed the biggest scandal of the Wilhelmine era (cf. Haeberle "Justitia;" Steakley "Iconography").

marginalized it. On the other hand, Hirschfeld was very interested in the various forms of sexuality and sex determination and looked for connections between them. Ulrichs had already started to construct a taxonomy of the sexes and implemented the urning as a third sex. Krafft-Ebing and others also devised different organizational structures of sexuality that showed the relation between heterosexual men and women and 'inverts.' Hirschfeld continued this line of work and developed what he referred to as *Zwischenstufenmodell* ('model of sexual intermediary stages'). His basic assumption was similar to Ulrichs' thought: human babies developed from physically and psychologically undifferentiated, hermaphroditic fetuses.[21] Psychological sex corresponded with the desire of the individual, and physiological sex corresponded with the somatic features of the individual; and both developed independently from each other. Although the fetus would usually develop into a somatic male or female paired with heterosexual desire (Hirschfeld called these types 'full' men or women), the development could also stop at some point and produce a type that deviated from the norm on some level. Hirschfeld argued that these sexual intermediary stages, 'Zwischenstufen', were almost infinitely diverse and it followed that man was generally not man *or* woman, but man *and* woman.[22] He maintained that 'full' men and women were ideal types, the poles on a continuum, but rarely met in real life. Most humans came in various hermaphroditic stages.

Following the publication of Krafft-Ebings *Psychopathia Sexualis*, Mehlmann attests to a discursive explosion on homosexuality (cf. 181). The main question that psychiatrists, neurologists, lawyers, and activists debated at the end of the 19th century and early 20th century was the origin of homosexuality: where does *it* come from? Who or what is responsible? Is *it* innate, a biological variation and therefore natural? Or, is homosexuality acquired? What is the role of education and social environment? While Ulrichs, Krafft-Ebing, Hirschfeld and others opted for a physiological-anatomical explanation, psychoanalyst Sigmund Freud and philosopher Otto Weininger developed models that explored psychological

---

21 "In der Uranlage sind alle Menschen körperlich und seelisch Zwitter" (Hirschfeld *Sappho und Sokrates* qtd. in Mehlmann *Unzuverlässig* 236).
22 "Der Mensch ist nicht Mann oder Weib, sondern Mann und Weib" (Hirschfeld "Die intersexuelle Konstitution" 9).

explanations or regarded character as decisive factors. Weininger (1880 Wien – 1903 Wien) questioned the causal relationship between the physiological-anatomical body and a psychological sex in his anti-Semitic and misogynist *Geschlecht und Charakter* (1903).[23] Building on a theory of 'bisexuality,' Weininger proposed a general mixture of the sexes in each individual, both on a somatic level, e.g. hermaphrodites, and on a psychological level, e.g. 'inverts.' Each 'mixing ratio' was understood as distinct, and echoes Hirschfeld's intermediary stages. As a result, Weininger argued in favor of individualized treatments of patients and multifaceted education of children. According to Freud (1856 Freiberg – 1939 London), each individual was born polymorphously perverse, i.e. with a libido that is not focused on a specific object. Rather, Freud identified five stages of psychosexual development in his *Drei Abhandlungen zur Sexualtheorie* (1905)[24] that guide the child's libido from polymorphously perverse to a heterosexual desire focused on genitalia and reproduction. Heterosexuality was therefore no longer innate or biological, but a result of social and psychological factors. Variations of a heterosexual, genital-oriented desire could be interpreted as arrests in the psychosexual development.

U.S. historian Elizabeth Reis describes a similar situation in the late 19th and early 20th centuries in the U. S.: The origin of homosexuality was heavily disputed and those arguing in favor of a congenital disposition, i.e. an innate biological explanation, were most likely conflating homosexuality with hermaphroditism and interpreting both as signs of a degeneration in sexual development. Following British sexologist Havelock Ellis' *Studies in the Psychology of Sex* (1897-1910), homosexuality was interpreted as a variation in the brain. Hermaphroditism, in that line of reasoning, was understood as a variation of the reproductive system (cf. Reis *Bodies* 59ff). Reis also identifies 'marriageability' and heterosexuality as important factors in the management of hermaphrodites since the 19th century: Interventional surgery on genitalia was "attempted [...] in the hope of making those organs serve the doctor's perception of patients' sexual and marital requirements" (45). Reis offers various incidents to show that the gonads as decisive factor in sex determination were under considerable

---

23 See Mehlmann for an elaboration of Weininger's concepts: 270-99.
24 Cf. Mehlmann 300-49.

doubt in the U.S. Following historian Alison Redick and refining Dreger's "age of gonads", Reis explains that "[i]n fact, a diverse and seemingly random approach typified doctors' reactions to such patients [i.e. patients with genital variations] since the seventeenth century" (859). On the other hand, she admits that although "[r]elying on the gonads to determine a patient's true sex was becoming increasingly debatable, [...] doctors in the 1930s still clung to the notion, if ambivalently" (101).

Summarizing the aforementioned treatment of hermaphroditism in Europe and the U.S. up to the 19th and early 20th centuries, approaches to hermaphroditism have been plenty and contradictory. While the legal category *hermaphrodite* vanished around 1800 in France and in 1900 in Germany, the medical concept of *hermaphroditism* was re-worked repeatedly and had been appropriated by the discourse on homosexuality by the end of the 19th century. Despite ongoing debates, no agreement on the 'true nature' of hermaphroditism was achieved and the hermaphrodite subject drifted back and forth between monster and marvel, between nature and myth, between true and pseudo, and between double or predominant sex. So far, missing from this sketch of legal, mythical, and medical discourses are the hermaphrodites' voices. The following analyses of two autobiographical texts will close this gap and study the voices of supposedly hermaphroditic subjects in interaction with surrounding and interconnected discourses.

Truth or Dare

The Memoirs of Herculine Barbin

'AT THE BOTTOM OF SEX, THERE IS TRUTH': LOCATING THE TEXT

In the late 1970s, Michel Foucault browsed the archives of the French Department of Public Hygiene and found himself drawn to a story published in a roughly 100 year old textbook by medical doctor Ambroise Tardieu. In 1874, Tardieu had published the second part of his treatise *Question médico-légale de l'identité dans ses rapports avec les vices de conformation des organs sexuels,* of which the first part had been published two years before. The text that enthralled Foucault to the degree that he began to research its history and eventually chose to re-publish it was the story of Herculine Barbin. While her[1] early years in a girls' school and convent in rural France received no public attention, Barbin first made the papers when the successful teacher at a girls' school officially changed her civil

---

1   Scholars use a variety of pronouns in reference to Barbin, e.g. Foucault mirrors Barbin's use of pronouns and alternates in his use of masculine and feminine pronouns; Judith Butler uses a slashed "s/he," and Morgan Holmes uses the bipotential pronoun "hir." The English language edition was translated by Richard McDougall, whom Holmes criticizes for having smoothed over pronoun ambiguities in Tardieu's introduction (cf. *Perilous* 82f). The editors, however, claim to "have followed Herculine's system [of pronoun use] wherever possible" (*Memoirs* xiii footnote 1). I aim to preserve the ambiguity that Barbin chose to evoke and switch between differently gendered pronouns. See Wing ("Simplified" 116) for examples of Barbin's play with pronouns.

status from female to male and began to live as a man. The document that first Tardieu and later Foucault published gives an account of her life story from the quiet early years, the gender transition in 1860, to the final years before his suicide in Paris in 1868.

Yet neither editor, Tardieu or Foucault, published the story on its own, but published it together with official medical reports. After having established the basic problem of the text as one of "true sex" (122^2), Tardieu explains that the "struggles and disturbances to which this unfortunate person was prey have been described by him in pages that are not surpassed in interest by any romantic novel. It is difficult to read a more harrowing story, told with a truer accent" (123). Yet Barbin's description alone does not satisfy the 19th century doctor and he continues, "[Barbin's] narrative may not contain a gripping truth, [but] we have, in the authentic and official documents that I shall annex to it, the proof that it is perfectly exact" (123). The second editor of the text, Foucault, did not have the original manuscript to hand but worked from Tardieu's edition. The latter had explained "not [to] hesitate to publish it almost in full" (123), but Foucault points out that the impact of the first editor of the text can only be speculated upon until the complete manuscript is found. He warns that Tardieu "neglected the recollections of Alexina's final years – everything that in his opinion consisted only of laments, recriminations, and incoherencies" (*Memoirs* 119) and Shirley Neuman adds that "precisely that content and rhetoric which, in the misogynist traditions of literature and medicine, have been associated with women's writing and women" ("Autobiography" 147) might have been omitted. Nevertheless (or maybe even because of this constellation) Foucault was fascinated by Barbin's account and announced that he would devote the next volume of *The History of Sexuality* to hermaphrodites (cf. *Memoirs* 119). While Foucault never wrote the volume, he re-published the memoirs under the title

---

2   Unless otherwise indicated, citations from Barbin's text as well as from the introduction and the documents contained in the dossier refer to the American edition, *Herculine Barbin: Being the Recently Discovered Memoirs of a Nineteenth-Century French Hermaphrodite* (1980), hereafter referred to as *Memoirs*.

Herculine Barbin, dite Alexina B. in France in 1978.[3] Moreover, he expanded the annexed dossier, the medical reports by Barbin's doctor Chesnet[4] and the pathologist E. Goujon,[5] and added a section on original names, dates and places, press reports, private letters and legal documents as well as a fictional re-working of the story by German psychiatrist Oscar Panizza, "Ein scandalöser Fall" ("A Scandal at the Convent" 1893). In 1980, an English-language edition followed, prefaced with an introductory essay by Foucault, and titled *Herculine Barbin: Being the Recently Discovered Memoirs of a Nineteenth-Century French Hermaphrodite*. In 1998, a German translation was edited by Wolfgang Schäffner and Joseph Vogl, who added more documents to the dossier and attached an epilogue. The German title became *Über Hermaphrodismus. Der Fall Barbin*. While the French title did not mention hermaphroditism at all, Foucault assigned Barbin the status of a hermaphrodite in the title of the American edition. In the German edition, then, Barbin's 'case' already serves as a prime example for hermaphroditism *as such*.

Foucault's publications generated numerous academic debates among literary scholars, scholars in Gender Studies, and historians of science, e.g. Alice Dreger chose the year of Barbin's death to begin her historical study on hermaphroditism because "Barbin shaped the biomedical treatment of human hermaphroditism for years to come" (*Hermaphrodites* 28f.); and *Middlesex* author Jeffrey Eugenides confides that the memoirs were his original source for his novel *Middlesex* (cf. van Moorhem 2003). Moreover, he references the memoirs in the novel when he lets his narrator Cal explain: "Her memoirs [...] make unsatisfactory reading, and it was after finishing them years ago that I first got the idea to write my own" (*Middlesex* 19, see also the chapter "Hermaphroditus ♥ *Middlesex*" of the

---

3   To my knowledge, Herculine Barbin's memoir is the earliest Western autobiographical representation of hermaphroditic experience. The French *Mémoire pour Anne Grandjean, connu sous le nom de Jean-Baptiste Grandjean* (Vermeil 1765) served as a document in a court trial and was not written by Grandjean him_herself (cf. Foucault *Abnormal* 55-80).

4   Chesnet "The Question of Identity; the Malformation of the External Genital Organs; Hypospadias; an Error About Sex." 1860. Barbin *Memoirs* 124-128.

5   E. Goujon "A Study of Incomplete Hermaphroditism in a Man." 1869. Barbin *Memoirs* 128-144.

present study). A general academic interest in 19th and early 20th century representations of hermaphroditism and gender variant individuals may also be acknowledged: Historian Herman Simon edited and re-published the 1907 memoirs of N.O. Body aka Karl M. Baer in 1993, *Aus eines Mannes Mädchenjahren*, and translated them into English in 2006, *Memoirs of a Man's Maiden Years*.[6] In 1994, a joint exhibition of the work of French photographer Nadar aka Félix Tournachon was shown in the Musée d'Orsay, Paris, and the Metropolitan Museum of Art, New York, including a series of nine photographs of a 'hermaphrodite' dating back to 1861. The photographs have been reprinted and are accompanied by two critical essays in a 2009 collection by Magali Le Mens and Jean-Luc Nancy. In 1995, literary scholar Anna Livia edited and translated the 1930 French novel *L'Ange et les Pervers* ('*The Angel and the Perverts*') by Lucie Delarue-Mardrus that focuses on the hermaphrodite Mario/Marion. In 2004, Gary Williams edited and published the fragments of Julia Ward Howe's novel *The Hermaphrodite* for the first time[7] and in 2013 Swedish scholar Inger Caisou-Rousseau edited the autobiography of Andreas Bruce, a Swedish gender variant person born in 1808.[8]

The structure of Foucault's edition of the text mirrors Tardieu's edition; Barbin's text is introduced by the respective editor and followed by some 'original' documents. Moreover, Foucault also explains that he chose not to publish every document from the archives that contained the name Adélaïde Barbin, but that it seemed "enough [to him] to publish the most significant ones" (*Memoirs* 120). His choice to annex Panizza's story appears similarly random or arbitrary when he refers to another "strange novel" in which the "story of Alexina can easily be made out" (120) and which he did not choose to re-publish.[9] For Foucault, Barbin's text serves

---

6   Hereafter referred to as *Maiden Years*. For an analysis see the following chapter "N.O. Body and the Making of a True Man."
7   Howe probably started work on the novel in the winter of 1846-47, but never finished it. In 2012, Williams and his colleague Renée Bergland edited the first critical reader on *The Hermaphrodite*.
8   The autobiography is not yet translated into English. See Holmqvist "Könsväxlingar" (7f) for a short analysis of the text in Swedish.
9   While Foucault did not publish the text, he indicates author, title and publication date (Dubarry, *L'Hermaphrodite*, 1899) and categorizes the novel as part of an

as a document of "the end of the nineteenth century, that century which was so powerfully haunted by the theme of the hermaphrodite" (xvii) and he again echoes Tardieu when he opens his introduction with the question: "Do we *truly* need a *true* sex?" (vii) and places the text in "one of those periods [around 1860 to 1870] when investigations of sexual identity were carried out with the most intensity, in an attempt not only to establish the true sex of hermaphrodites but also to identify, classify, and characterize the different types of perversions" (xif). Yet Foucault not only reads Barbin's text as a document, but classifies it as a "journal or rather [...] memoirs" (xi), comments on Barbin's writing style, "that elegant, affected, and allusive style that is somewhat turgid and outdated" (xii), and explains that the "narrative baffles every possible attempt to make an identification" (xii). On the one hand then, both editors treat the text as a revealing and informative document *on* the discourse of 'true' sex at a given time and place (and thereby ignore its position as a text *produced by* this very discourse). On the other hand, they note a general difference in quality between the official reports as documents and Barbin's text, which they position in the category (or somewhere in the vicinity) of fiction.

'THAT VAST DESIRE FOR THE UNKNOWN': QUESTIONING THE TEXT

So, what kind of questions can this text answer? Can a literary analysis of the text 'solve' the question of Barbin's sex, and maybe even determine hir 'true' sex? Surely not. However, the text presents itself in a way *as if* this were possible. From the very beginning of the text, Barbin tries to establish her reliability by pointing out her religious upbringing, "Houses that were truly pious, hearts that were pure and true, presided over my upbringing" (*Memoirs* 3), and her excellent memory with phrases like, "I was seven years old then, and the heartbreaking scene [...] is still vivid in my mind" (5) or, "I have never since forgotten the distressing incident [...]" (13). Although she uses pseudonyms throughout the text, and shortens or leaves out the names of cities, authorities, and institutions, she never tires of

---

"abundance of 'medico-libertine' literature in the final years of the century" (120).

invoking the autobiographical pact, as established by Phillipe Lejeune as "the identity ('identicalness') of the *name* (author-narrator-protagonist)" (*Autobiography* 14), and claims authenticity for hir text: "My skill as a writer cannot match that of those giants of drama [Alexandre Dumas, Paul Féval]. And then, remember that I am writing my personal story [...]" (*Memoirs* 35). Of course, the autobiographical pact, the identity between the name on the cover of the book and the narrator-protagonist, is impossible due to the text's posthumous publication via an editor. Yet Lejeune explains that pseudonyms (and, I would like to add, edited volumes) do not generally threaten the pact (cf. *On Autobiography* 12).[10] Moreover, the text matches the criteria established for the genre *autobiography* in large parts. Lejeune describes autobiography as a "[r]etrospective prose narrative written by a real person concerning his [sic!] own existence, where the focus is his [sic!] individual life, in particular the story of his [sic!] personality" (*On Autobiography* 4).[11] Repeatedly, Barbin, the author-narrator-protagonist, named Camille in the text, assures the reader that the text is written in a retrospective mode by a real person; it concerns hir own life and the story develops continuously and chronologically.[12] Moreover, the text draws heavily on exemplary

---

10 While Barbin's birth certificate had been changed from "Adélaïde Herculine Barbin" to "Abel Barbin" (cf. *Memoirs* 150) the narrator-protagonist in the text goes by "Camille" (17), a French name that may be used for both, male and female individuals. Crapanzano identifies up to five different selves for Barbin: "Barbin as the author of the text; Alexina as the narrator of the first, coherent part and Camille as her subject or narrated self; Herculine as the narrator of the fragments and Abel as his subject or narrated self" ("Self" 67). While I do understand Barbin's text as complex and multilayered, Crapanzano's distinction implies a separation between the different selves that I do not see realized in the text. Rather, I understand "Barbin" as a hybrid subject position manifested through a dynamic author-narrator-protagonist relationship.
11 Shirley Neuman and others have shown that theories of autobiography have often overlooked *gender* as a relevant category of analysis in the genre and that these "poetics assume a male subject of autobiography" (*Autobiography* 1). Lejeune's phrasing indicates that his scholarship may maintain this tradition.
12 Towards the end of the text, the part that covers Barbin's life as a man in Paris, the mode of writing changes to an erratic diary-like form, sometimes marked

representatives of the genre such as the *Confessions* by Augustine and Rousseau. Augustine wrote his *Confessions* between 397 and 400 AD and chronicled his life from sinful youth to his conversion to the Christian faith. Augustine's religious tone[13] is copied by Barbin, who often addresses God and proclaims her trust and faith, "O my God! What a fate was mine! But You willed it, no doubt, and I shall say no more" (*Memoirs* 87). Moreover, the text mimics Rousseau in his *Confessions of J. J. Rousseau* (1782). He opens with the following declaration:

I am resolved on an undertaking that has no model and will have no imitator. I want to show my fellow-men a man in all the truth of nature; and this man is to be myself. Myself alone. I feel my heart and I know men. I am not made like any that I have seen; I venture to believe that I was not made like any that exist. [...] I have told the good and the bad with equal frankness. I have concealed nothing that was ill, added nothing that was good, and if I have sometimes used some indifferent ornamention, this has only ever been to fill a void occasioned by my lack of memory; I may have supposed to be true what I knew could have been so, never what I knew to be false. (*Confessions* 5)

---

    with the date of writing. Scholars usually distinguish between these two parts as the coherent and conventional, autobiographical part (*Memoirs* 3-98) and the fragments (*Memoirs* 98-115; cf. Crapanzano "Self" 67). Neuman and Porter connect the different writing styles to the performance of a gender transition from female to male (cf. "Autobiography" 146f and "Figuration" 131). Barbin's text may then be said to embody the supposed duality of its author.

13 Augustine begins each chapter with a prayer to God, e.g. "I wish to act in truth, making my confession both in my heart before you and in this book before the many who will read it" (*Confessions* 207). Similarly, Barbin proclaims, "But You remain to me, my God! You have willed that I belong to no one here below [...] Your divine work! Though I am a sad disinherited creature, I can still lift up my eyes to You, for You at least will not reject me!" (*Memoirs* 93). Barbin's accounts of repeated transgressions of moral and religious codes of conduct paired with her confessional mode of writing may also be read in the tradition of spiritual autobiography. See Porter "Figuration" for an analysis of the *Memoirs* as a parody of the conversion narrative.

And Barbin echoes: "[T]his incredible journey, which no other living creature before me has taken! No matter how strict may be the sentence to which the future will condemn me, I intend to continue my difficult task" (*Memoirs* 35f). She claims to struggle with her highly singular and extraordinary story, but nevertheless claims to be reporting the truth as best as possible:

I am feeling a certain hesitation, for I am about to begin the hardest part of the task that I have imposed upon myself. I have to speak of things that, for a number of people, will be nothing but incredible nonsense because, in fact, they go beyond the limits of what is possible. It will be difficult for them, no doubt, to get an exact idea of what my feelings were in the midst of the extraordinary peculiarities of my life. There is only one thing that I can ask of them: that they be convinced of my sincerity above all. (15)

What may be read as a constraint to the truth, explains Lejeune, paradoxically increases rather than weakens the perceived authenticity of the autobiographical narrative (cf. *Autobiography* 25). She claims piety, shows a good memory, and is sincere, yet she still suffers from the problem that she has "to speak of things that [...] go beyond the limits of what is possible" (*Memoirs* 15). This problem of rendering the truth into speech, into discourse, is elaborated repeatedly: although she is able to "say for certain" (19) a number of things and recall various details of her life as a child and young student, she suffers due to the impossibility to describe her feelings truthfully: "I do not know what inexpressible uneasiness seized me [...]. It was pain, it was shame. What I felt – no words could express it" (25). Here, as in other examples ("My predicament cannot be expressed. [...] Possessed by feelings that would be difficult to describe" [32f]), she reframes her inability to explain or give an exact account of something as an impossible task, as something that is simply beyond words and therefore inexpressible or unsayable. Ultimately, the difficulties and obstacles that Barbin reports authenticate the text further. They render it true and emphasize a link between *autobiography* and a ritualized discourse that supposedly produces the truth about an individual, the *confession*. Both Augustine and Rousseau have exploited the tradition of the confession as a truth-producing discourse by titling their life narratives respectively. Barbin's text is titled "My Memoirs" in the English edition and "Mes

Souvenirs" in the French, but it is unclear whether this title is Barbin's invention or needs to be ascribed to one of the editors. *Confession*, explains Foucault, is a mode of the production of truth about an individual and dates back at least to the Middle Ages. He dismantles truth as an effect, a product of ritualized practices and not as something 'hidden' that could be 'revealed' (cf. *Will* 59ff). The religious confession or juridico-religious mode of truth production is marked by the following characteristics:

> The confession is a ritual of discourse in which the speaking subject is also the subject of the statement; it is also a ritual that unfolds within a power relationship, for one does not confess without the presence (or virtual presence) of a partner who is not simply the interlocutor but the authority who requires the confession, prescribes and appreciates it, and intervenes in order to judge, punish, forgive, console, and reconcile; a ritual in which the truth is corroborated by the obstacles and resistances it has had to surmount in order to be formulated; and finally, a ritual in which the expression alone, independently of its external consequences, produces intrinsic modifications in the person who articulates it: it exonerates, redeems, and purifies him; it unburdens him of his wrongs, liberates him, and promises him salvation. (*Will* 61f)

This notion of *confession* can be summed up as 1) the confession is always about a self; 2) the confession is made to an authority who judges the person who confesses; 3) the truth of the confession is secured by the difficulties in expressing it; and 4) the confession is a performative act that modifies the person who confesses. Next to the religious confession, Foucault points to other confessional practices that produce truth about the individual such as "interrogations, consultations, autobiographical narratives, [and] letters" (*Will* 63) that take place between "children and parents, students, and educators, patients and psychiatrists, delinquents and experts" (63). As I have argued above, Barbin's text presents itself in large parts as an autobiography and may therefore be read as participating in a confessionnal mode of truth production. Yet rather than falling into the trap of the confessional discourse and reading the text for its truth claims, I follow Judith Butler and suggest analyzing the text as a product of discursive conventions. Butler insisted that the confessional practice of writing a journal or memoir was embedded in specific discursive traditions and should not be misunderstood as 'true' (cf. *Gender* 93-110). Confessional writing, from this perspective, is a performative practice, an act, not the expression of a pre-discursive identity or a pre-discursive 'self.' While the text that is marketed and marked as a memoir or an autobiography claims to *reveal* the truth about Barbin, it must be read as *constructing* the thing it claims to describe. Butler agrees and calls Barbin's text "a kind of confessional production of the self" (*Gender* 99). In addition to the confession, Butler points to various other discourses that govern the production of the text, among them "the conventions of female homosexuality both encouraged and condemned by the convent and its religious ideology" (*Gender* 98) and "h/er nineteenth-century French education [that] involved schooling in the classics and French Romanticism" (*Gender* 98). As relevant literary conventions for Barbin's text, she identifies the sentimental novel, Christian legends, and Greek myth (cf. *Gender* 98f). Scholars have since followed Butler's suggestion and detected other literary traditions in the text such as the gothic novel (cf. Webb "Human") and the Book of Job (cf. Connolly "Voices"). With respect to the genre *autobiography*, Nathanial Wing argues that Barbin's identity construction fails or is ineffective because Barbin lacks "narrative models [...] that will confirm or valorize his/her desires" (Wing "Simplified" 110). Moreover, Vincent Crapanzo explains that "Barbin's life can be understood in terms of the loss of a genre – of those conventionalized discursive strategies by which a man (or woman) [...] could 'meaningfully' articulate his (her) life – or past – and give seemingly full expression to his (her) self" ("Self" 62). For Roger Porter "writing turns out to be *de-composition*" ("Figuration" 127) for Barbin because rather than producing a coherent and whole identity via autobiographical writing, the text fails to repair the fragmentation of her body and life.[14]

---

14 Some of these readings of *autobiography* as a restrictive and restricting genre that does not support a possibly disruptive change in life stand in contrast to the readings of other autobiographies of sex or gender variant people from the 19th century onwards. N.O. Body's memoir, published in 1907, would be a case in point. Moreover, these readings ignore both the narrative potential of a sex or gender change and the genres' capacity to make use of radical developments and drastic changes in a life. Speaking of one's life as marked by transgression and temptation, suffering, pain and disruption may then be read as conventional rather than exceptional. See Müller for an analysis of 19th century homosexual

So far, these approaches to the text have offered critical insights into the construction of a 'self' through autobiographical writing. Yet Barbin's text offers more than just an insight into the autobiographical mode of truth production about an individual. Rather, in my view, it serves as a reflection on different confessional practices or different modes of truth production: Barbin's reports of hir experiences with religious confessions question the juridico-religious mode of truth production. Hir accounts of medical consultations are manifestations of the medico-scientific mode of truth production and the text itself, the memoir, serves as an exploration of the autobiographical mode of truth production. Moreover, the medical reports that are annexed to the narrative add another layer in an analysis of different modes of truth production. As documents of a historically situated medico-scientific discourse they are liable to a specific generic tradition, i.e. the medical case study, and they may be read as being characterized by specific truth claims. In the following, I begin by turning to these reports and scrutinizing their truth claims. Afterwards, I turn to Barbin's text and analyze the description of the religious and the medical confessional practices ze participates in. As a last point, I analyze the text as part of the autobiographical mode of confession.

'We Are About to See': Reporting the Truth

Herculine Barbin first became the object of a medical case study by Dr. Chesnet in 1860.[15] The report that he published in a professional journal was the result of his examination of Barbin and had effected Barbin's change of civil status. The report largely follows the generic requirements of a case study as outlined by Julia Epstein (cf. *Altered*): first, the doctor introduces himself, "I, the undersigned, a doctor of medicine" (*Memoirs* 124) and establishes the authenticity of the following report. Then, he introduces the patient, including details about her personal life and family history, continues with her history of ailments and earlier treatments and

---

autobiographies. See Runte and Prosser for analyses of autobiographical writings by trans* people and Kilian for a more general analysis of the emplotment of sex changes in narrative, both fictional and autobiographical.

15 See my paper "Das geständige Geschlecht" for a more detailed analysis of the medical reports.

comes to the "facts" (125) resulting from his examination. The facts are then discussed in length:

What shall we conclude from the above facts? Is Alexina a woman? She has a vulva, labia majora, and a feminine urethra, independent of a sort of imperforate penis, which might be a monstrously developed clitoris. She has a vagina. True, it is very short, very narrow; but after all, what is it if it is not a vagina? These are completely feminine attributes. Yes, but Alexina has never menstruated; the whole outer part of her body is that of a man, and my explorations did not enable me to find a womb. Her tastes, her inclinations, draw her toward women. At night she has voluptuous sensations that are followed by a discharge of sperm [...]. Finally, to sum up the matter, ovoid bodies and spermatic cords are found by touch in a divided scrotum. These are the real proofs of sex. (127f)[16]

Despite these seemingly complex and sometimes contradictory findings, the doctor comes to a simple conclusion and announces in the end, "Alexina is a man, hermaphroditic, no doubt, but with an obvious predominance of masculine sexual characteristics" (*Memoirs* 128). Similarly, the autopsy report by Dr. E. Goujon follows generic conventions and is structured into a part called "preliminary information," i.e. information about the doctor and how he became acquainted with the case. This part also contains praise for the earlier report by Dr. Chesnet, which is cited in full. The following parts are titled "State of the External Genital Organs" and "Examination of the Internal Organs" and describe the 'findings' of the doctor. The last part is the "Discussion of the Preceding Facts" and even exceeds the conclusions of Chesnet. Goujon finds "hermaphroditism does not exist in man and the higher animals" (139).

A close reading of the reports, however, reveals them to be less convincing than claimed. Goujon's report especially is full of contradictions and incoherencies: in 1860, Chesnet had used Barbin's female first name "Alexina" and a feminine pronoun to refer to his patient who was then still living as a woman. In 1868, Goujon uses a female first name despite Barbin's legal and medical assignment to the male sex eight years before and produces sentences such as: "Alexina's testicle [...] had completely

---

16 See especially Wing ("Simplified") for an analysis of heteronormative assumptions in both reports.

descended" (144). Confusion is added when the female first name is combined with masculine pronouns: "Alexina possessed the organs that are characteristic of his sex" (143). Moreover, Goujon uses differently gendered terms to refer to Barbin such as "young man" (128) or "hermaphrodite" (130), and stresses Barbin's capacity "to play either the masculine or the feminine role in coitus, without distinction" (131). He also describes hir genitalia as "a large clitoris rather than a penis" (131) and points out that "it is difficult [...] to discover a more extreme mixture of the sexes" (129). Goujon also compares his analysis of Barbin's anatomy to similar 'cases' from the medical records and explains that "surgery is often all-powerful in remedying certain malformations that are designated under the name of hermaphroditism" (139).[17] Goujon, it seems, understands hermaphroditism as a "malformation" that can be "remedied" by surgery. Therefore, hermaphroditism must exist and he contradicts his own claim. Neuman argues with Laqueur and attributes the "confusion" ("Autobiography" 142) in the medical reports to the "tension between a same-sex model and a different-sex model for the human body" (142). While the doctors of the time claim to have found out and determined Barbin's true sex, their reports mirror uncertainty and may be said to multiply rather than simplify Barbin's sex.[18]

---

17 Examples are reports by Geoffroy Saint-Hilaire on a "hermaphrodite monk" (137), by "Schweikhard," by "Louis Casper" (138), by "Léon Le Fort" and by "Béclard" (139). These acts of name-dropping show, on the one hand, that hermaphroditism is a relevant topic in the medical discourse of the time. On the other hand, Goujoun shows his expertise and familiarity with the current state of research. Goujon's self-fashioning as an expert in the field continues when he dismisses comparative anatomy as an explanatory system for hermaphroditism. Instead, he turns to embryogeny, references two more experts, "Doctor Coste" (140) and "Professor Courty" (141), and promises "the knowledge necessary to resolve such questions" (140).

18 Dreger's research also shows that the two case studies did not have the effect desired by the proponents of the 'true sex' doctrine. She explains that "the medical men reporting the case of Sophie V. specifically referred to Barbin's suicide as a reason to worry about forcing an unfamiliar new sex on a hermaphrodite patient" (*Hermaphrodites* 29). Similarly, Franz von Neugebauer, a late 19th century expert on hermaphroditism, remarks in his discussion of

With this outcome, the reports may be said to confirm Foucault's thesis that the medical discourse on sex in the nineteenth century was part of "an entire machinery for producing true discourses concerning it" (*Will* 69). And rather than a deficiency there was "an excess, a redoubling, too much rather than not enough discourse" (64) on sex. Medicine was part of this "incitement to discourse" (17) on sex and the reason for the extraordinary interest in sex was the expectation that "the most secret and profound truths about the individual, that [...] what he is and what determines him" (Foucault *Memoirs* x) were to be 'found' in sex. Medicine, Foucault explains, had adapted the "ancient procedure of confession to the rules of scientific discourse" (*Will* 68) and connected truth, sex, and confession. The sexual confession, explains Foucault, came to be constituted in scientific terms, 1) "*Through a clinical codification of the inducement to speak*" (*Will* 65), i.e. the two, formerly distinct practices of physical examination and confession were combined and formed the medical consultation; 2) "*Through the postulate of a general and diffuse causality*" (65), i.e. sex was conceived as linked to everything in the body and the minds of patients. Whether there was a physical problem, nervousness, or a bad habit – sex could be the cause; 3) "*Through the principle of a latency intrinsic to sexuality*" (66), i.e. the truth about sexuality was supposed to be very difficult to determine. This was not because it was indecent to talk about it, but because it was inherent in the 'nature' of sexuality that it involved something that tried to stay hidden and undetermined – even to the person who wanted to say everything about it; 4) "*Through the method of interpretation*" (66f), i.e. following from the principle of latency, the sinner who confessed all his sins could never realize or understand the complete truth about them. Therefore, the confession needed to be interpreted by the person who listened and the listener became the person who explained the truth to the sinner-patient; and 5) "*Through the medicalization of the effects of confession*" (67), i.e. the confession was recodified as a therapeutic

---

Barbin's case that the experiences with gender reassignments (as in the Barbin case) do not support the 'true' sex doctrine: "Theoretisch sollte man annehmen, dass mit dem Momente, wo Alexina die soziale Stellung und die Rechte eines Mannes zuerkannt waren, ihre seelischen Qualen allmählich schwinden würden, dass er das moralische Gleichgewicht wiederlangen würde, die Erfahrung spricht jedoch dagegen" ("Interessante" 39f).

operation: "Spoken in time, to the proper party, and by the person who was both the bearer of it and responsible for it, the truth healed" (67). While the sinner was promised salvation after ze confessed hir sins, transgressions, or excessive behavior, the patient who participated in a medico-scientific examination and truth production was judged against the normal and the pathological (cf. 67). The determination of 'the truth' was a crucial part of the cure and necessary for the healing process. The medical interrogation is then one example of a confessional mode of truth production and the reports of Dr. Chesnet and Dr. Goujon show how simple a truth was constructed along the lines of discourse despite contradictory findings.

Ambivalent Truth:
The Juridico-Religious Mode of Confession

Turning from medical reports to Barbin's text, this analysis now focuses on the modes of truth production and confessional practices as presented by Barbin. From the beginning of the text, ze confesses to numerous transgresssions of the daily routines of the religious institutions ze grew up in.[19] Sexuality is a recurring topic of these confessions, such as hir sexual awakening in the arms of a nun (cf. *Memoirs* 32), the development of "*strange hallucinations*" (33) that haunt hir at night while lying awake in the girls' dormitory and finally hir "real passion" (48) for hir fellow teacher Sara. Barbin remarks casually that a "year slipped by" (52) while they explore their love and sexuality, before ze finally finds hir way to "the man

---

19 While Barbin at times claims to have led a solitary life during her youth, marked by difference and isolation, she also reports being the object of admiration of hir fellow students and enjoying the company of special friends (cf. *Memoirs* 26f). At age eleven, Barbin took to regularly visiting her 17 year old friend Lea in her dormitory after bed time (cf. 11). Aged 17, Barbin paid nightly visits to Thécla (cf. 27f), and as a teacher Barbin finally shared hir bed with fellow teacher Sara (cf. 47ff). All these transgressions were noted and critically remarked upon by the respective representatives of the pedagogical or religious institution. And while "the pious exhortations" (12), the repeated appeals to the "feeling of modesty" (28) and to the "proprieties that must be observed, even among *girls*" (56), regularly drew tears from the child and young adult, Barbin never changed the habit.

who, here below, occupies the place of God – the confessor" (54f). Knowing very well that ze was "usurping a place, a title, that human and divine laws forbade [hir]" (52), Barbin and Sara nevertheless dream of "belonging to each other forever, in the presence of heaven, that is to say, through marriage" (52). At the time, Barbin is living as a woman. Through the relationship to Sara though, Barbin seems to conceptualize hirself as male, as Neuman points out: "Alexina thinks of it [the relationship between Sara and Barbin] heterosexually. To make love to a woman is to be a man" ("Autobiography" 145).[20] Barbin talks about having made Sara hir "mistress" (*Memoirs* 54), stresses hir part in the relationship as dominant and active, and is even afraid of having impregnated Sara (cf. 51, 58, 64). Whether this fear is justified due to the nature of their sexual encounters or merely a standard marker of an illegitimate heterosexual affair cannot be clarified. While I agree with Neuman's observation that Barbin heterosexualizes the relationship with Sara and thereby renders hirself male, I think it is necessary to stress that Barbin's masculinization of hirself is strongly rooted in the 'nature' of their *relationship* – not in the 'nature' of hir *anatomy*. There is no evidence that Barbin's physical appearance lead hir to believe ze is male. Rather, I would argue, Barbin's male self-conception needs to be understood as an effect of a strong heterosexual norm that almost automatically turns Barbin male. This argument is supported by Sara's first reaction to Barbin's love confession: "'from the depths of my soul I love you as I have never loved before. […] I sometimes envy the lot of the man who will be your husband.' Struck by the strangeness of my words, Sara was afraid; […] she did not try to give them an impossible meaning" (50). Sara seems to have no means to process the love confession of a woman to a woman. Such a meaning would be "impossible." But later, the pious Sara has developed an effective way to make sense of the situation and takes pleasure in using masculine pronouns for Barbin (cf. 58). A heterosexual love affair, albeit illicit, seems a well-known pre-text for the two lovers. So, the heterosexualization of their relationship and Barbin's masculinization is a form of crisis management and based on performative actions in their relationship rather than a re-conceptualization of Barbin's anatomy. Furthermore, Barbin's use of

---

20 See Donoghue "Imagined" for an analysis of the conflation between 'lesbian' women and hermaphrodites in Britain in the 17th and 18th century.

pronouns for hirself changes throughout the French text and a definitive (linguistic) gender cannot be determined. Therefore, Epstein concludes, "Barbin's language itself reflects ambiguity and indecision" ("Either/Or" 115).

Aside from the confessional structure of the narrative as a whole, the first explicit confession scene in the text features Barbin, who decides to talk to a priest and confess "such enormities" and "weaknesses" (*Memoirs* 55) that the Abbé H. does not offer "words of peace" (55), but heaps scorn and insults upon Barbin (cf. 55). While Barbin repeatedly emphasizes Sara's piety and innocence, Sara is never said to confess their relationship to a priest. Rather, Barbin portrays Sara as the one who wants to hide their relationship due to her fear of scandal and ruin. Maybe the truth Sara has created for herself is enough to calm her conscience. Barbin, however, feels a need for confession, but is disappointed by its outcome: ze leaves the Abbé "with an embittered heart, completely resolved to break now with such a guide, whose unspeakable moral code was at best fit to estrange a weak and ignorant person from goodness" (55). Barbin is obviously dissatisfied with the "ferocious inflexibility" (55) of the Abbé and it becomes obvious that, for hir, salvation – the fourth aspect of Foucault's notion of confession – is an integral part of the process. The monk does not only deny Barbin salvation, he also defies the production of truth about hir, or, rather, Barbin chooses not to build an identity from the "scorn and insults" (55) ze is confronted with.

Sure enough Barbin abandons Abbé H. and turns to a different confessor: "I appeal here to the judgment of my readers in time to come. I appeal to that feeling that is lodged in the heart of every son of Adam. Was I guilty, criminal, because a gross mistake had assigned me a place in the world that should not have been mine?" (54) The reader as confessor is asked to provide the understanding and salvation ze longs for. One has to note, though, that the confession to the reader is different from the confession to the Abbé: in hir narrative to the reader, Barbin already hints at a "gross mistake" that ze is the victim of and that seems to be the reason for this "false, exceptional situation" (55). At the time when ze confessed to the Abbé, ze was legally assigned female and lived as a woman. As the content of the confession remains untold, it is not clear whether Barbin is only telling the Abbé about hir relationship with Sara or whether ze is also trying to legitimize their relationship by pointing to hir as yet unnamed 'situation.' In any case, the Abbé does not approve of their relationship and, for Barbin, the ritual misses its point: ze has told him what ze believed to be the truth and expects to be awarded salvation in return, which is refused. Whether the reader as confessor and judge will show more mercy or understanding is questionable: after all, Barbin's confession remains vague. Neither does ze offer an account of hir confession to the priest nor does ze explain hir predicament to the reader. While claiming to tell the truth, the summarized account of the first confession to the priest and the address to the reader veil the truth more than produce or show it.

The second explicit confession scene in the text takes place at Barbin's former school. Hir plan is "to unburden [hir]self quite frankly to this unknown confessor and to await his judgment" (61f). The exact content of hir "strange confession" (62) again remains untold. And from the reaction of the monk it cannot clearly be deduced whether Barbin is telling him ze is in fact male, as in 'possessing male physical characteristics,' or whether ze is only confessing hir love to and sexual relationship with Sara. Barbin reports his judgment as follows:

'I shall not tell you,' he said to me, 'what you know as well as I do, that is to say, you are here and now entitled to call yourself a man in society. Certainly you are, but how will you obtain the legal right to do so? At the price of the greatest scandals, perhaps. However, you cannot keep your present position, which is so full of danger. And so, the advice I am giving you is this: withdraw from the world and become a nun; but be very careful not to repeat the confession that you have made to me, for a convent of women would not admit you. This is the only course that I have to propose to you, and believe me, accept it.' (62)

On the one hand, the monk acknowledges Barbin's right to call himself a man. Unfortunately, Barbin does not tell us how he reaches this conclusion. After all, hir physical characteristics had already caused a certain anxiety or been the subject of joking remarks on different occasions (e.g. the development of facial hair and lack of well-rounded limbs [cf. 26]; lack of menstruation [cf. 39]; chronic ill health [cf. 26, 42]). Nevertheless, these aspects are not mentioned in the confession scene with the monk and it might well be that, rather than having re-read Barbin's physical characteristics as male, the monk confirms once again what Neuman had proposed earlier: "To make love to a woman is to be a man" ("Autobiography" 145). On the other hand, the monk advises Barbin to become a nun and to live as a woman – without sexual activity, but still as a woman. From my perspective, this judgment reveals that Barbin does not discuss hir anatomy with the monk at all. Rather, the topic of hir confession is the sexual intimacy ze enjoys with Sara and the monk bases his interpretation of Barbin's social status on hir transgressive sexual behavior.

Butler and also Wing explain why the love between Barbin and Sara was so scandalous that, on the one hand, it was not possible to talk about it while, on the other hand, they were able to share intimacies in public with few consequences: as two women, brought up in piety and in religious institutions, Barbin and Sara were expected to search out the love of their fellow "sisters" and "mothers" (Butler *Gender* 105). Wing points out that moral authorities like Madame P., Sara's mother, encourage their intimacy from the start and thereby facilitate their relationship (cf. Wing "Simplified" 113). Barbin and Sara's fault was not to love each other – it was to love each other *too much*. Butler maintains that their shared sexuality is therefore an effect, a product of the ambivalent structure of the rules of conduct for young women – and not related to their physical characteristics. In contrast to the heterosexualization of their love affair and Barbin's masculinization, this argument explicitly renders their affair homosexual and both of them female: in this case, Barbin and Sara were guilty of loving too much – a question of quantity and not quality. The monk seems to be caught between these different explanations and unable to decide or choose just one. He grants Barbin the right to call himself a man and renders their relationship 'heterosexual.' Yet he advises hir to live as a nun, which is only possible as a woman and at the same time 'homosexualizes' their relationship. The results of these confessions are therefore very ambivalent, even contradictory. Barbin's sex remains unclear, and the juridico-religious mode of confession is compromised in its ability to produce 'truth.'

Simple Truth: The Medico-Scientific Mode of Confession

Barbin's text gives an account of two extensive medical examinations during hir life. The first one already bears a number of the characteristics of the medico-scientific mode of truth production described by Foucault, but Barbin is not satisfied with the results: recurring pains in the groin lead Sara to call a doctor for Barbin, who strongly protests. The setting of the examination by Doctor T. already creates a rather dubious atmosphere. At six o'clock in the evening, without candles, the room was only "plunged in a half-light" (*Memoirs* 68) and the answers Barbin provides to the doctor's questions "bewildered" rather than "enlightened him" (68). Apparently, the truth about hir pains could not be brought to light simply by questioning; the doctor decides to make use of "certain privileges" and starts a physical examination of his patient. Barbin remains covered while the doctor's "hand was already slipping under [hir] sheet and coming to a stop at the sensitive place. It pressed upon it several times, as if to find there the solution to a difficult problem" (68). The fact that Barbin stresses and explains the change in the techniques of examination – from doctor-patient interview to a physical examination – indicate that previous consultations with medical experts, e.g. due to hir absent menses, did not necessarily involve a physical examination. Despite half-light and a patient under cover who wishes him "a hundred feet under the ground" (69), Doctor T. seems to 'find' what he was looking for and Barbin remarks that "it exceeded all his expectations" (69). The doctor is unable to phrase his discovery though as only "muffled exclamations" (68) and sentences in "fits and starts" (69) escape his throat. Wing seems convinced that the doctor discovers the truth about Barbin in his examination, which for Wing consists of Barbin's "status as an intersexual" ("Simplified" 118) as manifested in "anatomical variance [...] and fluid gender identity" (118). Wing further argues that the doctor's "speechlessness is not only a sign of his great astonishment, but of his inability to speak of a difference so radical as to confound his verbal/conceptual world" (118f). This interpretation seems supported by Barbin's narrative: "he was obliged to take the initiative that his title and his faith as an honest man demanded of him; [...] indecision was not permitted; it was a grave fault, not only morally but in the eyes of the law" (*Memoirs* 70). In contrast to Wing and Barbin hirself, I am not convinced of the 'truth' of the findings of the doctor and the necessary consequences.

First of all, the doctor always addresses Barbin as *"mademoiselle."* If we believe the editor's claims to authentic reproduction of the original manuscript, then the italics were added by Barbin himself, who also points out that the doctor looks at hir "with a half-smile" (69). This implication of a tongue-in-cheek-manner can be read in various ways. It could be an expression of his insecurity towards the new situation. It might also be a supportive gesture and indicate a partner in crime-mentality of the doctor as in 'I know who you are, and that is fine.' Or, it might simply be a part of Barbin's dramatization of the events. After all, ze is the one who blames the doctor for not acting on his findings and transfers all responsibility to him. Thereby, ze renders hirself a passive object and excuses hirself from responsibility.[21] Secondly, the course of action the doctor takes does not give a clear indication of his diagnosis: did he find Barbin to be a man? Or, as Wing suggests, did he find hir to be intersex? While the category 'intersex' did not exist at the time, 'hermaphrodite' or 'pseudo-hermaphrodite' were available. Yet I would argue that this is not what Barbin expects. Although ze is convinced that hir relationship with Sara and possibly also hir position at the girl's school is inappropriate, ze never explains the reason for this inappropriateness. Therefore, I contend that Barbin, the monk and the doctor share a similar dilemma: the systems of knowledge, the discourses that surround them, offer different ways of structuring the information they encounter. The monk could not decide whether Barbin was male or female, 'homo- or heterosexual' because there was evidence for both interpretations. Barbin seems aware of a certain distance between hir body and the body of other girls and women. Yet ze also suffers as a result of hir desire and passion for these girls and perceives them as transgressive. Similar to the monk, ze cannot place hir transgression: does the 'problem' reside in hir body and is it the source for hir transgressive desires? Or did hir transgressive desires shape hir body? As a doctor, Doctor T. has access to a different system of knowledge,

---

21 In a similar manner, Barbin holds Madame P. responsible when ze accuses her of not having investigated the matter any further for selfish reasons (cf. 70). According to Barbin, Madame P. "drove her naïveté so far as to believe that I was completely ignorant of my position ... That was absurdity pushed to the last degree!!" (70). Barbin repeatedly excuses hir own liability in this process but seldom extends hir forgiveness to others.

scientific-medical discourse, and Barbin expects him to finally decide on this wobbling question and to determine the 'truth.' Doctor T. tries to do just that but he is, of course, caught up in the medical discourse of his time. After the examination, he prescribes Barbin some remedies against the pains and urges Madame P. to send Barbin away – but without giving a full explanation. If he had come to the conclusion that Barbin was in fact male, he might have been able to phrase a clear diagnosis and to pronounce it. However, as it was, his examination did not provide the doctor with enough convincing information, or 'facts,' for such a step. Evidently, Barbin's physical characteristics gave him cause for some anxiety, but hir social position as a woman, as a teacher at a girls' school and an intimate friend of the pious Sara overruled these findings.[22] In hir narrative, Barbin recalls the following scene when meeting Doctor T. on one of hir walks with Sara: "I would nudge Sara with my elbow. As he passed, he would always greet me with a smile! What must he have thought when he saw us laughing, the pair of us!!! What a strange situation! ... His silence, his attitude in my regard, seemed a revolting enormity to me" (71). The "revolting enormity" ze claims to feel may be due to hir own feelings of inappropriateness. Ze cannot place or name hir feelings and neither can the doctor. As stated above, Wing explains this speechlessness with the doctor's inability to speak of a radical difference, an impossibility to speak of what is not allowed to exist. Here, Wing emphasizes and essentializes the difference of Barbin's anatomy and interprets the silence on these differences as a discursive negation of hermaphroditic – or, in his words, intersex – reality. I disagree with Wing's reading for a simple reason: I doubt the positive and distinct significance of the material body for Doctor T. As Neuman points out he was a nineteenth century doctor who performed

at a historical juncture when two contradictory paradigms defining masculinity, femininity, and the relation between them were culturally current. The *psychology* of

---

22 The report by Dr. Chesnet, who Barbin calls Dr. H. in hir narrative, also shows that within the medical discourse of the time, a number of characteristics were perceived as markers of 'true' sex, e.g. sexual desire was one aspect that was clearly understood as being connected to the sex of the person. Barbin's desire for women was perceived as a clear indicator for hir maleness (cf. *Memoirs* 127).

masculinity, femininity and heterosexuality, since the seventeenth century, had increasingly been defined in terms of the *differences* between the sexes. [...] At the same time, however, the medical discourse of sexual morphology was still formulated, as it had been from the time of Aristotle and Galen and through the Renaissance, in terms of *similarities* between the sexes. ("Autobiography" 141)

The doctor may have been surprised, perplexed or confused by Barbin's physiology, but not to a degree that he questions hir status as a woman. Within the paradigm of a one-sex model where the homology of bodies, their similar development, is emphasized, a continuum between forms of bodies is granted and variations support rather than weaken the paradigm. On the social level, Barbin performs successfully as a woman and the doctor has no reason to doubt that. While Barbin and Wing criticize him for his inaction, I agree with Neuman and deem it perfectly understandable within the medical discourse of the time.

Without a satisfying answer to hir questions, Barbin continues hir quest for 'truth,' for "counsel and protection" (76), and visits the bishop of hir hometown, Monsigneur de B. The content of Barbin's confession is not repeated, but ze assures the reader that it was "complete" (76) and the reaction of the bishop finally offers what Barbin claimed to be hoping for: "Everything that the Christian religion can offer by way of encouragement, consolation – I felt it then! ... The few moments that I spent in the presence of that very great man are perhaps the most beautiful ones of my life" (77). While the bishop is able to provide a form of relief from the immediate fear and sorrow, he delegates the details of the inquiry to a doctor: "'I don't know yet how all this is going to turn out. [...] I cannot be a judge in such a matter. I shall see my doctor this very day. I will come to an understanding with him about what course of action to take.'" Here, the religious confession is only the frame for the medico-scientific examination that is going to follow and that is supposed to finally 'bring to light' the truth about Barbin's sex and sexuality. The examination by Doctor H., "a man of science in the full sense of the word," is a prime example of the sexual confession as constituted in scientific terms. Doctor H. explains his approach to his patient Barbin:

'Here you must regard me not only as a doctor but also as a confessor. I must not only see for myself, I must also know everything you can tell me. This is a grave moment for you, more so than you think, perhaps. I must be able to answer for you with complete assurance, before Monsigneur first of all, and also, no doubt, before the law, which will appeal to my evidence.' (78)

Doctor H. makes clear that he sees his task in providing evidence to solve Barbin's problem and points to his twin role as doctor and confessor. As such, he subjects Barbin to a "thorough examination" (77) and initiates himself literally and metaphorically into what Barbin refers to as hir "dearest secrets" (78). A physical examination, however, is only a part of the whole process of the production of 'truth.' In addition, the doctor needs to know everything Barbin can tell him and assures hir that he will answer for hir. This process illustrates the differences between the religious and the medico-scientific mode of confession as Foucault describes them:

The truth did not reside solely in the subject who, by confessing, would reveal it wholly formed. It was constituted in two stages: present but incomplete, blind to itself, in the one who spoke, it could only reach completion in the one who assimilated and recorded it. It was the latter's function to verify this obscure truth: the revelation of confession had to be coupled with the decipherment of what it said. The one who listened was not simply the forgiving master, the judge who condemned or acquitted; he was the master of truth. (*Will* 66f)

Barbin needs to tell Doctor H. everything ze knows. But, Doctor H. is under no allusion that what ze tells him is already the 'truth.' Rather, the doctor is the one who needs to gather as much information as possible; he structures and organizes it and this information then leads to a final interpretation. Following the questioning and the examination, Barbin remarks: "science conceded that it was convinced" and Doctor H. announces his conclusion to Barbin's mother, "It's true that you've lost your daughter, [...] but you've found a son" (*Memoirs* 78).

The Monseigneur is informed about the doctor's 'findings,' underlines the latter's authority and proclaims: "'I have seen the doctor [...] and I know everything'" (80). This confirms the validity and significance of the scientific report. From the beginning, Doctor H. was confident that he could explain and justify his decision and never thought of the need to hide the truth to reduce any possible scandal. The former confessions all contained a moment of silencing and of covering up the respective decision literally and metaphorically. The scientifically produced truth now stands out in broad daylight and the church, the law, Barbin and hir mother, Sara and Madame P., and the whole city acknowledge it: a second medical examination confirms the first one, Barbin's civil status is legally changed or, from the doctor's perspective, 'corrected' from female to male, ze is given a new first name and after Barbin attends church dressed "as a man [...] the whole town was talking about it" (90). The local and regional newspapers pick up the story of the young man who grew up among girls and Barbin is "the subject of all the conversations at the seashore bathing establishment" (90). Despite its public attention, the truth of the story as such was not questioned at all. Only a few weeks later, Barbin states that "the stir caused by [hir] adventure was beginning to die down. The situation was better appreciated now that it stood out in broad daylight" (94). The medico-scientific mode of confession succeeded, so it seems, in establishing a simple truth about Barbin's sex. The doubts and ambivalences that former confessions carried with them were ruled out and the final and official truth declared: Barbin was a man. His new name and official civil status should finally provide him access to his 'true' place in society. Moreover, according to doctors, officials and newspapers, the "dénouement" (79; 88) is expected.

Unfortunately, the narrative does not end on this 'happy note' and Barbin soon proves to have grown very critical of the validity of the doctor's findings. Ze anticipates hir autopsy and explains:

[...] a few doctors will make a little stir around my corpse; they will shatter all the extinct mechanisms of its impulses, will draw new information from it, will analyze all the mysterious sufferings that were heaped up on a single human being. O princes of science, enlightened chemists, whose names resound throughout the world, analyze then, if that is possible, all the sorrows that have burned, devoured this heart down to its last fibers; all the scalding tears that have drowned it, squeezed it dry in their savage grasp! Discover how many wounds scathing contempt, abuse, vile mockery, bitter sarcasm, have inflicted upon it, and you will have discovered the secret that the tombstone pitilessly keeps! (103f)

Barbin doubts that the "princes of science" and "enlightened chemists" as ze ironically calls the doctors will be able to discover the truth about hir. After all, hir corpse might seem to provide new information for them, but to discover the "secret," ze demands to analyze the "sorrows," the "tears," and the "wounds" suffered from contempt, abuse, mockery, and sarcasm. The medico-scientific discourse, supposedly ruled by reason and an examination of the material body will not be able to follow hir advice. Here, Barbin aptly points to the failure of the discipline to capture lived experience and manages to reject the truth-producing power of the discourse even after hir death. Barbin's text, I conclude, has dismantled both the medico- scientific and the juridico-religious mode of truth production as inadequate. The value of their truth claims is consequently challenged and will be contrasted with the autobiographical mode of confession in the following part.

Impossible Truth:
The Autobiographical Mode of Confession

"Western man has become a confessing animal," explains Foucault, thinking of the imperative to confess everything from the most ordinary everyday experiences to horrible crimes and unspeakable abominations (*Will* 59). But the "obligation to confess is now [...] so deeply ingrained in us, that we no longer perceive it as the effect of a power that constrains us; on the contrary, it seems to us that truth, lodged in our most secret nature, 'demands' only to surface. [...] Confession frees, but power reduces one to silence" (60). This notion of confession, speech as liberating inverts the proverbial 'golden silence' and Foucault sees the discourse of confession mirrored in the development of literature. He argues, "we have passed from a pleasure to be recounted and heard, centering on the heroic or marvelous narration of 'trials' of bravery or sainthood, to a literature ordered according to the infinite task of extracting from the depths of oneself, in between the words, a truth which the very form of the confession holds out like a shimmering mirage" (59). Autobiographical writing or life narratives are exactly the kind of confessional literature that Foucault is describing here. A thorough self-examination should give way to the truth that is expected to be suppressed by censorship and taboos regarding speaking and thinking. Barbin's text bears witness to this obligation to confess: various transgressions are dutifully recorded, ecstatic dreams recounted, and arrogant pretensions pointed out. Nevertheless, ze is critical of the power of confession and after the medical diagnosis ze reflects doubtfully:

This inevitable outcome, which I had foreseen, had even desired, terrified me now like a revolting enormity. In short, I had provoked it, no doubt it was my duty to have done so; but who knows? Perhaps I had been wrong. Didn't this abrupt change, which was going to reveal me in such an unexpected way, offend all the laws of conventional behavior? ... Was it likely that society, which is so severe, so blind in its judgments, would give me credit for an impulse that might pass for honesty? [...] I was driven to it by the thought of duty that had to be fulfilled. I did not calculate. (*Memoirs* 79f)

Eventually, the confession that ze had urged on out of "duty" fails to liberate hir: ze loses hir job as a highly qualified teacher and hir successful career is over. Ze loses hir lover Sara, and ze loses the admiration of fellow teachers and the family ze lives with. Instead of producing an identity for Barbin, the truth rather robs hir of an identity and dismantles the discourse of truth; the confession in its various disguises (literary, medico-scientific, juridico-religious), reveals itself to be oppressive.

Following the moment of truth, the medical diagnosis, a conventional "dénouement" (79) is announced by the family's benefactor M. de Saint-M., but the text diverts from convention and refuses to participate in the confessional mode any longer. Rather, Barbin learns and explores the values of silence and secrecy: upon hir return to the boarding school, Sara's gaze reproaches Barbin for having made the confession: "'If you had wished,' said that gaze, 'we could have been happy for many days longer'" (80). And when Mme P. asks for an explanation, Barbin decides to withhold the truth and to lie to protect Sara: "Should I have answered with a brutal confession, thus withering that chaste flower whose perfume still intoxicated me? No, certainly not. [...] The secret of our love would have to be kept between God and myself" (83) – and the reader, one might want to add. Yet, despite Barbin's withholding of some details of their relationship, soon "hateful rumors circulated among the public" (91) and ze experiences again the negative consequences of the 'truth.'

Barbin then tries to escape to Paris, and the continuous narrative is replaced by fragments. The quest for identity that had lead Barbin to participate in various forms of confessional practices now seems to come to an end. Ze conjures images that emphasize hir singularity and describes the distance ze feels now towards man as "an abyss between them and myself, a barrier that cannot be crossed" (102). Ze rejects the status assigned hir by the medical experts and distances hirself from man – *man* read here in its double meaning as "male human" and as "mankind." Being unable to find a place in society, Barbin tries to connect to a 'higher' level and to transcend "earthly ties" (99): ze not only rejects masculinity and men, but also femininity and women, and aligns hirself with angels: "I soar above all your innumerable miseries, partaking of the nature of the angels; for, as you have said, my place is not in your narrow sphere. You have the earth, I have boundless space" (99). Neuman remarks with reference to the fragmented part of the text that "[m]ost particularly, Abel/Herculine no longer speaks of his body" ("Autobiography" 147) and explains that "[m]asculinity, as rhetoric, consists precisely in this disembodiment" (148). Yet Porter reads the fragmented part as evidence that "there is no true self because there is finally no clear gender" ("Figuration" 135). Moreover, he argues, "Barbin's *Memoirs* function as an unconscious parody of the crisis-and-conversion form" (134) and points out that the "conventional awakening to one's truest essence never takes place" (134). Barbin's rhetoric in the fragmented part is then an attempt "to break the norms of conventional autobiography" (134) and, linked to this, a violation of the obligation, the "duty," to confess. But, as Porter also notes, Barbin's text was never the "complete" confession that ze claims. Even in the coherently told, retrospective first part of the text, Barbin "prefers not to reveal too much, and is generally fascinated with illusions and buried truths" (130). Through allusions to and comparisons with drama, myth, and fiction the text stages Barbin's life, or rather hir life writing, as a narrative construction.[23] The *Memoirs*, concludes Porter, draw "a veil between autobiographer and reader, though the gesture encourages us to peer – we are turned into voyeurs, but discern little about what Herculine really felt at the time" (130). The truth about the autobiographical 'self' is revealed to be nothing but a normative literary convention. Barbin's text engages with different modes of truth production, but neither the medico-scientific, the juridico-religious, nor the autobiographical mode of confession succeed in establishing a lasting or convincing truth. By abandoning the requirements of the genre *autobiography* in the final part of the text, Barbin draws attention to the

---

23 The text repeatedly draws comparisons to mythical or religious figures and styles Barbin and other characters as actors in their own lives (cf. *Memoirs 18; 35;* 82; 87; 88; 89; 90; 96; 106; 114).

normative discourse and challenges its capacity to produce the truth about an individual. Ze calls hirself "a disinherited creature, a being without a name" (*Memoirs* 100) and turns literally and metaphorically a referent without a signifier, free-floating and unattached – unattachable.

'WHAT STRANGE BLINDNESS MADE ME HOLD ON UNTIL THE END?': CLOSING THE TEXT

Barbin's text dismantles the juridico-religious, the medico-scientific and the autobiographical modes of truth production. Ultimately, they all provoke the opposite of what they set out to achieve: instead of one 'true sex', Barbin was assigned a number of different sexes and the promised truth multiplied. The obligation to confess and to look for a truth has erased the possibility to continue "the happy limbo of a non-identity" (Foucault *Memoirs* xiii). While *autobiography* is a genre well-adapted to the narrative needs of a sex change, it remains tied to the confession and to the discourse of a singular 'truth,' the essence of a 'self.' This requirement is challenged and rejected by Barbin's text. Hir shifting identifications as a woman, as a man, as neither of the two, both or something else entirely, go well beyond the limits of the genre and render the search for the truth about Barbin futile. While ze did successfully escape the narrative requirements of a 'true sex' and identity, hir suicide tragically demonstrates the real life consequences of a 'true' sex doctrine. From this perspective, Foucault's sub-title for the English edition *Being the Recently Discovered Memoirs of a Nineteenth-Century French Hermaphrodite* seems an anachronistic sex assignment: neither Barbin hirself nor the doctors of hir time called hir a "hermaphrodite." Barbin's *Memoirs* live on and continue to lend themselves to new formations of the discourse on truth and identity. New readings of the text may generate new questions or provide new answers to the old ones. Thereby, the discursive process of the production of truth continues and what Barbin calls "that thirst for the unknown" (*Memoirs* 114) remains unsatisfied.

N.O. Body and the Making of a True Man

WHAT MAKES A MAN?

In November 1906, Magnus Hirschfeld, medical doctor, early sexologist and activist for gay rights, gave a talk at a medical society with the title "Three Cases of Erroneous Sex Determination."[1] Announced as a 'lecture with demonstration,' Hirschfeld did not come alone but brought along a number of artifacts and three of his patients. He started his talk with a critique on the legal situation of persons of doubtful sex: with the introduction of the new Civil Code (BGB) in 1900, he explained, the very useful paragraphs on hermaphroditism from the Prussian Civil Code (ALR, installed in 1794) had been abolished. Yet science had since proven, Hirschfeld argued, that 'true' hermaphroditism in humans was real and in existence (cf. "Drei Fälle" 614) and passed around photographs to illustrate his claim. While he admitted that 'true' hermaphroditism in humans was rare, 'doubtful sex' was a rather frequent occurrence and he referred to a list of cases collected by one of the leading experts on hermaphroditism, Franz von Neugebauer (cf. 614). The list contained roughly 1,200 cases and was published in different parts in Hirschfeld's *Yearbook of Sexual Intermediaries*.[2] Hirschfeld then introduced the audience to a patient he

---

1 The German title is "Drei Fälle von irrtümlicher Geschlechtsbestimmung" and the talk was published in the journal *Medizinische Reform: Halbmonatsschrift für soziale Hygiene und praktische Medizin* XIV.51 (1906): 614-7.

2 Neugebauer continuously expanded his collection and published it in 1908 as *Hermaphroditismus beim Menschen*. "Case 1061" in this study is an account of "Alexina B." i.e. Herculine Barbin including a long citation from Tardieu's

called Anna Laabs, whom he had diagnosed as a 'person with doubtful sex.' His description of the 'case' Laabs consists mainly of a medical report that he wrote for court to support Laabs' official transition from female to male and ends with a definitive conclusion: in reality, Anna Laabs was a man.[3] An analysis of the report, however, reveals that the evidence he offers was not as decisive as his final judgment might suggest. The report is structured in four parts: anamnesis, current situation, genitalia and sex drive, and epicrisis. This structure is borrowed from the famous questionnaire that Hirschfeld and the Scientific-Humanitarian Committee (WhK), the group that published the *Yearbook*, used to collect data on their 'patients' (cf. Hirschfeld "Objektive Diagnose" 26-35). The questionnaire shows that various factors were deemed influential for the determination of a person's sex and, for Hirschfeld, sex assignment was a complex procedure. He recounts Laabs' family history, summarizes her accounts of her childhood (wild; prefers playing outside; outstanding student), describes Laabs' physical appearance (height; weight; body form; hair growth; voice; breathing type etc.) and mental capacity and character (strong-minded; advanced abstract thinking skills; not emotional; not interested in acting, perfumes, or fashion; exhibits a preference for dark colors; 'male' handwriting). He emphasizes that Laabs is physically and mentally healthy, although suffering temporarily from insomnia due to inner conflicts. The third part is divided into a description of the genitalia and Laabs' sex drive or desire (aversion against sexual activity with men; sexual desire exclusively directed towards women). The examination of the genital tract led Hirschfeld and fellow doctors Georg Merzbach and Iwan Bloch to conclude: at the moment, the genitalia were of a quite masculine type.[4] The experts identified a 'penis' (4 cm; capable of erection). Moreover, they felt one 'testicle' in a 'split scrotum' and suspected the

---

French edition of the *Memoirs* (cf. 542ff). Separate entries exist for N.O. Body's *Maiden Years* (cf. 126) and for Hirschfeld's report on Anna Laabs (cf. 254). The identity of Laabs, Body and Baer is not revealed.

3   "[…], dass Laabs in Wirklichkeit Mann ist" ("Drei Fälle" 616).

4   "Die Geschlechtsteile, welche ausser von dem Unterzeichneten u.a. von Dr. med. G. Merzbach zu Berlin und Dr. med. J. Bloch zu Charlottenburg inspiziert wurden, zeigen nach übereinstimmender Diagnose zurzeit einen durchaus männlichen Typus" (615).

other to be inside the body. Yet, further examinations did not reveal a 'prostate gland' and the 'ejaculate' failed to contain any sperm. These findings, Myriam Spörri argues, are inconclusive and Hirschfeld's diagnosis failed to deliver the irrefutable evidence for Laabs' 'true' male sex.[5] Despite these diagnostic 'shortcomings,' Laabs' request was granted and her sex was officially changed from female to male.

Laabs, whose real name was first Martha Baer, then Karl M. Baer, wrote his memoirs and published them as *Aus eines Mannes Mädchenjahren* (*'Memoirs of a Man's Maiden Years'*[6]) in 1907. The account was published under the pseudonym N.O. Body and accompanied by a foreword by publisher and writer Rudolf Presber and an epilogue by Hirschfeld. *Maiden Years* tells the story of a young man, Norbert O. Body, who had been assigned female at birth and grew up as a girl, Nora O. Body. After falling in love with another woman, a doctor recognized Nora as 'truly' male and she transitioned to live on as Norbert and to marry the woman he had fallen in love with. The publication was accompanied by a number of reviews in newspapers and medical journals and the book went through at least six editions in the first year after publication. At a price of 2.50 mark apiece, it was affordable for a wide readership. An overall popularity and success of *Maiden Years* can be assumed as two movies loosely based on the text were made in the following years: *Aus eines Mannes Mädchenzeit* was produced in 1912 and *Aus eines Mannes Mädchenjahren* followed in

---

5   "Hirschfelds Schluss, dass es sich um Genitalien männlichen Geschlechts handelte, war jedoch streng wissenschaftlich nicht haltbar, denn im Ejakulat [...] konnten keine Spermien nachgewiesen werden. Spermien aber fungierten als Repräsentanten der Geschlechtsdrüsen und die Sicherstellung von Spermien garantierte dieser kausalen Logik zufolge die Existenz von Hoden und damit die zweifelsfreie Zuordnung zum männlichen Geschlecht. Hirschfelds Diagnose wurde damit den wissenschaftlichen Standards nicht gerecht. [...] Streng genommen ließe sich Hirschfelds Diagnose bloß als 'Wahrscheinlichkeitsdiagnose' bezeichnen, denn sekundäre Geschlechtsmerkmale, Genitalien und sexuelle Orientierung galten gemeinhin nur als 'unterstützende Momente' und 'Hilfsbefunde' – Supplemente, die auf die Geschlechtsdrüsen verweisen sollten, sie aber dennoch nicht gänzlich ersetzen konnten." (Spörri "N.O. Body" 251)

6   References to the English language edition hereafter referred to as *Maiden Years*; to the German edition *Mädchenjahre*.

1919. Both movies use the title of N.O. Body's narrative and some plot elements, but significantly alter the story, explains the later editor of the text historian Hermann Simon (cf. *Mädchenjahre* 195f). Simon republished the memoirs in German in 1993; an English translation followed in 2006. Moreover, Simon undertook extensive research to determine the identity of N.O. Body with Jewish functionary Karl M. Baer, born Martha Baer, and added a detailed essay on Baer's life and the publication history of the text to his edition. The English edition includes an introductory essay by Jewish literary scholar Sander L. Gilman.

Similar to Barbin's *Memoirs*, Body marks his text from the beginning as an autobiographical account written in the confessional mode: "This book tells a true story. In it, what was probably the strangest youth ever lived, shall speak with its own voice. This life needs to be believed, as strange as it may seem. But strangeness need not be equated with lies" (*Maiden Years* 7). Having claimed authenticity, Body then introduces the major conflict in the text: "In this book, I wish to speak of a life that lay like a burden on an obscure human being until a woman's soft white hands lifted the weight from him and transformed his sorrow into joie de vivre. It is the story of the confusion and conflicts that arose for me from my very own nature. I was born a boy, raised as a girl" (*Maiden Years* 7). Body here already foreshadows the conventional happy ending, i.e. a heterosexual marriage, and clears out moral doubts. Moreover, he establishes himself as 'naturally' male, a boy who had been mistaken for a girl after birth, but a boy nonetheless. Rudolf Presber prefaces Body's account, acts as a witness and confirms the authenticity of "this strange book, which contains an account only of things that have been experienced and nothing that has been invented" (*Maiden Years* 3). Moreover, he recommends it especially to "parents and educators in need of guidance" (*Maiden Years* 3). Magnus Hirschfeld continues this reasoning in the epilogue when he credits the memoir as "a substantial and valuable addition to the scientific literature on cases of erroneous sex determination. [...] this autobiography may claim general attention far beyond the world of medicine or law" (109). Baer, or rather Body, also emphasizes this aspect and explains: "I did not want to write this book, but others convinced me that I owed it to mankind as a contribution to modern psychology and that I should write it in the interest of science and truth" (108).⁷ In this mode, Body, Hirschfeld and Presber position the life story as a critical text in the discourses on pedagogy, psychology, and science in general.⁸ Likewise, various reviews stress the decency and scientific significance of the text: Hirschfeld's sister, Franziska Mann, herself a writer, praises the text in a review for the journal *Frauen-Rundschau* as the 'must-read' of the season, which bears special significance for parents, those concerned with child education, and humanity in general.⁹ P. Kempendorff seems to share Mann's judgment and echoes Presber's and Hirschfeld's claims to science and pedagogy. In addition, he proclaims in a long review for the conservative journal *Der Türmer: Monatsschrift für Gemüt und Geist* that the book touches the reader without causing sensation or shock. Moreover, he maintains that the book would not satisfy sexual desires.¹⁰ Together with Hirschfeld, Dr. Georg Merzbach had acted as a medical expert in Baer's transition and in his review of *Maiden Years* for the medical journal *Monatsschrift für Harnkrankheiten, Psychopathia Sexualis und Sexuelle Hygiene* he confirms

---

7   Throughout the text, Body positions himself as an expert in education and offers advice to teachers and parents on professional childcare, e.g. "[...] I have spoken of it [early sex play among peers] mainly to draw the attention of parents and teachers to how early sexual feelings may arise in some children" (*Maiden Years* 19; for further examples see 21, 23, 27, 107, 108).

8   Brenner reveals the emphasis on "respectability" and science as rhetoric strategies that provide "the license to talk openly about sexuality" ("Re-Dressing" 39). This argument agrees with Foucault's analysis of the "Incitement to Discourse" by pedagogy and other sciences (cf. *Will*, esp. 17-35).

9   "Diese seltsame Lebensgeschichte eines jungen Menschen wird binnen wenigen Wochen d a s Buch sein, welches man gelesen haben muß. [...] Das Buch des Herrn N.O. Body ist erlitten. Es will nicht auf seinen künstlerischen Wert hin zuerst betrachtet sein, sondern auf seinen Wert für die Menschheit. Und dieser Wert ist ein ganz bedeutender. [...] Gerade eine Zeit, die sich so viel mit der Aufklärungsfrage des Kindes beschäftigt, wird auch die Schilderung dieser Lebensgeschichte nicht übersehen können" (Mann "Review" 493f).

10 "Das Buch greift uns ans Herz. Es will nicht Sensation erregen; es wird auch dem Lüsternen, der nach ihm greift, wenig Befriedigung gewähren" (Kempendorff "Review" 498).

the maleness of the young woman and sees it proven 'beyond doubt.'[11] In summary, contemporary public opinion, Presber, Hirschfeld, and Body himself all agree on Body's unequivocal male sex.

Literary scholars, however, have since argued that Body's narrative identity is not without ambiguity: Andreas Hartmann identifies ruptures and breaks in Body's male self-identification (cf. "Geschlecht" 196f); Myriam Spörri shows that Body's maleness is neither coherent nor continuously produced and explains that, as a consequence, gender evolves as a multi-dimensional effect.[12] David Brenner calls *Maiden Years* a "marketing coup" ("Re-Dressing" 38) and argues that "the author proves himself a master of *Trivialliteratur*, drawing constantly on a hodgepodge of nineteenth-century genres: the autobiographical confessional, the narrative of uplift, the romance, the detective story, and the Freudian case history" (36). He adds the "rags-to-riches-story" (38) to his analysis of the textual genres and ultimately finds the text to be "polysemic and multigeneric" (36). Moreover, Brenner attests the text a "pleasure of multiple identities" and a "considerable investment in the activities of identity formation" (41).

The different positions on Baer's/Body's identity as either essentially and unequivocally male or as a many-faceted construct are also reflected in the debate about Baer's pseudonym *N.O. Body*: Rudolf Presber had claimed that all names and places in the text "had to be concealed out of discretion and out of consideration for the living and the dead who erred, and because of the young person's understandable shyness" (*Maiden Years* 4), and

---

11 "Erst nach mehr denn zwanzig Jahren der Enttäuschungen, der seelischen und äußeren Qualen, nahte diesem Opfer der irrtümlichen Geschlechtsbestimmung, die Referent in mehreren analogen Fällen zu beobachten Gelegenheit hatte, die Stunde der Erlösung, nachdem Dr. Hirschfeld und Referent nach gemeinsamer sorgfältiger Untersuchung die Zugehörigkeit dieses jungen Mädchens zum männlichen Geschlechte unzweifelhaft festgestellt hatten" (Merzbach "Review" 102).

12 "Verschiedene Hinweise, die verstreut im Text liegen, stellen jedoch die Kohärenz der männlichen Geschlechtsidentität in Frage und lassen damit Geschlecht nicht ein-, sondern mehrdimensional erscheinen: N.O. Body hat sich keineswegs immer nur als Knabe, als männliches Individuum begriffen. Vielmehr schwankte er zwischen weiblicher und männlicher Identität hin und her" (Spörri "N.O. Body" 256).

editor Simon remarks, "*Naturally*, [...] Baer had no desire to be identified by everyone as the author of the autobiography" (*Maiden Years* 122, emphasis added).¹³ In contrast, Brenner sees Body "indulge in public spectacle, a type of performance intimately familiar to a person engaged in role reversal and 're-dressing'" (41). Of course, the publication under pseudonym seems, on the one hand, to protect the identity of the author. On the other hand, the pseudonym is another referent for the person Karl (born Martha) Baer, whom Hirschfeld referred to as Anna Laabs, and Spörri reads the multiplicity of names as a mirror or a product of the ambiguous sexual identity of the author.¹⁴ Fabienne Imlinger contends that Baer's use of the telling pseudonym at once reproduces and undermines the gendered practices of naming (cf. "Kein Körper"). At first, in my view, Baer's identity seems disguised to a good extent by the use of the pseudonym, by changing place names, and by masking his family as French and Catholic rather than Jewish.¹⁵ At the same time, however, Karl M. Baer does not seem to strive for complete anonymity. He continues Martha Baer's life, public and private, in Berlin¹⁶ and accompanies Hirschfeld to his talk in

---

13 Similarly, an anonymous reviewer in a pedagogic journal explains that the use of a pseudonym was acceptable given the circumstances and highlights Presber's and Hirschfeld's position as authenticating witnesses of the account: "Der Verfasser verbirgt sich aus Gründen, die man anerkennen muss, hinter einem Decknamen [...] Die Bürgschaft gegenüber der Öffentlichkeit übernimmt aber der bekannte Schriftsteller Rudolf Presber [...]. Ein Nachwort stammt von Dr. med. Magnus Hirschfeld [...]" (U. "Review" 320).

14 "Diese Vielzahl an Namen kann als Spiegel, aber auch als Produkt der unklaren geschlechtlichen Identität interpretiert werden" (Spörri "N. O. Body" 259).

15 "'French' was viewed in Baer's time as a racial category as well as a political one," explains Gilman (*Maiden Years* xix), and Body's translation of Jewishness into Catholicism, he suggests, may be motivated by contemporary anti-Semitic discourse: "For Baer and for the world in which he loved, the 'damaged' genitalia of the male Jew, damaged through circumcision [...] meant that the male Jew is already neither truly male nor actually female" (xxi).

16 For example, Karl Baer continues to attend the meetings of a circle of young Zionist intellectuals that Martha Baer had participated in earlier. Of course, the sex change does not go unnoticed among the members of this circle and they know Baer to be the author of *Maiden Years* (cf. *Maiden Years 128*).

1906, where he participates in a question and answer session with the audience (cf. Hirschfeld "Drei Fälle" 616). Although editor Simon maintains that Baer's change of civil status was not discussed in public, he admits that Baer "himself seems at first to have been somewhat open about the whole affair of his changed identity" (*Maiden Years* 128). In the second half of the century, historians of sexology[17] and researchers of local history in Arolsen, Baer's place of birth, acknowledge the identity of Baer and N.O. Body in their respective works.[18] Certainly, anonymity is one aspect of a pseudonym, but this aspect may not be what moved Baer to the

>Furthermore, Karl dedicates a copy of his autobiography to the poet Theodor Zlocisti, whose poem he uses as an introduction to *Maiden Years* (cf. 128f and Simon "Kein Ende"). The university library in Berlin changes the entry in the catalogue for *Maiden Years* from "Body, N.O." to "Baer, Karl" (cf. *Mädchenjahre* 196). In addition, Karl Baer continues the work of Martha Baer and publishes articles on the white slave trade and women's rights in Eastern Europe: Simon notes three articles/books that appeared in 1908 – a full year after Baer's transition. An article called "Mädchenhandel" appeared in Presber's journal *Arena* signed with the name "M. Baer." An article signed "K. M. Baer-Berlin" is published in Hirschfeld's *Zeitschrift für Sexualwissenschaft*. And, a book by "M. Baer" called *Der internationale Mächenhandel* (cf. *Maiden Years* 134f). In 1920, Baer starts to work for the B'nai B'rith lodges in Berlin – the same Jewish organization that had paid for Martha Baer's education as a teacher of domestic science in Hamburg in 1903 and that had sent her as a social worker to Galicia the following year. Martha and Karl were both active members of the Jewish community and their identity to many not more than an open secret.

17 Manfred Herzer and James Steakley edited Hirschfeld's memoir *Von einst bis jetzt. Geschichte einer homosexuellen Bewegung 1897-1922* in 1986. Hirschfeld mentions the memoirs by N.O. Body, but does not lift the pseudonym. Nevertheless, Herzer and Steakley note in the register to the text: "Body, N.O. (d. i. Karl Baer)" (193).

18 Simon notes: "Daß Baer Hermaphrodit gewesen sei, ist der Heimatgeschichtsforschung bekannt. So findet sich in der von ihrem Vater stammenden genealogischen Kartei Ingeborg Moldenhauers (Arolsen) zu [Karl] Baer die Eintragung: 'Hermaphrodit, wurde von den Eltern als Mädchen erzogen, dann später als Mann. Sie (er) schrieb unter dem Pseudonym N. O. Body'" (*Mädchenjahre* note 67, 241).

decision. After all, *N.O. Body* is a telling name that invites speculations about the author rather than subduing them, e.g. the pseudonym disguises the sex of the author, a practice that was not uncommon among nineteenth century women writers. The Brontë sisters, for example, opted for epicene, i.e. unisex, names (Currer, Acton, and Ellis Bell), while Mary Ann Evans (George Eliot) chose a pseudonym that was clearly gendered and indicated male authorship.[19] Baer chooses a pseudonym that refers to the female Nora O. Body as well as to the male Norbert O. Body and Sander L. Gilman comments: "'N.O. Body' is a most appropriate pseudonym for Karl M. Baer (1885-1956) to have used when he sat down to pen his autobiography. For being 'nobody' was his way of seeing his body" (*Maiden Years* vii). Gilman explains that Baer felt alienated from his body "as it was male as well as female, Jewish as well as German" (vii). Hermann Simon links the pen name to the narrator's concealed Jewishness and argues that Baer had a passage from a Zionist novel[20] in mind when he chose the pseudonym and highlights the use of the pseudonym for the religious dimension of Baer's identity. Brenner opens another dimension when he establishes a parallel between Karl M. Baer and Bertha Pappenheim. Both were activists and worked for the rights of (Jewish) women. Pappenheim became famous when Sigmund Freud and Josef Breuer published her case study under the pseudonym "Anna O." in 1895 in *Studien über Hysterie* and Brenner claims that "it is no coincidence that Baer dubs himself Nora O. Body" ("Re-dressing" 33). Another reading is suggested by Myriam Spörri who aligns Body's female first name "Nora" to Henrik Ibsen's play *A Doll's House* about Nora, wife and mother, and her struggle for emancipation (cf. "N.O. Body" note 111, 260). In addition, Imlinger points to Homer's use of "nobody" as an astute pseudonym that saves Odysseus from the cyclops

---

19 See Judd "Pseudonyms" for an analysis of the use of pseudonyms by British women writers. See also Hahn *Autorschaft* for an exemplary analysis of Jewish women writers and pseudonym use.

20 Simon quotes from Theodor Herzl's *Altneuland* first published in 1902: "'Wanted: an educated, desperate young man willing to make a last experiment with his life. Apply N.O. Body, this office.' One of the men says, 'But I should like to know who this Mr. Body is, with his queer tastes.' 'It is no one.' 'No one?' 'N.O. Body, nobody. Means no one in English'" (qtd. in *Maiden Years* 199).

Polyphemus (cf. "Kein Körper"). With respect to the effects of the pseudonym for *Maiden Years*, I would like to add that the 'false name' does not as such threaten the autobiographical pact (cf. Lejeune *Autobiography* 12). In *Maiden Years*, its use may even support the discourse of respectability that Brenner identified. From this perspective, it may be read as adding to rather than diminishing the credibility of the author-narrator-protagonist. Moreover, the use of a pseudonym was standard in medical case studies and likens the autobiography to exactly that genre: the 'patient' tells their story to the doctor, Hirschfeld, who publishes the account and validates it by his professional authority. Thereby, the reliability, authenticity, and decency of the account are enforced rather than weakened. In this light, the decision to use the pseudonym *N.O. Body* may be read as a rhetorical strategy that multiplied and increased, rather than subdued, interest in and speculations about the (sexual) identity of the author.

The incoherent and changing construction of a male and a female narrative identity for N.O. Body, the ambiguous pseudonym, and Hirschfeld's ill-founded medical report are aspects that could have incited a debate about Baer's sex. This debate, however, never did take place. All contemporary reviews and even a parody of the account in the satiric journal *Lustige Blätter*[21] agree on Baer's (and Body's) unequivocal male identity. This finding, the lack of a discourse on doubtful sex, I contend, is an effect of two aspects: on the one hand, Body's use of narration and focalization erases every potential to disrupt or question his masculinity. On the other hand, sexologists of the early 20th century had already collected and grouped such a vast number of perversions and aberrations of sexual types that the gonads as a single decisive criterion for a sex had lost their influence.

---

21 The parody ignores Body's hermaphroditism and exaggerates his stereotypical masculinity: The misrecognized man who works as a handmaid in a hotel fathers twins annually. 'She' drinks more than any 'man' and carries the heaviest suitcases and furniture. When 'she' is found out to be 'he,' the maid is promoted to the position of a butler and earns six times as much (cf. Hochstetter "Aus eines Mannes Dienstmädchenjahren").

NARRATION AND FOCALIZATION

Mythical Intertexts

German editor Hermann Simon begins his biographical essay on Baer's life with a personal anecdote: as a child, he remembers, his mother heard that the family friend Karl M. Baer "had been born in Eastern Europe, the son of devout Jewish parents who had registered him as a girl in order to prevent him from being conscripted into the army" (*Maiden Years* 116). The initial "M.", the mother was told, stood for Baer's girl name "Martha." The explanation fascinates Simon and is the starting point of his research on Baer. Years later, he has collected numerous details about the life of Karl M. Baer, and contradicts the story by his great aunt and grandfather. Simon's biographical work shows Baer to have been born neither in Eastern Europe nor in Bergheim, a fictional mountain town in Saxony where N.O. Body sets his place of birth in *Maiden Years*. Instead, Baer was born in Arolsen, a small town in Lower-Saxony. Simon compares his findings to the story that Baer constructs in his autobiography and confirms the basic plot line of *Maiden Years*: Baer is assigned female at birth, lives his childhood and teenage years as a girl and officially changes his sex when he is 21 years old. His family is Jewish; one of the many facts Baer changes in the autobiography. However, the reason for his female upbringing was not fear from conscription but rather the "physical properties of the newborn" (*Maiden Years* 9), explains Body in his autobiography. The faked story, however, mirrors the Greek myth of Achilles who was disguised as a woman by his mother Thetis to prevent him from being recruited.[22] A prophecy has Achilles secure the Greeks' success over Troy and so Odysseus is sent out for him. Odysseus finds Achilles among the women of Scyros and, as predicted, he becomes the greatest hero in the battle over Troy. So far, the myth highlights masculinity and strength and justifies the female upbringing of a man. Earlier, Thetis had also dipped Achilles in the river Styx to make him invulnerable. In doing so, she was interrupted and his heel, the part where she held the infant, remained unprotected. One day, Achilles was attacked with a

---

22 See Hard *Handbook* and Hornblower *Classical* for accounts of classical myth.

poisoned arrow and a small injury to his proverbial heel killed the hero.[23] Here, an analogy could be drawn between the 'weaknesses of Achilles, his heel, to Baer's 'weakness,' his genitals that were deemed "strange" (9) by the midwife. The hyper-masculinity of Achilles is therefore extended to Baer, who shares not only the female upbringing but also a physical 'weakness.' In *Maiden Years*, the adult narrator Norbert remembers reading some "Legends of Antiquity" (32) when he was ten years old and living as Nora. Young Nora, Norbert maintains, readily identified with the Greek hero: "Then, by chance, I read the story of Achilles, whose mother gave him female garments. With feverish excitement, I read the legend to the end. I rejoiced. I was saved! [...] Yes, that was how it was and how it had to be: I was a prince who was being raised far away from his parents" (32). While Nora seemed to have celebrated this explanation for her experiences of difference and distance, the adult narrator-focalizer Norbert disqualifies Nora's identification with Achilles by commenting, "at the age of ten, I had lost all sense of reality" (32).

The myth of Achilles is only one of several intertextual references in *Maiden Years*. Body also names the legend of Oedipus, the son of the king of Ithaca, who was abandoned in the woods by his parents and grew up with adoptive parents (cf. 32), and the fairy tale of the Ugly Duckling (cf. 36).[24] Both stories have the young hero grow up in difficult situations while slowly discovering their 'true' value, talents, and beauty. Body also refers metaphorically to the story of Cupid and Psyche, and again shows familiarity with classical myth: at the beginning of her apprenticeship, Nora is ashamed to undress in front of her co-workers and she washes early in the evenings when everyone else is out. One night some of the girls come back early and "a crowd of Psyches, with their lamps in their hands, stared at me, poor half-naked Cupid" (63). Body self-identifies as the male god of love who falls in love with the mortal beauty Psyche and only visits her in the dark so as not to betray his own beauty. Although Psyche has never

---

23 Similarly, Herculine Barbin alludes to the myth of Achilles when ze remembers that "some people went so far as to accuse my mother of having concealed my true sex in order to save me from conscription" (*Memoirs* 90) and the "newspapers" compared hir to "Achilles spinning at the feet of Omphale" (90).

24 Hartmann also points to the bible as an intertext and emphasizes Nora's identification with Jesus, who suffered for the world (cf. "Geschlecht" 200).

seen her lover, she is enchanted and conceives a child. One night, Psyche waits for Cupid with a lamp and finds him to be a god. The lovers then have to endure numerous adventures and crises until Psyche is immortalized as well and they can marry and live happily ever after. The relationship between Cupid and Psyche is sexually charged from the beginning and Body's account of the event eroticizes the relation between Nora as Cupid and her co-workers as Psyches. In analogy to the myth of Achilles, Body is again masculinized through the account.

The allusion to the myth of Hermaphroditus, however, might complicate Body's male self-fashioning: according to Ovid, the young and beautiful Hermaphroditus set out to explore the woods and mountains near Caria, present day Turkey. He stopped at a pool, undressed and refreshed in the waters. Nymph Salmacis watched the boy, was overcome by lust and tried to seduce him. He turned her down, but Salmacis violently embraced him and called to the gods to unite them forever. The gods granted her wish and merged their bodies. Now Hermaphroditus, half male and half female, asked the gods to enchant the pool so that everyone who entered the pool would be similarly transformed. Body does not mention the myth explicitly, but alludes to it by having young Nora sit repeatedly by the fountain in the courtyard of her house. The fountain, Norbert explains twice, bears a special significance during Nora's youth (cf. 13 and 33) and he remembers an incident from his childhood:

I am thinking of summer evenings. [...] I was sitting with my parents on the bench, when the splashing of the fountain, which lay in the twilight of the summer evening, drifted by my ear. Surely, I was the son of a king. The ordinary old fountain had become a glorious well of healing. I drank the first sip and presented the water to my faithful burghers of Bergheim. The tinkling of the glass breaking on the flagstones wakes me up and, unfortunately, my mother as well. (32f)

The young Nora's perspective on the event is evident in her identification with "the son of a king" and she is the only one who drinks from this "glorious well of healing" that is likened to Salmacis' pool with its transformative powers. The scene is framed, though, by Norbert's introductory phrase and his description of Nora's memory as a dream. While Achilles, Oedipus, and Cupid represent masculine ideals, Hermaphroditus stands for effeminacy and androgyny. As Michael

Groneberg points out, readings and translations of the myth often prove misogynistic by devaluing femininity (cf. "Mythen" 96). His reading emphasizes the desirability of the two bodies that are merged: the male youth as well as the young nymph were legitimate sexual objects in Greek Antiquity and their union could be read as a sexual ideal. Furthermore, the union of the bodies might be read as a heterosexual copulation that eternally unites male and female (cf. 100). The significance of Hermaphroditus' parents adds to this reading: Aphrodite was the Goddess of love, beauty and sexuality, and Hermes was not only a messenger but also a phallic God referred to by *herma* ('pillars') adorned with penises that were used as road signs. Sexuality and fertility were the attributes of these Gods.[25] This indicates that their son Hermaphroditus may symbolize a perfect heterosexual union, rather than an effeminate boy. So, while the myth of Hermaphroditus seems to complicate Body's identification with hegemonic masculinity at first, it may also be read as reproducing a normative discourse on heterosexuality.

Sexuality, or to be more precise heterosexuality, is also a major topic in the myth of Cupid and Psyche. Through Body's identification with Cupid, he is not only masculinized but the relationship to his co-workers is also heterosexualized. Nominally, Nora Body, a young woman, shares the bedroom with three female co-workers. The intimacies they share when they discuss "sexual matters," hold "beauty competitions" and compare "[b]odies and busts" while Nora trembles "with excitement" (64) evoke erotic attraction, and Norbert kindles this reading when he wonders whether he (as Nora) "alone perhaps felt like a lesbian" (64). So, while sexual attraction is freely admitted, he then rejects the possibility of same-sex desire and attributes Nora's desire to "a purely aesthetic joy" and to an "artistic taste" (64). With the help of Cupid and Psyche, the relation between Nora and her co-workers is erotically charged, but simultaneously re-written into a heterosexual relation. "[L]esbian love" (65) seems out of the question.[26] Intertextual references and allusions, then, offer little

---

25 See Melville's translation of Ovid's *Metamorphoses* for the myth and "Hermaphroditus ♥ *Middlesex*" for a more thorough discussion.

26 In contrast to Cupid, Achilles is not known for his love to a woman but for his feelings for fellow warrior Patroclus. Whether this relationship was sexual or platonic is disputed and David M. Halperin remarks: "Homer, to be sure, does

potential to unsettle Body's heterosexual male self-fashioning. Moreover, Norbert's position as the male and adult narrator of the account overrules Nora's childish perspectives time and again as will become more evident in the following sections.

Gender

Next to myth, Norbert, the post-transition male adult, narrator and major focalizer, employs memories of his life as a girl to illustrate his innate maleness. The following passage is a memory of Nora's fifth birthday:

There lay a doll, as big as I was. So that was the wonderful thing my godmother had promised me? I could have cried, but just in time my eyes fell on a hobbyhorse, which my godmother, who had guessed my preferences, had added to the presents. [...] Only then was I truly happy. Without saying thank you, and entirely ignoring the doll, I galloped away on my proud steed and, contemptuously, left everything else lying there. So even then I had no interest in girls' toys and a distinct inclination toward games for boys. (20)

Nora, the young girl, is the focalizer at the beginning of the passage when she approaches the table with her presents ("as big as I was"). The focalization then gradually changes to the perspective of the adult narrator Norbert, when he judges and explains the behavior of his own five-year old self. It is Norbert who finally comments, "even than I had no interest in girls' toys and a distinct inclination toward games for boys", and interprets the choice of Nora's toys as an early expression of an innate maleness. Nora's perspective is missing and so is an explanation for the behavior of Nora's friend Hilde, who shared Nora's hobby although "her mother thought hobbyhorses were not really suitable toys for a girl" (21). This narrative strategy is repeated numerous times in the book: Norbert re-interprets, comments on, qualifies and judges the experiences of his younger self Nora.

---

not portray Achilles and Patroclus as lovers [...], but he also did little to rule out such an interpretation" ("Achilles and Patroclus" *Oxford Classical Dictionary*).

Nora, it seems, was indeed female-identified. As a nine year old, she is sent to a girls' school. She proves untalented with needlework,[27] is scolded by her teacher as "being clumsy as a boy" (30) and from then on the object of ridicule and insults by her schoolmates: "'Go away, you nasty boy, you, we don't play with boys' I did not understand her at all. 'You're a proper boy, we know that for sure. And Fräulein Stieler says so, too, and that's why you can't knit. Go away and play with boys!'" (30). Young Nora is hurt, irritated, especially after Norbert had remarked earlier: "I believe that at that time, I had entirely lost my awareness of the physical difference between myself and other little girls, or did not understand the meaning of it" (29). The insults by her friends renew Nora's doubts about her sex:

In the evening, when I was alone in my room, I looked at my body. It was simply not true! I was not a boy! Mama called me her little girl [...] I certainly was a girl; that is why I was so often sad about tearing my clothing when I climbed trees. [...] I [...] was entirely convinced that I was a girl, just a bit different from most, which did not appear strange to me. Since my nature was different from all theirs, why should my body not be so, too? (31)

The young Nora does acknowledge a difference between herself and other girls and to bridge this difference she constructs an analogy from her wild "nature" to her "body." If she was different in "nature," i.e. her preference for adventurous games and 'boys'' toys, why should she not be different in "body" as well? This quite differentiated self-analysis bears evidence for Nora's self-perception as a masculine girl. She does not negate her masculine preferences, but rather embraces them, and incorporates these preferences into a masculine female identity. But again, it is from the perspective of the adult Norbert that her self-concept is rated and re-assessed as evidence for an innate maleness and he explains: "Being brought up as a girl, being called by a girl's name had had a suggestive influence on me" (31). The self-concept of the young Nora as a masculine

---

27 As a teenage apprentice, Nora, the "unknown salesgirl" (70), collects warm clothing for homeless people. She loses her "loathing of the needle and female handiwork" (70) and spends many nights washing and sewing the clothes. Apparently, her earlier clumsiness at "female handiwork" needs to be attributed to a lack of motivation rather than to a lack of ability.

girl is thereby re-written as the effects of education and socialization on a young boy.

Another revealing memory is Norbert's account of Nora's apprenticeship as a salesgirl at a fashion shop. She is very unhappy with the work and suffers as a result of derogatory remarks from her male co-workers about her lack of feminine features. Her female co-workers, though, the Psyches that she shares a room with, offer comfort and support: "'You poor little thing, you needn't be ashamed because you're so skinny!'" (63) Nora's own doubts about her femaleness are thereby redirected and given an anatomical explanation: "They only thought I was thin and as lacking in breasts as a ten-year-old" (63). To veil other possibly masculine features of her body, Nora is already used to applying all kinds of tricks: She changes her washer-woman every eight weeks, so that the lack of menstruation would not be noticed (cf. 67), she removes her facial hair (cf. 50, 82), and her deep voice is paradoxically called a symptom of her lack of physical development and related to consumption (cf. 56). Thus, Nora is aware of physical differences between her and other girls. Yet, she also finds arguments that explain these differences without challenging her femaleness: "Gradually, I was losing the feeling that I was a boy altogether. I had read in a pseudoscientific book that in anemic and poorly developed girls, menstruation did not begin before the twenties. Thus, I came to believe sometimes that I was an abnormal girl" (64). Here, Nora again acknowledges her status as an outsider. She is not a typical girl, but this is something she is used to. So, the femaleness she claims is that of an "abnormal girl" – girl, nevertheless.

As a seventeen year old, then, Nora is admitted to university in Berlin by means of a stipend (cf. 74). She studies political economy and shows an interest in charity organizations and women's rights. Her report of this time reveals her self-confidence and changes the perspective on her suffering as an apprentice girl:

I was admitted as a student. I shall pass over the details of the following period and only mention that I did not find my studies difficult, that the professors respected me, and that I was popular with my fellow students. The work caused me indescribable joy. I was liberated from my yoke, saved from the suffering! In the sphere of learning, my pains, worries, and doubts about my sex faded. The intellectual pursuits, which I took up with great enthusiasm, soothed my overstrained nerves, and I began to feel like a human being among other human beings. Not like a person of equal value, but like someone who should be valued differently from the others. (75f.)

Nora poses here as a successful student and explains that her work liberated her from "doubts about her sex." Some of the suffering during her apprenticeship can thereby be attributed to a general rejection of the job and her social position. Nora was always among the best at her school. Only the ruin of her father's business made it necessary for her to find a paid job and she always felt superior among her co-workers at the fashion shop. Now that she is a student, her social rank is re-established and her worries – even about her sex – fade. Nora, or rather Norbert, continues to boast about her success at university:

In my spare time, I wrote a series of articles on the subject 'The Best Way of Organizing Charitable Societies.' The articles were accepted for publication by a respected journal. Dr. M., an authority in the field, had asked incredulously, 'What? A young girl of seventeen is supposed to have written these lines? Impossible. I do not think that any woman can possibly write like that.' Similar things were often said to me. Therefore, there must be something specifically masculine about my intellectual activity, which women who write do not usually possess. (76)

Dr. M.'s statement is used by Norbert as a double-edged sword: on the one hand, the value of the articles is increased by expressing surprise that a young and a female person has written them. Both, Nora's age and her gender, are deemed exceptional. On the other hand, Norbert uses the sexist remark to question Nora's femaleness and to argue his point that Nora, i.e. himself as a girl, always already displayed male "intellectual activity." This 'double-edgedness' gets clearer with a comparison of Nora's and Norbert's views on women's rights and feminism: During her apprenticeship, Nora comes into contact with books on women's rights and explains, full of enthusiasm, that "the demands were justified, [and] exactly in agreement with my feelings […]. I felt the physical and mental equal of men and saw no reason why they should be privileged and have better chances of getting an education than I, and other women, had" (69). Here, Nora identifies readily with "other women" and expresses a firm belief in the mental and physical equality of men and women. Following the boast about Nora's masculine intellectual activity, the focalization switches again to male-identified Norbert:

I should like to underline once again the view that I gained during my girlhood – in other words, from such a precise knowledge of women, one that other men can hardly gain. My thesis is: 'Women are not inferior to men but, rather, different.' They are certainly capable of achieving as much as men in scholarly endeavor, albeit in different ways. The only difference lies in the method. (76)

While Nora's perspective had emphasized the equality between men and women, Norbert's focus is on the difference between them. He distances himself from his former girl-self and aligns himself with "other men." From this perspective, Norbert still argues against the inferiority of women, but stresses certain differences "in the method." Nora's success in her studies and her political activism is thereby attributed to her innate maleness and reverses the arguments of the women's rights activist: Theoretically, women can still achieve similar things as men. But, from Norbert's perspective, Nora has never been a woman, and her success is therefore the success of the man she has always been. However, Nora's experience of her time at university, her enthusiasm for education and learning and her subsequent work for a charity organization may also reveal the narrator's disguised proximity to contemporary Jewish middle-class values. As Kaplan points out, Jewish women were among the earliest female students at German universities. Their studies were often and preferably followed by a career in social work (cf. *Making*).

What can be concluded from the aforementioned is that Nora feels awkward about her body throughout childhood and puberty. She is not feminine and hardly meets the expectations of a girl and young woman. Nevertheless, Nora makes a lot of friends, girls and boys, during childhood, is successful at school and later popular among her fellow students. The lack of femininity and "development" provoke recurring doubts about her sex, but she integrates these into the identity of an "abnormal girl." When the focalization switches to Norbert, he re-assesses Nora's childhood memories and turns the "abnormal girl" into a misjudged boy. This re-assessment produces the narrative of a seemingly continuous and coherent male sex for Norbert Body, but stands in contrast to Nora's perspective. Nora's masculine, in Norbert's perspective 'deficient,' female identity prepares the ground for the rewriting of her identity into a male one. The male self, Norbert, appropriates Nora's perspective in retrospect, denies her experiences and turns the masculine girl and young woman into a boy and man.

Desire

From the very beginning of *Maiden Years*, Norbert presented the love to a woman, to Hanna, as the transformative power in his life and marriage as his ultimate goal. As Nora, he had felt attracted to girls from a young age on: covered by the branches of an old tree, Norbert remembers, that Hilde, Lene and Nora share kisses, caresses, intimacies and finally the revelation that "Nora is very different from us" (18). This result does not at all lead to repulsion but seems rather to increase Nora's attraction because "from then on I was the darling of the two girls, who quarreled over being allowed to be close to me" (18). The detailed description of the three naked girls hiding under the tree is justified by the adult Norbert as being significant for two reasons: on the one hand, these games make Nora aware of a physical difference between her and the other girls. On the other hand, Norbert wants "to draw the attention of parents and teachers to how early sexual feelings may arise in some children" (19). Awakening sexuality was therefore the driving force behind these games, and the description of the scene legitimated as part of the pedagogical impetus of the text. This is continued in Nora's recounting of her first orgasm during a climbing exercise at school that leads to a "hot, hitherto unknown, intoxicatingly pleasant feeling [that] shook me, a shudder ran through my body" (52). Similar accounts of orgasms during the visit of a female dentist (cf. 52f), while dreaming of a neighboring girl (54), or of "women who played in wide waters, soft white bodies, whose curving lines I saw breaking the surface of the blue waves" (56f) take up the topic of child and teenage sexuality and are framed by Norbert's pedagogical remarks.

The topic is developed during the accounts of Nora's apprenticeship at the fashion shop. Recurring erotic dreams of women and the arousal when she massages the breast of one of her co-workers establish Nora's sexual desire as directed exclusively towards women. Nevertheless, she negates the possibility of "lesbian love" (65) and explains: "We admired this love, which we thought was more delicate and without pain, but we hardly believed in it" (65). This narrative strategy works in two ways: On the one hand erotic fantasies are exploited by giving insights into intimate all-female situations. On the other hand, Body refrains from the description of explicit sexual acts and frames his account as a study with pedagogical value. Moreover, female homosexuality is addressed but rejected as an explanation for Nora's constant arousal on the grounds that the girls "hardly believed in it", i.e. they had no idea what love between women could be like; they lacked a narrative.

During her studies, Nora's attraction to women continues and she is the object of erotic advances by quite a number of them: the American girl Harriet who is "a hotly sensuous, passionate creature" (77), the Friesian who is "slavishly devoted" (78) to Nora and loves her hands (cf. 78), and blond-haired and blued-eyed Lucie from Hamburg (cf. 79ff). At the end of a summer spent at a beach resort with Lucie's family, the two take a long walk and Body charges the situation with erotic allusion while refraining from explicit sexual content:

With our arms wrapped tightly around each other, we walked to the beach. It had grown dark, as dark as it can be only on a summer evening when the moon is shining and painting trembling circles on the deep green water. We walked along the soft sand of the dunes, toward the water. The tide was in. The waves came slowly closer, gobbling up the fine lines in the yellow sand as if with greedy lips. Lucie pressed close to me. I put my arm around her shoulder and lightly caressed her hair. It was quite silent on the beach. Now and again, when a boat drifted past or the dying sound of oars reached us from afar, the waves increased their murmur. Otherwise there was no sound, no life. [...] But life raced through our veins, wilder and fiercer than ever. Lucie flung herself onto the sand. I wanted to stretch out next to her, but she pressed me passionately to her, so that our bodies lay closely touching. And in a touching soft voice, she murmured again and again, 'I am so fond of you, I long for you so!' 'I am fond of you, too, from the bottom of my heart, and I am here with you,' I replied. 'So how can you still long for me?' 'I don't know but I feel a longing. I want to be very close to you. Do you know how? I am ashamed.' With hot, trembling lips, she kissed my hands. Ecstatic passion took possession of me then, and I covered her mouth with burning kisses. A ship passed by very close to the shore. We walked home, lost in dreamy thoughts. My hand lay around her waist, the rhythm of her steps gently rocking my body. (83f)

The waves, the soft sand and the moon at this warm, quiet, and dark night set the atmosphere for this erotic encounter. Both are mutually attracted, but have considerable difficulty explaining the "longing". Again, they seem to lack a pretext, a narrative that would structure the desire of a woman for a woman until "passion" takes over and they exchange "burning kisses." The scene ends here and ensuing activities are not spelled out. In doing so, Body's account still adheres to the rules of decency and refrains from explicit sexual descriptions.[28] Also, "passion" is rendered an active force that subdues Nora and excuses and legitimates her behavior.

Despite the shared passion, Nora leaves Lucie and begins to work for a German-American newspaper. She is asked to travel to Poland and other parts of Eastern Europe and to report on the social position of women. Nora attends lectures and conferences, meets with women's organizations, industrialists, party leaders and is a welcomed and celebrated speaker wherever she goes: "I achieved cult status," boasts Body. "People asked for my autograph and on some evenings I sold my signature a dozen times for a good cause" (87). While a newspaper comments on one of Nora's lectures: "'Nora O.B. is an excellent speaker who combines masculine determination with feminine charm'" (89), Norbert attributes Nora's overwhelming success as a public speaker to "an unconscious sensuous attraction" (87) and describes Nora's effect on women: "The wife of a parliamentarian once said to me: 'When you speak, you exude a strange aura, such as I have never felt in another female speaker. I only feel something similar when my husband speaks'" (87). Again, Norbert rewrites the "feminine charm" into a male "aura" and turns same-sex desire into heterosexual desire. This strategy is continued and expanded when Norbert recounts incidents that show Nora repeatedly as the object of desire for her hosts: "Quite often I had to share a room with my hostess when her husband was away on a journey. Once I had to share a bed with a young girl. [...] The girl kissed me wildly, but no intimate relations ensued. She just felt the man in me. There is a knowledge of the body that is stronger than all logic" (89, similar cf. 77). On the one hand, Body remains within the discourse of romantic friendship between women when he describes the more or less intimate

---

28 While Body often admits sexual desire in *Maiden Years*, he mostly claims abstinence. Hirschfeld contradicts this claim to respectability and reports that Laabs admitted repeated intercourse with women (cf. "Drei Fälle" 616).

moments in bedrooms and beds when kisses and caresses are exchanged. Romantic friendship between women was understood as completely asexual, as women per se lacked active sexual desire, and was thereby safely contained within the rules of conduct for women.[29] On the other hand, he provokes a re-reading of the same practices as sexual practices when he points out that "no intimate relations ensued." Furthermore, Body negates the possibility of same-sex desire in women by rendering the attraction heterosexual.

Body's contradictory perspective on homosexuality is exemplified in another situation: Nora meets an American girl named Harriet in a student group, who is "particularly friendly" (77) to Nora, kisses her often and presses her "hands to her breasts in bursts of passion" (77). While Nora "enjoyed doing this," and the girl "excited [Nora's] sense to the point of wild ecstasy" (77), she feels let down as her "senses remained unsatisfied." But when the girl arrives one afternoon in her bedroom, throws herself on top of Nora, and kisses her, Nora feels repelled by the "hysterical convulsions" of the girl's body. So, while Nora enjoys Harriet's attention and feels "wild ecstasy," she is nevertheless put off by inappropriate "hysterics" (77). The situation does not end with this scene, though, because Nora changes her mind and "return[s] her kisses" (77). While Nora does not approve of Harriet's desire for and active pursuit of another woman, she has no difficulty admitting her own desire for the girl, and legitimates these double standards as follows: "I also believed that she was only attracted to women and that I would be repulsive to her as a man" (77). As a "man", Nora's desire for Harriet is heterosexual, and only Harriet's desire remains somehow suspicious. But Norbert comes to Harriet's moral rescue, commenting on the situation and finding a liberating excuse for Harriet as well: "In reality, Harriet was a normal girl

---

29 Lillian Faderman, *Surpassing*, unearthed the changing history of relationships between women from the 16th century until the end of the 20th century and elaborates on the concept of 'romantic friendship.' Brigitte Eriksson and Faderman, *Lesbians*, focus on the situation of lesbian women in Germany from 1890 to 1920. In *Lesbian-Feminism* they edited stories and autobiographical writings from the time. See also Karin Hausen's seminal essay "Family and Role-Division" on the development of sexual stereotypes in 19th century German bourgeois families.

who had never felt attracted to women and who later made a normal marriage. It was the man in me to whom she instinctively felt physically attracted" (77). Retrospectively, both partners in the act are turned heterosexual and thereby "normal." This scene shows again the two-fold narrative strategy that exploits erotic fantasies such as same-sex desire while simultaneously re-writing them as heterosexual to claim respectability. It also demonstrates the status of same-sex desire compared to opposite-sex desire: one is "normal," the other does not even have a name. All these incidents construct Body's desire as being exclusively directed towards women, and the switches in focalization between Nora and Norbert render the desire asexual by positioning it within the discourse of romantic friendship, or heterosexualizing the desire and normalizing it.

When Nora finally meets Hanna, the discourse of romantic friendship is abandoned and they submit to an "overpowering natural force" (93) that leads them irresistibly to each other and unites them forever as Norbert explains full of pathos (cf. 93). While 'passion' had acted earlier as an excuse for sexual activity, this "natural force" is even stronger and Nora's self-concept as a masculine woman crumbles:

Worries and doubts tortured me again and again. What was I really? A man? Oh, God, no. That would have been indescribable joy. But miracles no longer happen nowadays. I knew nothing more. My whole life seemed like a powerful illusion that covered up the truth. Everyone considered me to be a woman; even my dear friend called me Nora. How could I ever have thought I was a man? I was an abnormally formed girl, that was all. But this feeling? I did not know; neither of us did. Could this joyous, compelling power be a vice? Could being intoxicated with the purest of joys, the most beautiful thing in life be a vice? (93)

This attraction is more than "aesthetic pleasure" or "artistic taste." Nora claims to feel "the purest of joys," but seems unable to comprehend this feeling as the "lesbian love" she had heard about earlier. The relationship between Nora and Hanna would not necessarily be a crime under contemporary legislation, but at least a "vice." And, in Nora's eyes, "the purest of joys" should be a virtue. They do not see a way out of this, "no salvation" (97), and therefore decide to die: "We wished to be joined forever. As life was unable to grant us that joy, we wished to go to our deaths together" (97). The plan was not executed, but it shows that they could not imagine living together as two women.

In this desperate situation, Nora goes to church and considers confessing her "ill-fated, hopeless love" (98). When she smells the incense, she decides against the religious confession and leaves the church. The following day, she has a minor accident and is forced to call a doctor. The man understands immediately that his patient is not only suffering from an injured foot and asks "in a kind, fatherly tone of voice, '[...] Wouldn't you like to unburden your heart to me? Perhaps you will feel relieved afterward!'" (99). Nora remembers that a "doctor was bound to silence by his professional duty" (99) and recalls her desire to confess. Instead of the clerical authority, she decides to talk to the doctor and explains a "heavy burden was gradually lifted from my soul as I at last spoke openly of what had depressed me for so long" (99). This confession scene again recalls Foucault's analysis of the medico-scientific process of truth production (cf. *Will*): Nora tells her story to the doctor, he listens, he asks further questions and after a thorough physical examination, the doctor proclaims the relieving 'truth':

There was no reason to be sad. My love for my lady friend was no vice, and, by the way, as far as love was concerned there was no vice, perhaps only in sensuousness, it was a natural feeling. 'If you wish to be close to your friend and you can secure a future for her, then go ahead and marry her! You are as much a man as I am!' Only a minor operation [...] was needed. [...] I should take courage; the authorities could not deny permission for my transformation, and then I could marry my lady friend with a clear conscience. (99)

This declaration is the miracle Nora had ruled out earlier. *Her*, or rather *his* desires were no vice, but absolutely "natural" and the "abnormal" girl is turned into a very "natural" man. Nora's reaction is designed as a revelation: "It was as though dark veils had been torn from my eyes. The doctor was right. Physically, I was a man. And I had often been told that I had the spirit of a man" (99). Nora's identity with varying degrees of masculinity in a female is now officially turned into the identity of a heterosexual man. The complex structure she had constructed and that had worked until she felt unable to imagine two women living together is reduced to one simple structure – that of a heterosexual man. Hanna is equally happy and, equipped with scientific certificates, the authorities grant Nora's petition and she has her "change" (100, 101). Here, Nora lives through all stages in the confession process described by Foucault. Most importantly, and in contrast to Herculine Barbin, Nora is transformed and "healed" by the confession. While Barbin's suffering begins with hir transition, Body feels liberated.

Over the course of the narrative, the focalization had gradually developed from childhood and teenage memories of young Nora, commented on by the adult Norbert, to the full perspective of Norbert. He is the narrator and, according to the doctor's judgment, the only focalizer. Nora's perspective only shines through from time to time: "I now wanted to break with my life as a woman and become a man at last" (101). This indicates that Body does not immediately identify as a man, rather, she is aware that she needs to *learn* to be a man. Over the following weeks, Nora practices the social rules of masculinity: she cuts her hair, starts to wear men's clothing, and has to remember to raise her hat when she greets ladies on the street. Norbert argues that his "attitudes and opinions were always masculine" (105) and therefore his "outlook" did not change much, but he does acknowledge that "some new aspects have, however, been revealed" (105) to him.

N.O. Body's claim to a male sex is therefore quite differentiated: he does acknowledge that masculinity as well as femininity is, to a certain extent, learned, or acquired. Nora's childhood and teenage experiences show preferences for activities with a masculine connotation or coding, her anatomy and physical development give rise to recurring suspicion and she is attested superior, i.e. 'male', mental capacity. Nevertheless, Nora constructs a (masculine) female identity for herself. Thus, I suggest, an undervalued factor in N.O. Body's claim to a male sexual identity is neither anatomy nor mental capacity or behavior. Rather, Nora's sexual desire for women, the "natural force", leads to the transformation and is the crucial factor in the determination of sex. On the one hand, 'desire' is rendered a biological category when Body aligns it with 'nature.' On the other hand, 'desire' is a category that is structured as sexual attraction between members of opposite sexes; for Body, its default setting is strictly heterosexual. While Hirschfeld maintains that the sex drive was undifferentiated[30] and Body has heard about "lesbian love," the concept remains vague and heterosexuality is the norm that Body aspires to. The opposing perspectives of Nora and Norbert stand next to each other throughout long passages of the text and prepare the ground for a possibly complex and changing sexual identity of the protagonist. In the end, however, Norbert remains the only focalizer and his perspective dominates the entire text. The narrative structure that combined two opposing or differing aspects such as male and female in the pseudonym and the focalization, or the construction of credibility and scientific value in combination with myth, eroticism and sexuality is therefore reduced to a single, one-dimensional structure.

The reduction of the double-layered to a one-dimensional perspective, the re-writing of Nora's experiences into Norbert's, stands in contrast to the bundle of malleable characteristics that N.O. Body employs to mold his sexual identity. *Maiden Years* shows that characteristics such as anatomy, desire, mental capacity, or behavior lend themselves equally to a male or a female identity. The same events and practices are judged differently by the opposing perspectives of Nora and Norbert and the process of re-writing Nora's experiences and perspective into Norbert's provides evidence for a complex construction of sexual identity that is neither continuous nor without ambiguity. In this light, N.O. Body's text is evidence for a multidimensional constructedness of (sexual) identities. Instead of the expression of a positivist-essentialist sex based on a single characteristic such as the gonads, N.O. Body constructs his identity from a bundle of characteristics: anatomy is just one characteristic among others; and the emphasis on desire as a determining characteristic reveals the impact of the heterosexual norm on N.O. Body. He clearly performs, constructs and writes his sex to conform to it. Thereby, questions of sex and sexual identity are intricately linked to desire and sexuality.

---

30 "Es spricht vieles dafür, dass überhaupt dem Geschlechtstriebe ursprünglich keine bestimmte Richtung angeboren war" (Hirschfeld "Diagnose" 15).

SEXOLOGY

The strong link between sexual identity and desire in the early 20th century is not surprising given the contemporary discourse of sexology: in 1899, in the first issue of the *Yearbook*, Hirschfeld outlines his theory of sexual identity and explains that differences between the two sexes, male and female, exist in degree (i.e. in quantity) rather than in kind (i.e. in quality), and that mental and physical qualities are mixed in each individual. This leads him to conclude that there may exist men with female genitalia and women with male genitalia.[31] Moreover, he claims, the distinction between man and woman is complex and full of exceptions[32] and suggests a model that explains sexual identity as the result of a combination of five characteristics: gonads,[33] genitalia,[34] secondary sex characteristics,[35] mental

---

31 "Das wertvollste Ergebnis der Forschungen auf homosexuellem Gebiet ist die Ermittelung, dass zwischen Mann und Weib in allen geistigen und körperlichen Punkten nur graduelle, quantitative Unterschiede bestehen, dass zwischen ihnen nach allen Richtungen Mischformen in ausserordentlicher Mannigfaltigkeit vorkommen, an deren Grenzen, so paradox es klingen mag, Männer mit weiblichen und Frauen mit männlichen Geschlechsteilen existieren." (Hirschfeld "Diagnose" 4)

32 "Im übrigen ist die Unterscheidung zwischen Mann und Weib keineswegs in allen Punkten so leicht, wie es uns durch die Kleidung gemacht wird. Es giebt [sic] so viele Ausnahmen, dass es schwer ist, Regeln aufzustellen. Je umfassender die anthropologischen Untersuchungen sind, um so unbestimmter und verwickelter werden die Resultate" (Hirschfeld "Diagnose" 7).

33 "I. In den Bildungsstätten der Keimzellen. Beim Weibe: Eierstock für Eizellen. Beim Manne: Hoden für Samenzellen" (Hirschfeld "Diagnose" 8).

34 "II. In den Aus- und Einfuhrwegen der Keimzellen. Beim Weibe: Eileiter; Gebärmutter; Scheide. Beim Manne: Nebenhode, Samenleiter, Glied" (Hirschfeld "Diagnose" 8).

35 "III. In körperlichen Eigentümlichkeiten, die mit der ersten Reifung und Abstossung der Ei- und Samenzellen eintreten. Beim Weibe: Wachstum der Brüste. Eintritt der Periode, Haupthaar auf dem Scheitel. Beim Manne: Wachstum des Kehlkopfs, (Stimmwechsel), Wachsen der Barthaare" (Hirschfeld "Diagnose" 8f).

capacity,[36] and sex drive.[37] Yet these groups of characteristics may be differentiated and manifested differently in any individual and lead to variations and crossings between the groups.[38] With this complex diagnostic network, Hirschfeld's model of sexual differentiation is far from the gonad-based binary model that Dr. Chesnet had applied in 1860 to determine Barbin's sex. Hirschfeld and his colleagues developed their perspectives over the following years; e.g. in 1904, Dutch doctor von Römer calculated that theoretically there were up to 687,875 sexual types – but he admits that some of them were rather unlikely and settles on the possibility of 687 types.[39] In this context of plurality and diversity, *man* and *woman* were reduced to theoretical poles on an almost endless continuum and Hartmann concludes that the sheer abundance of variations had rendered the ideal of a clear and simple sexual binary suspect.[40] Moreover, Hirschfeld's model allowed for the development of a sex in a given

---

36 "IV. In geistigen Unterschieden. Unter andern: Das Weib reproduktiver, anhaltender, treuer, praktischer, gemütvoller, reizbarer, kindlicher, äusserlicher, kleinlicher als der Mann. Der Mann aktiver, produktiver, wechselnder, unternehmungslustiger, ehrgeiziger, härter, abstrakter als das Weib" (Hirschfeld "Diagnose" 9).

37 "V. Im Geschlechtstrieb. Das Weib fühlt sich vom Manne, der Mann vom Weibe angezogen" (Hirschfeld "Diagnose" 9).

38 "In allen fünf Gruppen kommt es nun aber vor, dass gewisse Teile zu weit fortschreiten, andere zu früh stehen bleiben. Es entstehen dadurch zahlreiche Übergänge und Abweichungen, die umso häufiger sind, je später die Gruppe zur Differenzierung gelangte" (Hirschfeld "Diagnose" 15).

39 "Mit diesen Variationen können nun wieder die Verschiedenheiten der körperlich-psychischen Variationen kombiniert werden, und so finden wir als mögliche Variationen, d. h. als sexuelle Zwischenstufen, die ungeheuere [sic] Anzahl von 1625 X 423 = 687875 Variationen. Natürlich werden darunter auch absolut undenkbare Kombinationen zu finden sein, aber wenn auch nur 1/1000 davon wirklich besteht, so wären das doch schon 687 Zwischenstufenformen." (v. Römer "Vorläufige Mitteilungen" 847)

40 "Das Spektrum der Besonderheiten zerrieb die Illusion einer einfachen, klar konturierten sexuellen Normalität und stellte den Alltag insgesamt in ein latent hermaphroditisches und pseudo-hermaphroditisches Zwischenreich" ("Geschlecht" 192).

individual *over time*. There were, he argued, cases of hermaphroditism where the sex of the newborn could not be determined after birth; in most of these cases, though, an exact determination was possible following puberty.[41] While sex in the age of gonads was innate and fixed and determined solely by the type of gonad in a body (pre- or post-puberty), Hirschfeld's multidimensional framework of intermediary stages offered more flexibility and enabled an individual to *become* a sex during puberty. Anna Laabs, i.e. Baer, serves as Hirschfeld's prime example for such a case: the genital examination had revealed that *at that moment* the genitalia were of a quite masculine type[42] and, in 1906, he assigned Laabs *male without doubt*.[43] For Hirschfeld, this diagnosis does not necessarily imply that Laabs had always already been clearly male and Norbert's pre-puberty identification as female Nora is completely in accordance and even supports Hirschfeld's model of sexual development.

While pre-puberty Nora somehow 'suffered' from doubts about her sex, Body's post-puberty sexual identity seems clearly male. In the epilogue, however, Hirschfeld complicates this rather straightforward explanation somewhat. He describes Body's sexual development as a struggle, a negotiation and an interaction between different factors:

We further see an absolutely classical example of the struggle between a congenital disposition and external influences, between the inherited and the acquired. We observe how, with elemental force, certain inner impulses break through barriers that

---

41 "Die bisherigen Fälle, bei denen auch nach der Reife das Geschlecht noch unbestimmt ist, stellen gewiss grosse Raritäten dar. Neben diesen gibt es aber eine *ungleich grössere* Gruppe von Personen zweifelhaften Geschlechts, nämlich diejenigen, deren Geschlechtszugehörigkeit bei der Geburt unsicher, sich erst im postpubischen Alter nach einer oder der anderen Richtung entscheidet" (Hirschfeld "Drei Fälle" 614).

42 "Die Geschlechtsteile [...] zeigen nach übereinstimmender Diagnose *zurzeit* einen durchaus männlichen Typus" ("Drei Fälle" 615, emphasis added).

43 "Es kann nach allem nicht dem geringsten Zweifel unterliegen, dass es sich bei Anna Laabs um einen Fall von irrtümlicher Geschlechtsbestimmung handelt. Sowohl der Genitalbefund als die sekundären Geschlechtscharaktere, sowie der Geschlechtstrieb stellen es in ihrer Gesamtheit sicher, dass Laabs in Wirklichkeit Mann ist." ("Drei Fälle" 616)

education and environment have erected, and how in spite of everything, in the end it is the spirit that molds life. The following holds true in the field of sexuality. *The sex of a person lies more in his mind than in his body*, or to express myself in more medical terms, it lies more in the brain than in the genitals. (*Maiden Years* 109f)[44]

Hirschfeld's explanation that sex lies more in the "mind" or the "brain" than in the "body" or the "genitals" is surprising given Body's story: he had claimed that his female upbringing was the result of an erreur de sex. The midwife and local doctor had misinterpreted the genitalia of the newborn and it took the experienced doctor who recognized the post-puberty genitals as 'truly' male. The explanation Hirschfeld offers is somewhat different and it is reminiscent of the concepts by Ulrichs and Krafft-Ebing, who maintained that *urning* and *invert*, respectively, were variations of the soul or the psyche. As Foucault pointed out the "nineteenth-century homosexual became a personage, a past, a case history, and a childhood, in addition to being a type of life, a life form, and a morphology, with an indiscreet anatomy and possibly a mysterious physiology" (*Will* 43). Far from being limited to certain sexual practices or desires, homosexual individuals differed from heterosexuals not only in every aspect of their 'doing' but also in their 'being', i.e. the "morphology", "anatomy", and "physiology" of homosexuals was supposedly different from that of heterosexuals. Ulrichs, Krafft-Ebing, Hirschfeld and others label homosexuality *psychological hermaphroditism* and thereby describe homosexuality as just another form of hermaphroditism, just another form of an intermediary stage. Both concepts are likened to one another and when psychiatrists, neurologists, lawyers, and activists debate the 'origin of' or 'reason for' homosexuality at the end of the 19th and early 20th centuries, hermaph-

---

44 "Wir sehen des weiteren in geradezu klassischer Weise den Kampf zwischen angeborenen Anlagen und äußeren Einflüssen, zwischen Ererbtem und Erworbenem. Wir beobachten, wie mit elementarer Gewalt gewisse innere Triebe die Schranken durchbrechen, welche Erziehung und Umgebung errichteten, wie trotz allem es schließlich doch der Geist ist, welcher sich das Leben formt. Das gilt namentlich auf dem Felde der Sexualität. *Das Geschlecht des Menschen ruht vielmehr in seiner Seele als in seinem Körper* oder, um mich einer mehr medizinischen Ausdrucksweise zu bedienen, viel mehr im Gehirn als in den Genitalien." (Mädchenjahre 163f)

roditism is regularly used as an explanatory structure. As a result, by the end of the 19th century, homosexuality is discussed in terms of hermaphroditism and Sander Gilman concludes for *Maiden Years*: "By then, the hermaphrodite had become not only a model for, but also the etiology of, homosexuality" (*Maiden Years* xiv). Thus, the model that Hirschfeld uses to diagnose Body/Laabs/Baer, his model of sexual intermediary stages, obliterates hermaphroditism as a distinct category and explains it in terms of homosexuality.

At the time, homosexuality was, of course, still a vice, and, more than that, a crime to be punished under the notorious §175. Between 1906 and 1907, six military officers had committed suicide after having been blackmailed for homosexual practices, while in the preceding three years almost twenty officers were convicted of homosexual offences by military courts . Moreover, what came to be known as the Harden-Eulenburg affair[45] was already simmering beneath the surface: journalist Maximilian Harden 'knew' Philipp Prince of Eulenburg-Hertefeld, diplomat and advisor to Kaiser Wilhelm II, to be involved in homosexual practices and had already been threatening him with a public scandal since 1902. In 1906, Harden published a series of suggestive articles and a political affair began that led to a series of lawsuits and counter-lawsuits. Hirschfeld, the advocate for the rights of homosexuals and renowned sexologist, had to participate in these trials as an expert witness, but, according to Haeberle, his performance did not add to his reputation.[46] In 1907, the year *Maiden Years* was published, respectable 'men' (and women, I assume) still cringed at the mere thought of homosexuality (and some preferred suicide to a public scandal).

Thus, one problem that Hirschfeld and his colleagues were faced with in their struggle for the de-criminalization of homosexuality was the lack of

---

45 For a full discussion of the affair see Haeberle "Justitia," Steakley "Iconography," Jungblut *Famose Kerle*.

46 "[…], der angeblich wissenschaftlich geführte Nachweis von Heterosexualität oder 'unbewusster Homosexualität' erschien vielen Beobachtern, nicht nur dem breiten Publikum, als ein windiger Hokuspokus und Hirschfeld als ein 'Perversitätenschnüffler', der edlen Gefühlen niedrige Triebe unterschob. Aber nicht nur die 'Begutachtung' mißfiel, sondern am Ende erschien sogar die Sexualwissenschaft an sich […] in diesem Sinne suspekt" (Haeberle "Justitia" n.p.).

'hard' evidence for their theory: while physical hermaphroditism could be visualized, psychological hermaphroditism, i.e. homosexuality, was hard to grasp.[47] When Hirschfeld describes Body in broad terms as a sexual intermediary without specifying the exact diagnosis, he transfers the persuasive power of physical hermaphroditism to the concept of psychological hermaphroditism, i.e. homosexuality. He argues: "We now know that cases like the one described here are only extreme forms of intermediate sexual stages," and adds en passant, "which, to a lesser extent, occur in a great variety of physical and mental forms" (*Maiden Years* 110). Here, he likens Body's alleged physical hermaphroditism to psychological hermaphroditism. Moreover, when Hirschfeld gave his talk on hermaphroditism in 1906, he did not only pass around pictures of hermaphroditic individuals, he also passed around a wax figure of Laabs' genitalia and the audience held a three-dimensional copy of Laabs' genitalia, 'hard' evidence, in their hands, while listening to the case study. He also invited the audience to talk to Laabs and to ask questions: although Laabs was *by now* a man, he was living proof for Hirschfeld's model of sexual intermediary stages.[48]

Moreover, the specific desire that was legitimated in the case of N.O. Body/ Anna Laabs was not homosexual desire but strictly heterosexual desire. Body, Presber, befriended reviewers such as Hirschfeld's sister Franziska Mann and colleague Merzbach, and not least Hirschfeld himself had positioned the text (and N.O. Body) as a model of respectability.

---

47 Mehlmann argues similarly when she points to the lack of evidence for 'aberrations' of the soul: "Im Unterschied zu den hermaphroditischen Missbildungen [sic!] stellt sich für Hirschfeld jedoch das Problem des anatomischen Nachweises 'seelischer' Bildungsabweichungen" (*Unzuverlässig* 237).

48 Kathrin Peters (cf. *Rätselbilder* 158ff) and Sabine Mehlmann (cf. *Unzuverlässige* 235ff) analyze Hirschfeld's understanding of science and describe Hirschfeld's own research as predominantly empirical and positivistic: He conducts surveys and interview studies; he collects pictures, all sorts of artifacts and documents, and thereby tries to gather (or produce) evidence, proof for his theories. A 'hermaphrodite,' in this sense, may be understood as visual evidence for a mixture of the sexes and, supposedly, as an obvious, an evident case of an intermediary stage.

Lesbian desire was negated and ruled out by everyone involved and Hirschfeld reports Laabs to be the model of the bourgeois man whose ultimate goal was to marry the woman he loved.[49] Laabs' change of civil status, then, produces a heterosexual man, a conventional marriage and frees everyone from the 'burden' of a doubtful sexual identity and suspicious, unnamed desires. Thus, both sexology, the somehow shady and a little less than respectable academic discipline, and Magnus Hirschfeld, the wise and experienced doctor of N.O. Body's account, perform as the liberators of subjugated masculinity and as the advocates of normative bourgeois sexuality. N.O. Body's case, I conclude, was used by Hirschfeld in two ways: to promote the reputation of the academic discipline that he stood for and to illustrate the 'natural' and supposedly self-evident difference of homosexuals visually. The latter was the key argument for the de-criminalization of homosexuality. If homosexual desire was neither a choice nor a vice, it should not be punishable or in need of treatment.

In light of this analysis, I suggest revising Spörri's argumentation somewhat: in her analysis of *Maiden Years* and the discourse of sexology, she explains that hermaphrodites existed only in the moment of diagnosis, were then assigned one of two 'true' sexes, labeled 'pseudo-hermaphrodites' and thereby erased once they were constructed.[50] The discursive negation of 'true hermaphrodites,' she concludes, led to the non-existence of hermaphroditic identities.[51] I suggest that this argument does not apply to N.O. Body. Medical experts do not render N.O. Body a 'pseudo-hermaphrodite', and assign him a 'true' sex. Rather, Hirschfeld acknowledges a mixture of the sexes in N.O. Body, but he re-locates this mixture from the

---

49 "Als höchstes Ideal steht ihr eine dauernde eheliche Verbindung vor Augen. Sie beabsichtigt nach Umänderung ihrer Metrik mit einer Dame die Ehe einzugehen, mit der sie sich als verlobt betrachtet (Hirschfeld "Drei Fälle" 616).

50 "Der Hermaphrodit existierte einzig im Moment der Diagnose und wurde sodann auf dem Hintergrund einer binär organisierten Geschlechterordnung vereindeutigt und in diese Ordnung zurückgeführt" (Spörri "N. O. Body" 253).

51 "Darin lässt sich auch ein gewichtiger Unterschied zur Diagnose der Homosexualität festmachen: Homosexuelle Identitäten wurden von der Sexualwissenschaft mitkonstruiert, während die Kategorie des Hermaphroditen wieder zum Verschwinden gebracht wurde und damit auch keine hermaphroditischen Identitäten entstanden" (Spörri "N. O. Body" note 56, 253).

gonads to the brain, from the body to the mind. While he discusses hermaphroditism in his talks and in his publications, he does not address it as a category in its own right, but deconstructs it as just one of the many manifestations of sexual intermediaries. N.O. Body is thereby not denied the status of a hermaphrodite, but he is likened to a psychological hermaphrodite, i.e. a homosexual. Paradoxically, at the same time, N.O. Body rhetorically crafts his desire for women as a heterosexual desire, uses it as an argument for his unequivocal maleness, and is supported in this argument by Hirschfeld's report. When, as I have argued, hermaphroditism and homosexuality were likened and hermaphroditism described in terms of homosexuality, the focus was shifted from *sex* to *sexuality*. N.O. Body's account might not have provoked a debate on sex, I believe, because it was understood as a contribution to the debate on sexuality and desire. Moreover, it was not homosexuality that was being legitimated in the account, but heterosexuality, and a debate was therefore unnecessary.

MANNING THE BINARY

The 'fact' of N.O. Body's/Baer's unequivocal male sex was not questioned in contemporary discourses, but the reason or the origin of this sex remained somewhat in doubt: was it because Body had been physically and psychologically male from the beginning as Norbert claims in his memoirs? Did his innate masculinity express itself in the struggle between Nora and Norbert's perspective, which the latter clearly decided for himself? In that sense the strong and reassuring voice of the heterosexual man who, it seemed, succeeded quite easily in silencing his former girl self confirms the bourgeois order of the sexes. The naturalized, hierarchical binary between male and female may then be read as mirrored in the misogynist structure of the text that shows the 'man' in full control of his text while the female perspective is erased, belittled, and re-written. Yet the reason for Body's/Baer's male sex may not be the reproduction of an essentialized binary sexual order but rather its opposite; the decomposition and confusion of this very order. After all, sexology had already rid itself of rigid categories and relied on a multitude of criteria to determine a sex. A few years earlier, when the gonads still carried a more determined meaning, Body's self-fashioning might have been questioned more rigorously. But for Hirschfeld the exception was the new norm and 'full' men and women were little more than theoretical constructs. From this perspective, Body's claim to the male sex was justified as much (or as little) as anyone else's because the category *male* had lost its exclusive and stable character. Hirschfeld's epilogue and Body's memoirs cater to both readings: *Maiden Years* serves as a prime example of the norm of the exception, the intermediary stage as the rule; at the same time, the text confirms and reproduces a naturalized binary sexual order. *Maiden Years*, I suggest, stands between these two readings and it may be that the public success of the text was due to its particular 'nature' between transgression and approval of the binary order. Moreover, after reading the book, the question 'what makes a man?' still remains.

PART II: Intersex Narratives

At a Glance II: Intersex History

The following chapter provides a historical sketch of the discursive debates on intersex from the 20th to the early 21st century. On the one hand, its purpose is to connect the two parts of this study on hermaphroditism and intersex. On the other hand, the historiography is presented to contextualize the following analyses. As my focus in this chapter is less on originality than on comprehensiveness, especially in the pre-1990 era, I draw heavily on accounts written by other scholars and will now introduce some major sources: while historian of science Alice Dreger has written numerous articles and books on hermaphroditism in 19th century Europe (cf. *Hermaphrodites*), she has also published on the intersex movement in the U.S. in the late 20th century (cf. "Consent" and with April Herndon "Progress"). Historian Elisabeth Reis focuses on a period from colonial America to the 1960s in her study on intersex in the U.S. (cf. *Bodies*). The early 20th century is covered in studies by Geertje Mak (cf. "Self") and Alison Redick (cf. "Hopkins"). Two historical studies by Ulrike Klöppel (cf. *XXOXY*) and Heinz-Jürgen Voß (cf. *Making*) that focus on the history of hermaphroditism and sex determination in Germany are also helpful. Both studies connect their findings to transatlantic developments and offer informative insights into the workings of globalized discourses in the natural sciences. The entanglement of the natural sciences with cultural norms is the focus of feminist biologist Anne Fausto-Sterling (cf. *Myths*; *Sexing*) and psychologist Suzanne Kessler (cf. *Lessons*). Furthermore, medical anthropologist Katrina Karkazis (cf. *Fixing*) and sociologist Sharon Preves (cf. *Identity*) combine their respective studies on the experiences of intersex by intersex adults, parents of intersex children and doctors working with intersex patients, with extensive analyses of the historical context.

Literary scholar Iain Morland critically engages with the emergence of intersex activism and the ethical critique on the medical treatment of intersex (cf. "Injustice"; "Postmodern"; "Plastic"; "Intimate"; "Critique"; "Five").

NAMING THE PARTS: *HERMAPHRODITISM* AND *INTERSEX* (1900-1940S)

With the implementation of the *Prussian Civil Code* (ALR) in 1794, the *hermaphrodite* ceased to be only a legal subject: the medical expert was introduced to the mode of objectification and informed the judge about the appropriate decision on the sex of the hermaphrodite. Over the course of the 19th century, the medical field gained influence as a science and, with the codification of the new civil code (BGB) in 1900, the hermaphrodite vanished completely as a legal subject. Instead the hermaphrodite was turned into a medical subject: by the early 20th century, medical experts were examining hermaphrodites and determining their 'true' sexes according to different, sometimes opposing, systems of categorization. Often, the former legal hermaphrodite, who was allowed to choose between one of two sexes, was now found to be or to have one clear and distinct 'true' sex. This sex sometimes needed augmentation or reinforcement and, since the 1850s, surgeries on hermaphroditic bodies have been used to shape well-defined, single-sexed bodies.

Around the same time, the distinction between *true hermaphrodites* and *pseudohermaphrodites*, and the focus on the gonads in the medical realm, had decisively diminished the number of bodies considered 'truly' hermaphroditic. The strong assumption that each body had or was exactly one sex, albeit veiled, caused a certain dissatisfaction with the current terminology that implied a kind of mythical bisexuality, androgyny, or a blend of two sexes in one body – whether this mixture was 'true' or 'pseudo.' Dreger explains that, by the early 19th century all over Europe, "medical men would begin to argue that the very word 'hermaphrodite' needed to be done away with altogether" (*Hermaphrodites* 154). She mentions French surgeon and gynecologist Samuel Pozzi who, in 1911, suggested the terms *androgynoids* and *gyn-androids* to replace the, in his understanding, misleading terms *true* and *pseudohermaphrodite*. In 1914,

Scottish gynecologist and obstetrician David Berry Hart introduced new terminology to circumvent the term *hermaphrodite*. He referred to characteristics related to sexual development as *sex-ensemble* and differentiated between "typical male or female sex-ensembles" and "atypical male or female sex-ensembles" (Dreger *Hermaphrodites* 154-7). The criterion 'gonad' was still sex-decisive in his taxonomy, and the terminology reflected his belief that men and women were fundamentally different and that each individual was exactly one or the other.

Neither Pozzi's nor Hart's suggestions gained general acceptance, but when German zoologist and geneticist Richard Goldschmidt coined the terms *intersex* and *intersexual* in 1916[1] in his work on sex determination in a moth called *Lymantria dispar*, the medical establishment was eager to take up these fresh terms and leave the *hermaphrodite*, with its mythical baggage of in-between or double-sexes, behind. Voß points out that Goldschmidt was critical of the excessive usage of his terms, as Goldschmidt had conceptualized them as being distinct from hermaphroditism, and not as synonymous.[2] While the new terms were not necessarily used according to their intended coinage – Hirschfeld, for example, titles a 1923 essay on homosexuality "Die intersexuelle Konstitution" ('The Intersex Condition') and continues the conflation of hermaphroditism and homosexuality – the 'old' terms, *hermaphroditism* and *pseudohermaphroditism*, did not cease to exist, but continued to be used interchangeably. Voß shows that their usage was (and still is) common (cf. *Making* 216).

Advances in the first half of the 20th century in various disciplines made claims to one single and discrete sex for every body more difficult: the field of endocrinology, the study of hormones, had begun to take shape with castration experiments in male chickens since 1849, but emerged as a distinct discipline only after 1905 when the term *hormone* was coined by

---

1   Hausman dates Goldschmidt's use of the term "in the 1920s" (*Changing* 78).

2   Voß explains that Goldschmidt uses the term *intersex* to describe the mix of male and female characteristics in an individual with either XX or XY chromosomal sex. *Hermaphrodites* were individuals who produced both male and female gametes, i.e. egg and sperm (cf. *Making* 215).

London professor of physiology Ernest Henry Starling.[3] According to Fausto-Sterling, transplantation experiments on animals and humans by Eugen Steinach and others shaped the field between 1905 and 1915, but she refers to the years between 1920 and 1940 as the "heyday for endocrinology" (*Sexing* 177): in this period, research succeeded in identifying, purifying, and measuring discrete hormones that so far had been loosely referred to as "male" or "female hormones." The multiple workings of these groups of hormones were scrutinized and described and, in 1935, were named "estrogens" and "androgens." Early on, they had been found to play a role in sex determination and were therefore dubbed *sex hormones* – a term that still sticks to them despite findings that show this term to be both limiting and misleading. Critique voiced by Fausto-Sterling and others points to various functions of this group of hormones in "the processes of cell growth, cell differentiation, cell physiology, and programmed cell death" and she concludes: "They are, in short, powerful growth hormones affecting most, if not all, of the body's organ systems" (193). In addition, the gendered terms *estrogens* and *androgens* for the *sex hormones* divert attention from the fact that both substances are produced and needed in both 'male' and 'female' bodies. Moreover, the production of these hormones is by no means limited to the sexed regions of the body such as the gonads, but takes place in various locations for example the adrenal glands.

Next to endocrinology, research on chromosomes received wider attention after the turn of the century. While early studies of inheritance patterns in pea plants by monk and scientist Gregor Johann Mendel (1822-1884) had been ignored until the late 1890s, his work was then rediscovered and in 1905, English scholar William Bateson coined the term *genetics* to refer to the research on biological inheritance. In the same year, American biologists Nettie Maria Stevens and Edmund Beecher Wilson independently identified X and Y chromosomes and described the chromosomal basis for sex determination.[4]

---

3   See Fausto-Sterling, *Sexing* 147-194, for the history of endocrinology with respect to sex determination. For an extensive analysis see Oudshoorn *Beyond*.

4   Voß elaborates the current studies on chromosomes and their supposed relevance in sex determination (cf. *Revisited* 237-82).

The findings in endocrinology and genetics, the chromosomally and hormonally determined sex, added to the challenges of the gonadal sex determination and Dreger proclaimed the end of the age of gonads when, in 1915, British gynecologist William Blair Bell (1871-1936) suggested that "the time for a gonadal definition of every body's true sex had now passed" (Dreger *Hermaphrodites* 159). With the loss of this definite and definitive anatomical criterion for sex, sex determination got more difficult for doctors and Blair Bell advised his colleagues: "our opinion of the gender [of a given patient] should be adapted to the peculiar circumstances and to our modern knowledge of the complexity of sex, and [...] surgical procedures should in these special cases be carried out to establish more completely the obvious sex of the individual" (qtd. in Dreger *Hermaphrodites* 166). According to Dreger, this is the first mentioning of 'gender' in a text on hermaphroditism/intersex. Moreover, I want to point to Bell's idea of the "obvious sex": having refuted the idea of gonadal sex, he might hint at chromosomal and endocrinological sex when he refers to the "modern knowledge of the complexity of sex," but in the end he asks surgeons "to establish more completely the *obvious* sex" (emphasis added). Apparently, the quest for the 'true' sex of an individual had been replaced by a pragmatic wish for the 'obvious sex.' Reis names the determinants for the 'obvious sex' when she explains: "what remained consistent throughout the first half of the twentieth century was doctor's commitment to heterosexual marriage and, increasingly, to surgery devoted to guaranteeing the union of two differently sexed bodies by the creation of 'perfected' men and women" (*Bodies* 85).

However, she points out that surgery was usually undertaken not only with the consent of the adult patients, but on their request, and describes a case when Hugh Hampton Young, leading urologist at the Johns Hopkins University in the 1920s and 30s, operated on a patient he believed to be male after he found 'testicles' in her abdomen. The patient insisted on her femaleness, had the 'testicles' removed, the 'vagina' lengthened, married a man, and, Young remarked, "is apparently living happily as a woman, although, [...] probably a man" (Young qtd. in Reis *Bodies* 109). Hausman also discusses doctors' treatments of intersex individuals during this period and concludes: "It is important to understand how contested the treatment of intersexual patients was, and how tenacious the ideas of the physicians were concerning the constitutive aspects of a proper male or a proper female" (*Changing* 91). With reference to Young she recounts another 'case' where he excised the 'penis' of a young orphan who was assigned the female sex when seven years old due to "some internal female organs." At age sixteen, the 'girl' announced the wish to continue life as a man as soon as 'she' was out of the orphanage. Despite the decided wish of the 'patient', Young undertook a second operation and removed 'her' 'testicles.' The case shows that Young clings to the gonadal definition of sex and ignores the wish of the 'patient.' Apparently, the doctor did not follow one clear line in the treatment of his intersex patients. Sometimes he did or did not perform surgeries according to the desire of the patient; sometimes he acted according to his own judgment and against the will of the patient.

What can be concluded from the above is that endocrinology and genetics complicated rather than simplified the diagnosis of a sex by the doctor. Moreover, the categories 'sexuality' and 'desire' made the question of the 'true' sex of an intersex person very difficult to determine and the focus shifted to 'obvious sex.' Reis summarizes aptly: in the 1920s and 30s, "[m]edical opinion held that there was no one right way to manage intersex" (113).

BALTIMORE PROTOCOLS (1940S-1980S)

Historian of science Alison Redick observes a continuing inconsistency in the management of intersex until the 1950s and refers to the time between 1916 and 1955 as the 'era of idiosyncrasy' (cf. "Hopkins" 290). Based on an analysis of medical case studies from this period, she documents a "complete absence of medical protocols" (290). Conflicts between gonadal and psychological sex in young adults led to moral-ethical questions such as: what is the significance of testicles found in a person who identifies as female? And, is it a homosexual act when a female-identified person with testicles has sex with a man? Or, is it a homosexual act when the same person has sex with a woman? Without an adequate explanatory pattern, a theoretical framework to deal with such 'cases', doctors, Redick explains, "simply dealt with [intersex] on a case-by-case basis" ("Hopkins" 290).

During the 1940s, a "new analytical instrument" amended the diagnostic techniques of doctors. Next to hormonal and chromosomal testing, biopsies, and external examinations, "psychological testing" (Reis *Bodies* 121) became part of the diagnosis of sex. Up to the 1930s, patients were allowed to voice their opinions on their gender identity, but now psychological testing 'measured' a person's male or female identity, including their sexual orientation.[5] With tests such as the Wechsler-Bellevue Intelligence test, the Rorschach inkblot test, the Minnesota Multiphasic Personality Inventory test, the New Stanford Achievement test, the Otis Speed Test of Intelligence, the Otis Higher Intelligence Examination, or the Terman-Miles Attitude-Interest Analysis Test, verification of such a delicate matter as personal identity was handed back to science and the patient's perspective lost influence (cf. Reis *Bodies* 120; 131). The rise of psychology had far reaching consequences for the management of intersex: in a first step, an individual's male or female *psychological sex*[6]

---

5   See Mak ("Self") for a similar argument.

6   The terms *sex* and *gender* were not yet available. Money and the Hampsons introduced the terms *gender* and *gender role* in 1955 to emphasize the social dimension of sexual identity. They borrowed the term from linguistics, described *gender* as analogous to language acquisition and thereby opposed it to biological theories of psychosexual development. But Klöppel also explains that the 'social dimension' of Money's *gender* concept is limited to education through the parents and the body image of the individual. Therefore, she argues, Money's concept differed significantly from the understanding of *gender* in today's gender and queer studies (cf. Klöppel *XXOXY* 310; 324). Furthermore, she points out that the Baltimore team used terms like *psychological sex*, *psychosexual identity* and *gender role* interchangeably and did not develop distinct definitions of these concepts. Building on Money's ideas, psychiatrist Robert Stoller and sociologist Harold Garfinkel and their team from the University of California have been working on a concept called *core gender identity* that was distinct from Money's *gender identity* since 1958. In the following years, Stoller published numerous essays on the topic and in 1968 his seminal *Sex and Gender: On the Development of Masculinity and Femininity* and put down the distinction between *gender* as social and *sex* as biological that remained a doctrine until Judith Butler's deconstruction of the dichotomy in *Gender Trouble* in 1990 (cf. Klöppel *XXOXY* 499-503; Hausman *Changing* 102-9. On the contribution of John Money see also Goldie *The Man*; Downing et al. *Fuckology*).

was determined. Then, the genitals were surgically shaped to match the *psychological sex*. While the 19th century had the gonadal sex as the determining factor, gonads were now overruled by psychology. The diagnosis was therefore turned upside down and in some cases the psychological approach led to sex assignments that contradicted and opposed the gonadal sex. Surgeries and high hormone dosages were administered to 'fix' the external genitalia and secondary sex characteristics to correspond with the psychological sex, and, on the outside, the intersex person looked the same as their psychological sex – finally, doctors seemed to have found a way to 'heal' intersex, i.e. to make it go away.

From today's perspective, Reis points out that there were significant drawbacks to this new approach: for one, the criteria for masculinity and femininity were firmly rooted in 19th century gender roles when "submissiveness, compliance, and passivity reminiscent of [...] the 'cult of true womanhood' defined femaleness for these doctors" (*Bodies* 120).[7] Needless to say, desire for the 'opposite' sex was also understood as necessary for a successful male or female identity. Moreover, the focus on psychological sex facilitated a rise in genital surgery: there was no medical need for these surgeries, it has to be noted; they were done for cosmetic, i.e. social reasons. A psychological 'woman,' according to test results, should not have a clitoris that was 'bigger' than deemed 'appropriate.' Ergo, clitoris reduction, clitoris amputation, or clitorectomy, the removal of the clitoris, became a regular procedure in 'feminizing' surgeries for psychological 'females.' The ability to urinate standing was perceived as crucial for psychological 'males' so the lengthening or rerouting of urethras became a standard procedure in masculinizing surgeries. Both procedures regularly led to a significant loss in sexual sensitivity and to repeated or sometimes chronic inflammation of the genital tract (cf. Klöppel *XXOXY* 314ff).[8]

Another consequence of the psychological approach was the idea of the 'sex of rearing' as a determining factor. As a PhD student during the 1940s, psychologist John Money, then at Harvard University, had found that most

---

7   On the cult of true womanhood see Welter "Cult."
8   Intersex people have reported the various consequences of these treatments in numerous publications see, for example, Dreger (ed.) *Intersex*, Preves *Identity*, Karkazis *Fixing*.

'patients' identified with their sex of rearing. Whatever a certain gonadal, hormonal, or chromosomal make up would indicate; a male or female upbringing would often overrule these factors. For the first time in the history of science, there seemed to be proof that nurture was more decisive than nature. Leading endocrinologist at Johns Hopkins University, Baltimore, Lawson Wilkins had a pronounced interest in intersex[9] and formed an interdisciplinary team to find a way to 'manage' intersex according to the latest results in research. As early as 1950, Klöppel points out, he had proposed that intersex children should be assigned a sex based on the appearance of their external genitalia. Cosmetic surgical interventions and hormone treatment, he argued, should bolster up the assigned sex. Wilkins' voice already had some influence in the field, but he lacked a convincing theory to back up his recommendations (cf. Klöppel *XXOXY* 308). Together with senior psychologists Joan Hampson and her husband John Hampson, John Money became a part of the team and refined his gender development theory. Together with the Hampsons, Money published a series of five articles in 1955 and 1956 and established what later became known as the Baltimore Protocols.[10] Redick explains that these protocols were understood as "the ideal theoretical framework for standardizing intersex treatment" ("Hopkins" 292) and shows that the protocols were implemented into medical textbooks as early as 1957, i.e. right after their first publication (cf. "Hopkins" 295, see also Karkazis *Fixing* 47-62).

---

9   Lawson Wilkins specialized on Congenital Adrenal Hyperplasia (CAH) and developed a cortisone treatment to suppress virilization in CAH subjects in 1951 (cf. Klöppel *XXOXY* 308f). His research interest is, it seems, to produce normative bodies.

10 See the list of articles by John Money, Joan Hampson, and John Hampson in the bibliography. Although published in co-authorship, Redick found evidence in Money's archive indicating that he was the one "who wrote the protocols" ("Hopkins" 294). Also, while Money continued to publish and research on intersex and gender development, the Hampsons withdrew from the field. Money personally claims responsibility for the papers in his autobiography: "Responsibility for their design and writing was mine, but the published authorship was shared" (*First Person* 35).

Money's analysis of case studies indicated that the 'sex of rearing' was more decisive than somatic sex, i.e. gonadal, chromosomal, or hormonal. Based on these data, Money concluded, the human baby was born without a set or fixed sexual identity. While a newborn would be born psychosexually undifferentiated, a 'healthy' i.e. stable, coherent and distinct gender identity would be acquired and learned in social interaction. The hypothesis that was later popularized under the label "psychosexual neutrality at birth,"[11] led Money to develop medical guidelines for the management of newborns with so-called ambiguous genitalia. The assumption was that children needed to be reared as consistently and with as little ambiguity as possible to develop a distinctively 'male' or 'female' identity. To assure a consistent and unambiguous upbringing through the parents, Money believed it to be crucial that the external genitalia matched those of the assigned sex as closely as possible. Furthermore, an enlarged clitoris or a miniature penis would make it difficult for parents to raise their children as either consistently male or consistently female. Also, Money warned, children would recognize their physical differences when growing up, would suffer from ridicule by other kids, and would have difficulty integrating their physiognomy into their identity. Therefore, he deemed it absolutely crucial that a) the genitalia of the newborn had to be surgically remodeled to appear as 'standard' as possible; b) the parents of the newborn were not to be told that there might be a 'problem' with the sex of their newborn. Doctors should rather reassure parents that their baby was 'clearly' a boy or a girl, but that their baby's sexual differentiation, manifested in their genitalia, was not 'finished', and that their bodily features needed some augmentation (cf. Klöppel *XXOXY* 313f; Karkazis *Fixing* 59).

While Money did acknowledge that social factors played an important role in gender development, Redick points out that Money's model was not "purely culturalist" and she explains that, according to Money, gender was imprinted into an individual "like a native language" ("Hopkins" 292). He described a three-part process: from the fetus that interacts with hormones in uteruo, which leads to a preformation of a gender threshold, to the

---

11 Karkazis states that it is unclear who started to refer to Money's theory as "psychosexual neutrality" and she explains: "Money and his colleagues use the phrase *undifferentiated at birth*, but it is not obvious that they understood this to mean 'neutral'" (*Fixing* 300).

newborn that interacts with a human environment during a critical period of eighteen months after birth, when a gender is imprinted, and finally to a continuous process of social interaction that reinforces a specific gender role (cf. 292f). Redick concludes that Money's idea of 'learning' a gender depends on a neurological process that prepares the ground for the imprinting process.[12] Klöppel also shows that Money and the Hampsons developed the idea of a critical period for gender imprinting in analogy to Konrad Lorenz' work on young graylag geese, which was popularized in the 1930s.[13] Via this analogy, the critical period for gender imprinting became a biologically determined and therefore 'natural' process. Moreover, the notion of developmental stages was in accordance with contemporary theories of cognitive development based on e.g. Jean Piaget (cf. Klöppel *XXOXY* 323).

While genital surgery on intersex individuals was routinely performed even before Money's approach, the 'psychosexual neutrality at birth'-dogma dramatically changed the moment in time for the operation: in the 1930s and 40s, psychological testing had shown a patient to be of one or the other psychological sex. Surgery was then chosen to emphasize the

---

12 In an autobiographical essay published in 1997, Money explains "[t]he general tendency is to want to say that gender identity is either biological or not biological – to which my jocular response is that if it's not biological, then it must be spookological or occult, for there is a biology of learning and remembering, and it does affect the brain, doesn't it?" ("Serendipity" 302) Money felt that his gender identity theory was often misunderstood and he criticized the idea of a solely cultural production of gender: "In political and popular usage, and in much of social scientific usage also, gender has been conceptually neutered by being divorced from genital and procreative sex. However, it is not scientifically feasible to separate the coital and procreative role of a person from everything else about that person that is masculine, feminine, or androgynous" ("Serendipity" 303).

13 In her analysis of the implementation of the Baltimore protocols in Germany, Klöppel shows that the use of Lorenz' imprinting concept in particular invited critique: instinct driven actions in birds, argues e.g. Hedwig Wallis from the pediatric clinic in Hamburg-Eppendorf, could not be transferred onto mammals such as humans (cf. Klöppel *XXOXY* 483f).

assigned sex.[14] With Money's approach, the surgery was supposed to take place as early as possible. Infants could, of course, not be psychologically tested. Their sex of rearing was therefore determined by the shape of their external genitalia, or, to be more precise, by the genitalia's potential for a masculinizing or a feminizing surgery. In 1955, Money and his colleagues explained: "For neonatal and very young hermaphrodites, our recommendation is that sex will be assigned primarily on the basis of the external genitals and how well they lend themselves to surgical reconstruction in conformity with assigned sex" (Money et al. "Hermaphroditism" 290). From then on, the appearance of the genitals at birth and the skill of the surgeon determined the sex of the newborn. Sharon E. Preves sums up the effects of Money's recommendation: "As a result, the overwhelming majority of intersex children are assigned female" (*Identity* 56). In a 1993 interview in Johns Hopkins Magazine, intersex specialist John Gearhart comments cynically on the frequent feminization of intersex newborns: "You can make a hole [vagina], but you can't make a pole [penis]" (qtd. in Preves *Identity* 56).

Before Money's approach received due criticism, he popularized his notion of gender formation in talk shows and popular publications. As Suzanne Kessler admits self-critically in her study *Lessons from the Intersexed* (1998), feminists and gender theorists initially embraced the approach as they understood it as support for their premise that biology was indeed not destiny. At the time, Kessler argues, "gender researchers were blinded to a number of unexamined and deeply conservative assumptions embedded in Money's argument" (*Lessons* 7), and she asks why theorists that claimed to use social constructivist approaches did not challenge

---

14 While the Baltimore team has repeatedly claimed a paradigm shift from a 'true sex policy' based on gonadal sex to an 'optimal gender policy', analyses of the history of the medical discourse show that gonadal sex had become a contested criterion long before 1915. Klöppel deconstructs Baltimore's self-fashioning as a rhetoric strategy and explains that their 'best sex' or 'optimal gender'-approach matched the medical discourse at the time very well. The novelty in their approach was the systematic combination of surgical and hormonal intervention with the assumption of psychosexual malleability (cf. *XXOXY* 334).

Money's emphasis on the shape of genitalia as an indicator for gender.[15] The Baltimore protocols dominated the discourse on intersex from the 1950s to the late 1980s and critique was scarce. But eventually Money's paradigms were challenged, as will be outlined in the following chapter.

EARLY INTERSEX ACTIVISM AND POLITICS (1980s-2005)

The course of action developed by the Baltimore protocols determined the medical treatment of infants whose genital appearance did not easily match the expected form of either male or female genitalia from the mid-1950s onwards. At first, critique was rare and teams of surgeons, pediatricians, and endocrinologists in hospitals throughout the United States and Western Europe adopted the model. Suzanne Kessler sums up the instructions for treatment: "The experts must insure that the parents have no doubt about whether their child is male or female; the genitals must be made to match the assigned gender as soon as possible; gender-appropriate hormones must be administered at puberty; and intersexed children must be kept informed about their situation with age-appropriate explanations" (*Lessons* 14). While the protocols of the 1950s suggest "age-appropriate explanations," the ethical implications of medical practices had not yet come under scrutiny. The modern notion of 'informed consent' was not established before the early 1970s[16] and during intersex treatment, patients, i.e. intersex

---

15 See David A. Rubin for an analysis of "intersexuality's [...] role in the development of gender as a concept in twentieth-century American biomedicine, feminism, and their globalizing circuits" ("Unnamed" 883). He criticizes both the heterosexist assumptions within the Baltimore framework and the lack of criticism towards these assumptions within feminist theories.

16 Based on the Hippocratic Oath, the doctor-patient relationship in the Western world throughout the 19th century was dominated by a beneficence model of care: as experts, doctors supposedly knew the 'best' treatment for their patients and patients simply needed to trust their doctors to act on their behalf and in their best interests. The "doctor knows best"-model was influential throughout the first half of the twentieth century and specifically advised doctors to withhold information from patients if that information might 'upset' the patient.

children, were almost always kept in ignorance (cf. Karkazis *Fixing* 216-235). Moreover, parents were often specifically instructed by doctors not to discuss intersex with their children but to raise them as 'unambiguously' as possible (cf. Karkazis *Fixing* 179-215). Kessler studied physicians' decision-making in intersex infants and revealed social criteria to be central. She found that decisions were often "based on parental reaction and the medical team's perception of the infant's societal adjustment prospects given the way the child's genitals look or could be made to look" (*Lessons* 20).[17] In contrast to these findings, physicians veil such socio-cultural criteria in the interaction with parents and perpetuate "the notion that good medical decisions are based on interpretations of the infant's real 'sex' rather than on cultural understandings of gender" (*Lessons* 17). They imply that "it is not the gender of the child that is ambiguous but the genitals," argues Kessler and treatment involves "completing" "unfinished" organs or "surgically correct[ing]" "maldeveloped" genitalia (*Lessons* 22f). While the patients, i.e. the intersex infants, are obviously not competent and cannot give informed consent, full disclosure is often withheld from parents as well. Simultaneously, the management based on the protocols advises parents not to talk to friends or family and reinforces its complete control of

---

In the course of civil rights movements of the 1960s and 70s, this medical practice was challenged and patients' rights demanded. Faden and Beauchamp (*History* 89-100) and Annas explain how a series of court opinions in the early 1970s established the principle of informed consent in the U.S. and lead the American Hospital Association to the declaration of "A Patients' Bill of Rights" in early 1973 – a document that Annas characterizes as "vague and general" ("National" 695), but as the first of its kind. 'Informed consent' requires a competent patient to decide freely on any medical treatment or procedure based on full disclosure of his_her case. The doctor needs to provide information in a way that the patient understands the proposed mode of treatment along with its risks and benefits, possible alternative modes of treatment irrespective of insurance policies, and expected problems of recuperation.

17 Intersex activist Cheryl Chase argues that 90% of intersex infants are assigned female as removal of tissue is deemed 'easier' than the construction of a new structure (cf. "Hermaphrodites" 302). While Chase does not offer a source for this exact ratio, the overall argument is not disputed (see also Preves *Identity* 56, Holmes *Perilous* 67f, and Gearhart above).

the discourse. Rhetorical strategies such as silencing the parents and keeping the patients in ignorance contributed to an atmosphere of stigma and shame surrounding intersex. Furthermore, intersex was said to be extremely rare[18] and parents and patients had only their doctors to talk to (cf. Preves *Identity* 125-8; see also Karkazis *Fixing* 22-6, 89-178). As an effect, the Baltimore protocols contained intersex safely within medical discourse and prevented a spread to other discourses for almost four decades.

Scholarly texts on the history of intersex note only scattered evidence for discussions of intersex outside of medical discourse during the 1980s: *Ms.* is a liberal feminist magazine that was founded in the early 1970s. With an article on female genital mutilation (FGM) in African countries, *Ms.* magazine co-founder Gloria Steinem and Robin Morgan banded together recent feminist critiques of this practice in March 1980. In a letter to the editor, feminist biologists Ruth Hubbard and Patricia Farnes pointed out that the practice of clitoridectomy was not limited to so-called Third World countries, but also part of a procedure "to 'repair' by 'plastic surgery' so-called genital ambiguities" (Hubbard/Farnes qtd. in Chase "Hermaphrodites" 312) in the United States. According to intersex activist Cheryl Chase, this critique on the management of intersex based on the Baltimore protocols was the first of its kind. At the time, western feminists ignored the similarities between FGM and intersex treatment and Hubbard's and Farnes' call to follow-up studies on the effect of clitoridectomies on girls' psychosexual development went unheard.

In 1985, another feminist biologist, Anne Fausto-Sterling, addresses intersex in her study on biological differences between men and women, *Myths of Gender*.[19] Fausto-Sterling discusses both nurture-centered approaches like John Money's and nature-centered approaches like

---

18 For a discussion of intersex frequency between John Money and Anne Fausto-Sterling see below.

19 *Myths of Gender* critically reviews research on genetic differences, on hormonal differences, and studies on brain differences (second edition). Her analyses reveal a myriad of interactions between the socio-cultural and the biological realm and culminate in the claim: "Bodies, minds, and cultures interact in such complex and profound ways that we cannot strip them down and compare them separately" (270).

Imperato-McGuinley's.[20] In a chapter on hormones and aggression, she comments on the effects of clitoridectomy in three-year-old girls. While bluntly criticizing the post-surgical appearance of the genitalia ("If the surgery results in genitalia that looks like those shown in Money and Ehrhardt's book, then these particular psychologists are in need of an anatomy lesson!" [138]), she also points out that the "subtle effects of genital surgery on behavior, and even the likelihood of mutilation fears, cannot be lightly dismissed. Yet nowhere are these possible effects adequately discussed" (*Myths* 138).

In the same year, Suzanne Kessler conducts interviews with six intersex experts (one clinical geneticist, three endocrinologists, one psychoendocrinologist, and one urologist) and analyzes the implications of their understanding of gender reflected in their approach towards intersex. Kessler, a psychologist by training, had co-authored *Gender: An Ethnomethodological Approach* already in 1978 together with Wendy McKenna and elaborated their perspective on gender as a social construct. While their focus in *Gender* is on transsexuality, intersex is mentioned about a dozen times and Kessler's work on intersex in the 1980s can be seen as an elaboration of her earlier work. Kessler published a first report on her research in *Signs* in 1990, while the book-length *Lessons From the Intersexed* followed in 1998. Also in 1990, Julia Epstein published an article on the history of hermaphroditism, "Either/Or – Neither/Both," in the journal *Genders* and continued this work in *Altered Conditions* in 1995.

---

20 Endocrinologist Julianne Imperato-McGuinley and her team studied a remote village in Santo-Domingo with a relatively high percentage of individuals that show 5α-Reductase deficiency (5-ARD). Individuals with XY chromosomes and 5-ARD lack an enzyme that converts the androgen dihydrotestosterone and whose external genitalia may look more female than male. During puberty, these individuals may experience virilization due to an increased testosterone level. Imperato-McGuinley found that 16 out of 18 individuals raised female transitioned to the male gender in puberty. She concluded that hormones, and therefore 'nature', determine the psychological sex. Her studies oppose Money's theory of psychosexual neutrality and were cited by Milton Diamond in his arguments against Money's approach. Fausto-Sterling critically reviews both approaches and shows shortcomings of both (cf. *Myths* 85-9). *Middlesex* protagonist Callie is depicted as living with 5-ARD.

Fausto-Sterling and Kessler, two feminist scholars, approach intersex critically in the second half of the 1980s and continue to do so throughout the 1990s. They question medical assumptions about gender, challenge the current treatment, and ask for psychological support rather than invasive surgery to manage intersex. Although Fausto-Sterling and Kessler approach intersex from different disciplines, they share an investment in feminism and critically evaluate approaches that deny socio-cultural implications in the construction of sex. Their publications, however, by now classics in the field of feminist science and gender studies, did not incite public turmoil or a rethinking of the medical management of intersex at the time.[21] Despite Kessler's often cited conclusion that genital ambiguity is "corrected not because it is threatening to the infant's life but because it is threatening to the infant's culture" (*Lessons* 25), the Baltimore protocols were held firmly in place.

It was only in 1993 that intersex received attention outside of specialized scholarly and/or medical debates. Fausto-Sterling published a provocative essay titled "The Five Sexes: Why Male and Female Are Not Enough" in *The Sciences*, the magazine of the New York Academy of Sciences. The article was reprinted in the *New York Times* (March 12, 1993: A29) as "How Many Sexes Are There?" and triggered a number of reactions from readers in both publications. The subsequent issue of *The Sciences* printed five letters from readers and a response by Fausto-Sterling. The *NYT* repeatedly returned to the article over the next couple of years, e.g. an advertisement by the Catholic League for Religious and Civil Rights in 1995 read, "It is maddening to listen to discussions of 'five genders' when every sane person knows there are but two sexes, both of which are rooted in nature" (qtd. in Fausto-Sterling *Sexing* 78).

In her article, Fausto-Sterling had argued that the notion of "a two-party sexual system" was "in defiance of nature" ("Five Sexes" n.p.) and criticized unchallenged, heteronormative assumptions that governed legal and medical practices. Speaking from the position of a biologist, she explained there were "many gradations running from female to male; and [...] one can argue that along that spectrum lie at least five sexes – and

---

21 Morland discusses the impact of Fausto-Sterling's early critique in *Myths of Gender* (1985) and Kessler's 1990 *Signs* article and shows how their critique rewrites "intersex treatment as a discursively produced injustice" ("Five" 53).

perhaps even more." Taking up Victorian terminology she named three groups of intersex bodies ("herms": true hermaphrodites with both ovarian and testicular tissue; "merms": male pseudohermaphrodites with testes and aspects of female anatomy; "ferms": female pseudohermaphrodites with ovaries and aspects of male anatomy[22]) and declared them "additional sexes each in its own right." Fausto-Sterling offered brief glimpses of historical approaches to intersex and characterized the contemporary treatment of intersex, based on the Baltimore protocols, as "a clear example of what the French historian Michel Foucault has called biopower." Within this reasoning, intersex bodies were not treated for health reasons, but due to the "cultural need to maintain clear distinctions between the sexes." In the final paragraphs, Fausto-Sterling asks the reader to "imagine a world in which [...] the sexes have multiplied beyond currently imaginable limits [...] a world of shared powers. [...] in a culture that had overcome sexual division." These visions of her "utopia" mark her strong feminist conviction and align the politics of intersex treatment with the politics of gender equality. Moreover, Fausto-Sterling addressed alternative models for treatment, demanded that surgical interventions be held off until the age of consent, and pointed to case studies of intersex individuals who grew up without surgery.[23]

---

22 Morland refers to Fausto-Sterling's terminology as a "herminology" ("Five" 38) and science fiction novelist Melissa Scott uses the terminology and the concept of a society with five sexes in *Shadow Man* (1995).

23 Fausto-Sterling remarks "there is not a psychotic or a suicide in the lot" and is probably referring to the study by Kessler "Construction" and *Lessons*. In the early 1990s, follow up studies with intersex individuals were more than rare. John Money had reported on seventeen individuals who had undergone clitoridectomy in 1961: Twelve of them lived as women. Of the twelve, three did not offer any information on genital sensation. Four women seemed "inexperienced in orgasm," five women seemed to have experienced orgasm, and Money concludes: "The point of these data on orgasm and clitorectomy is not, however, that some clitorectomized patients did not experience orgasm. On the contrary, the point is that the capacity for orgasm proved compatible with clitorectomy and surgical feminization of the genitalia in some, if not all, of these patients" (Money qtd. in Fausto-Sterling *Sexing* 297). See also Fausto-

The reactions to this article were diverse: one reader referred to Fausto-Sterling's argument as "bizarre" and "deranged" (Bird "Letter" n.p.). Another asked about the possibility of self-impregnation, and John Money commented that it was "reckless to conjecture that on the campus of Brown University there are 240 students with a birth defect of the sex organs" (Money "Letter" n.p.). While Fausto-Sterling had pointed out that the frequency of intersex is difficult to determine and depends on the varying definitions of intersex conditions, Money's language reflects his understanding of intersex as an anatomical 'defect' that needs correction and clearly pathologizes intersex anatomy. Suzanne Kessler's argument shifts attention to the feminist aspects of Fausto-Sterling's text and criticizes her focus on biology to dismantle the heteronormative order: "in everyday life," Kessler argues, "gender [...] is performed regardless of the configuration of the flesh under the clothes" ("Letter" n.p.). Fausto-Sterling's argumentation for a continuum of sexes rests on descriptions of human biology and questions the adequacy of these descriptions but not the practice of description as such. Morland elaborates on this aspect and explains: "this is the wrong kind of question to ask, because it presumes the possibility of a descriptive correspondence between the identification of one's genitalia (penis, vagina, clitoris, etc.), and one's identity as a member of a sex (male, female, hermaphrodite, 'merm', etc.)" ("Five" 39). Intersex genitalia should not indicate more or less of a sex than non-intersex genitalia and he concludes that intersex and non-intersex individuals could identify as male, female, or intersex. From this perspective, Fausto-Sterling's re-reading of intersex anatomy for the sake of feminist politics reinforces rather than challenges an essentialist understanding of sex. Despite this criticism, or rather because of it, Fausto-Sterling's article is credited by virtually all intersex chronologists as having triggered the intersex advocacy movement. Yet the reason for the lasting impact is not its feminist critique on the Baltimore standards and Money's sour reply, but another letter by a writer using the pseudonym Cheryl Chase.

Headed "Intersexual Rights", Cheryl Chase's letter is printed as the first of five letters from readers and it opens with a blow: "As an intersexual I found Anne Fausto-Sterling's article [...] of intense personal interest"

Sterling *Sexing* 85; Kessler *Lessons* 52-76; Karkazis *Fixing*; Klöppel *XXOXY* 316; Preves *Identity*.

(Chase "Letter" n.p.). Up until then, intersex discourse had been dominated by doctors, biologists, and more recently some feminists. Chase's statement in this letter marks the first public intersex voice in the debate. Claiming a label that until then referred to passive patients, receivers of treatment, Chase confidently points to a blind spot in the discourse and offers to "provide some perspective on the experience." Chase continues by describing the devastating effects of genital surgery and hormone replacement therapy, pointing to the psychological effects of ongoing treatment and commenting on the absence of follow-up studies. She also relates her critique to the normative ideals of contemporary western culture and its "hatred and fear of sexuality." Towards the end of her letter, Chase discusses Fausto-Sterling's choice of terminology and anticipates later discussions on labels and language. In her closing paragraph, Chase finally addresses intersex people and announces a support group: "I encourage intersexuals and people close to them to write to us at the Intersex Society of North America, Post Office Box 31791, San Francisco, California 94131, where we are assembling a support group and documenting our lives" ("Letters" n.p.). The letter is reported to be the founding document of the intersex movement (cf. Preves *Identity* 92f) and it foreshadows one of the movement's central activities: telling stories. Chase later admits that using plural pronouns such as "we" and "us" was a deliberate strategy to attract attention to the group that, at the time of writing, had only one member – Chase herself. Furthermore, the use of plural pronouns in combination with Chase's identification with the label "intersexual" turned the medicalized term into an identity label for people with various intersex experiences.

Although the Intersex Society of North America (ISNA) was not the first support group for people with atypical sex differentiation,[24] ISNA

---

24 Preves notes the Turner's Syndrome Society, founded in Minneapolis in 1987, as the first support group for intersex people. Other diagnosis-specific and locally organized groups were founded over the following years in North America and worldwide (cf. *Identity* 92). Internet communication facilitated connecting these diverse groups, and intersex support groups nowadays are organized both on local and global levels. See for example the *Organisation Intersex International* (OII, www.oiiinternational.com) founded in Quebec,

differed from other groups in its overtly political goals. Cheryl Chase explains ISNA's twofold aims in a 1998 article that chronicles the emergence of intersex activism:

ISNA's most immediate goal has been to create a community of intersex people who could provide peer support to deal with shame, stigma, grief, and rage as well as with practical issues such as how to obtain old medical records or locate a sympathetic psychotherapist or endocrinologist. [...] ISNA's longer-term and more fundamental goal, however, is to change the way intersex infants are treated. ("Hermaphrodites" 306)

And Chase continues by describing the difference to diagnosis-specific groups:

When I first began organizing ISNA, I met leaders of the Turner's Syndrome Society [...] I was inspired by their accomplishments [...], but I wanted ISNA to have a different focus. I was [...] more interested in challenging its [intersexuality's M.K.] medicalization entirely, and more interested still in politicizing a pan-intersexual identity across the divisions of particular etiologies in order to destabilize more effectively the heteronormative assumptions underlying the violence directed at our bodies. ("Hermaphrodites" 307)

Although Chase insists on the double aim of peer support and medical reform from the beginning, in the first few years, ISNA's activities centered on the issue of community building.[25] She links her activism to an emerging transgender movement that focused on a critique of heteronormative structures, and reports that moving to San Francisco in 1992 helped her to

---

Canada, in 2003 by Curtis E. Hinkle with its various local chapters that connect activists both locally and globally.

25 The shift in focus from peer support to medical reform is reflected in ISNA's self-description on their website. In January 1998, ISNA self-characterizes as "a peer support, education, and advocacy group founded and operated by and for intersexuals: individuals born with an anatomy or physiology which differs from cultural ideals of male and female" (internetarchive.org, crawled isna.org 20. Jan, 1998). Ten years later, in 2008, ISNA is introduced as "devoted to systemic change to end shame, secrecy, and unwanted genital surgeries for people born with an anatomy that someone decided is not standard for male or female" (isna.org, accessed 07.08.2013).

connect with transgender activists like Kate Bornstein and the activists from Transgender Nation.[26] While medical discourse used "intersexuality" as an umbrella term for what was in their eyes a diverse group of only loosely connected diagnoses, Chase adopts this broad label to emphasize similarities between intersex experiences.

ISNA quickly began to establish a network to facilitate interaction and communication between intersex people. An e-mail mail list was established in November 1994; the first newsletter *Hermaphrodites with Attitude*, full of personal intersex narratives, was published in the winter of the same year, regular meetings of support groups have been organized since 1995, and the website www.isna.org, with a connected site for personal narratives called "Intersex Voices", went online in January 1996. In the same year, a video called *Hermaphrodites Speak!* was produced, featuring ten intersex people who volunteered their personal stories. Simultaneously, Chase and fellow activists began to organize political campaigns. By writing letters to magazines and medical journals that featured articles on intersex such as the *Johns Hopkins Magazine*, the *Journal of Urology*, or the *SF Bay Times*, activists started to publicly voice their criticism and to challenge the reports on intersex spread by medical experts. Also in 1996, ISNA activists picketed a symposium of plastic surgeons in New York in May and held a demonstration before the Annual Meeting of the American Academy of Pediatricians in Boston.[27] ISNA's activities were diverse and well-documented in their newsletter and online: the website developed into a research resource for anybody interested in the topic, videos were made, handbooks for parents and teachers were designed and distributed, t-shirts with the "Hermaphrodites with Attitude"-logo were available by donation, sponsors were sought, individual doctors and medical associations were contacted directly, and Cheryl Chase, ISNA's "fearless leader" (*HWA* summer 1998:8), together with an ever changing

---

26 In her account of the emergence of intersex activism, Karkazis distinguishes between intersex support groups (cf. *Fixing* 243-5) and intersex activism (245-63), the latter describing the history of ISNA.

27 Activists had offered to discuss their experiences with surgeons, but were denied access and AAP officials had "no interest in meeting with any Hermaphrodites with Attitude" ("Special Issue" *Chrysalis* 50). For reports on both events see Beck "Streets," Holmes "Growing Up," and Holmes "Deciding."

and ever growing board of directors and advisors, planned and plotted the agenda and politics of the organization. International cooperation with intersex groups from all parts of the world were developed, and with more and more support and advocacy groups in the US, intersex peer support turned into a viable social movement with a political agenda. The top priority on their list was (and is) to change the medical treatment of individuals with intersex. ISNA's mission statement therefore reads: "The Intersex Society of North America (ISNA) is devoted to systemic change to end shame, secrecy, and unwanted genital surgeries for people born with an anatomy that someone decided is not standard for male or female" (isna.org). Note that it reads "systemic change." The statement makes clear that ISNA aims at the medical paradigm of intersex treatment.

In 1995, Congress introduced a law to ban female genital mutilation in the U.S. and ISNA intervened because the law specifically exempted surgeries for so-called "medical purposes" (Federal Prohibition of Female Genital Mutilation Act of 1995). The law was passed in 1996 and ISNA's critique received little response. In 1997, after Milton Diamond and John Colapinto had published their accounts of the "cornerstone David Reimer case" (Preves *Identity* 156), Cheryl Chase and other activists used the media hype to draw attention to the practice of non-consensual surgeries on intersex infants (cf. Chase "Portrait").[28] Slowly, the opposition of individual doctors to the activists' claims wore off. In 1998, historian of science Alice Dreger edited a special issue on intersex for the *Journal of Clinical Ethics*, and in May 2000, Chase was invited to speak at the meeting of the Lawson Wilkins Pediatric Society. Earlier that year, pediatric urologist Ian Aaronson had founded the North American Task Force on Intersex (NAFTI) with Cheryl Chase as one of its members. The task force was a rather loose network of medical experts from various fields and selected activists, and participants did not necessarily agree on the best practice in intersex treatment (cf. Preves *Identity* 150f). Nevertheless, it was the first organization where doctors and some activists collaborated. In Arizona in 2002, Chase informed the First World Congress on the Hormonal and Genetic Basis for Sexual Differentiation Disorder about the "agenda of the intersex patient advocacy movement" (Chase "Agenda"),

---

28 See "Facts and Figures of Speech in Science and Activism" for more information on the Reimer 'case'.

and her invitation to the congress marks, on the one hand, the slow change in medical discourse, and, on the other hand, Chase's growing effort to collaborate with rather than confront the medical establishment. ISNA had changed their strategy: they started as a peer support group for "intersexuals" who called themselves "hermaphrodites with attitude," formed alliances with "transsexual sister Susan Stryker" (*HWA* 1995: 11) and demonstrated with activists from "Transgender Menace" in 1996. Four years later, the use of the term *hermaphrodite* and the use of *intersexual* as an identity category had significantly dropped in ISNA publications and given way to a less "essentializing" (Dreger/Herndon "Progress" 209) terminology. As Dreger and Herndon, both of them "academic feminists" and former directors of ISNA, explain, it can be "dehumanizing to equate people with one aspect of their physicality" and they align the change in terminology to the politics of disability rights groups (cf. 209). In her talk in 2002, Chase bears testimony to this approach and repeatedly refers to intersex individuals as "patients", refutes assertions that intersex is about gender, calls the intersex rights movement the "intersex patient advocacy movement", and asserts that "[m]edicine has an important part to play in lessening the pain of living with intersex conditions" (Chase "Agenda" 2f). Moreover, ISNA had used *intersexual* as a noun indicating an identity on their website until 2000. In 2001, the name of their newsletter *Hermaphrodites with Attitude* was changed to *ISNA News*. Former ISNA activist Morgan Holmes comments cynically on ISNA's activities: "[...] the intersex movement [...] has become not just a few voices crying 'foul' in the medical wilderness, but a slick media-driven and consumer/lobby movement" (Holmes *Perilous* 125).

While intersex organizations generally shared ISNA's overall goal of changing the medical standard of care and supported the paradigm shift to what ISNA called a patient-centered approach, ISNA's adoption of pathologizing terminology, its increasing distance to identity based politics, and its cooperation with surgeons estranged some activists and allies. This process culminated in another shift in terminology in 2005.

NAMING OTHER PARTS: *INTERSEX* AND *DSD* (2005 AND COUNTING)

In 2005, Alice Dreger, Cheryl Chase, and three 'supportive' medical doctors published a paper in the *Journal of Pediatric Endocrinology & Metabolism* criticizing current intersex terminology. They argue that all terminology based on the root *hermaphrodit** should be abandoned as they deem it "illogical, outdated, and harmful" ("Changing" 729). In consequence they suggest a rigid change in nomenclature and advocate for diagnosis specific terminology plus a new umbrella term "disorders of sexual differentiation" (733). The critique of the 'old' terminology voiced in a medical journal was taken well by the medical establishment, as the proceedings of an international conference in the same year show. Hosted by the Lawson Wilkins Pediatric Endocrine Society and the European Society for Paediatric Endocrinology, fifty representatives from different institutions were invited to Chicago in October 2005 to discuss the status of intersex treatment. Among the interdisciplinary medical experts (pediatric endocrinologists, pediatric urologists, psychiatrists, psychologists, and geneticists) were also two intersex activists: Cheryl Chase from ISNA and Barbara Thomas from the German support group XY-Frauen. The "Consensus Statement on Management of Intersex Disorders" was published both in *Pediatrics*, the journal of the American Academy of Pediatrics, and in *Archives of Child Disease* affiliated with the European Academy of Pediatrics in 2006 and summarizes the results from the conference. Referring to the "potentially pejorative" and "confusing" character of terms like "hermaphroditism", "pseudohermaphroditism", and "intersex" and quoting Dreger et al. 2005, authors suggest the term "disorders of sex development" (DSD) to refer to "congenital conditions in which development of chromosomal, gonadal, or anatomic sex is atypical" (Lee et al. "Consensus" 488). Thereby, the Chicago Conference basically takes up the critique on terminology voiced by ISNA activists earlier. Both the new terminology and further results of the conference continue to be discussed in online forums, at conferences and in letters to the journals. Recently, Feder ("Imperatives"), Spurgas ("(Un)Queering"), Reis ("Divergence") and Karkazis (*Fixing* 259-63) have summed up major positions in the debate. Reis describes the conference as "pathbreaking, specifically because intersex adults were included in the policy-making process at all" (Reis "Divergence" 538). Furthermore, she adds, experts agreed on the need for a more conservative approach to surgery. Nevertheless, Reis also examines the critique of the term "disorder" voiced by activists such as Peter Trinkle (support group Bodies Like Ours) and Morgan Holmes (formerly ISNA), who reject the term for its pathologizing character and its limited value for identity formation. Advocates of the term, like ISNA, stress that "DSD is much less charged than 'intersex,' and that it makes our message of patient-centered care much more accessible to parents and doctors" ("Why" isna.org). Since 1999, explains ISNA on their website, they had decided to work "primarily on medical reform" ("Why" isna.org), and to focus "strategically on educating medical professionals" ("What" isna.org). ISNA had consciously dropped the peer support from its agenda and concentrated all its activities on medical reform. Suggesting the medical term *disorder* in the first place and embracing the acronym *DSD* was just a logical step in their politics of cooperation and compromise.[29]

Following the Chicago Conference, which implemented the new DSD nomenclature and led to considerable disagreement among intersex activists, collaboration between ISNA and doctors intensified. In 2006, a so-called Consortium on the Management of Disorders of Sex Development, an independent group of doctors and ISNA activists, produced two books that applied the DSD terminology and collected ISNA's ideas on patient-centered care, *Clinical Guidelines for the Management of Disorders of Sex Development in Childhood* and the *Handbook for Parents*. With the move from *intersex* to *DSD*, and the strategic cooperation with medical experts, ISNA began to understand itself

---

29 Results from the Chicago Conference were discussed both online and in print see, for example, the proceedings from ISNA's DSD Symposium in October 2006 and Barbara Thomas' "Report on Chicago Consensus Conference 2005" (aissg.org). Critics include David Cameron (formerly ISNA), Esther Morris Leidolf (President and founder of MRKH.org), Sherri Groveman Morris (founder of the United States branch of the Androgen Insensitivity Syndrome Support Group), and Curtis Hinkle (founder of Organization Intersex International). Emi Koyama (director of Intersex Initiative) supports the new terminology. The controversy is well-documented on the websites of the Intersex Initiative and the Androgen Insensitivity Syndrome Support Group AISSG.

as an impediment or as inappropriate for its primary purpose. With its history of identity-based politics and public protest, some doctors were still hesitating to cooperate with the activists. Consequently, ISNA activists started to build a new organization, Accord Alliance, "with a mission to promote integrated, comprehensive approaches to care that enhance the overall health and well-being of persons with DSDs and their families" (isna.org). In 2008, when Accord Alliance (AA), officially started to take up its work, ISNA closed its doors. Assets and funds, states ISNA on its homepage, were transferred to Accord Alliance "with the comfort and knowledge that its work will continue" (isna.org). While the Intersex Society of North America bore the term *intersex* proudly in its name, Accord Alliance emphasizes cooperation and agreement without mentioning a cause. On their homepage, AA promises "better care, better outcomes, better lives" (accordalliance.org) and explains that there "is a strong need for an organization like Accord Alliance to assume the role of a convenor of stakeholders across the health care system and DSD communities" (accordalliance.org). Part of the legacy of ISNA is therefore visible in the politics of the new organization, but apart from that, any reference to the history of Accord Alliance is missing: as of February 2015, the AA website mentions the terms *intersex* and *hermaphroditism* only in their FAQ section; ISNA is not mentioned at all, although the two handbooks issued by ISNA in 2006 are still promoted as valuable resources on AA's website; neither former ISNA director Cheryl Chase nor long-time activist Alice Dreger are part of the directory.

The Consensus meeting in 2005 provided clinical guidelines for the treatment of intersex conditions, and philosopher and former ISNA member Ellen Feder summarizes the development from *intersex* to *DSD* as a change in conceptualization from "disorders like no other" to "disorders like many others" (Feder "Imperatives" 227). In her analysis of the guidelines as normalization, she asks whether "intersex [has] taken on the status of an identity, or [whether it is] a condition that is merely incidental to one's person" (226).[30] The history of the intersex movement shows that activists have answered this question differently. In 1993, ISNA began to build an

---

30 Spurgas argues correspondingly that the shift in terminology and change in politics is a shift from *"intersex-as-queer"* ("(Un)Queering" 99) to *"intersex-as-pathology"* (107). See also Holmes *Perilous* 123.

intersex community based on shared experiences of shame, secrecy and unwanted surgery. Fifteen years later, the same organization abandoned identity-based politics and started a new organization to close ranks with the medical establishment. When ISNA shut its doors in 2008, other organizations had already taken over and today 'the' intersex movement consists of various organizations ranging from local or regional diagnosis-specific groups and parents groups, to international groups focusing on legal advice and human rights issues, and to groups interested in collaboration with queer, LGBT or disability groups. The movement and its actors work both virtually and in personal meetings. The aims and strategies of each group are specific, and while some groups focus on peer and family support, others focus on raising awareness (public, legal or medical) to reach their goals. Both the politics of cooperation and confrontation are part of activists' struggles and strategic alliances are formed whenever useful.

At the bottom of these debates, I would argue, lies the question of the respective concept of intersex: what *is* intersex? Is it an identity or a condition? What are its defining characteristics? Who has the power to define and to name them? And, who interprets and evaluates these characteristics? In the following, I will address these questions by analyzing the negotiations and the struggle over the concept *intersex* in medical, activist and fictional contexts. My responses will not offer a definitive statement on the 'nature' of intersex, but critically analyze different perspectives on intersex in their respective discursive contexts.

Facts and Figures of Speech in Science and Activism

LOOK WHO'S TALKING: DAVID REIMER'S STORY

1997 was a remarkable year in intersex history: together with the psychologist H. Keith Sigmundson, biologist Milton Diamond published an "up-date to a case originally accepted as a 'classic' in fields ranging from medicine to the humanities" (Diamond "Reassignment" n.p.); journalist John Colapinto accompanied the publication with his magazine article "The True Story of John/Joan," and intersex activists Cheryl Chase and Martha Coventry guest edited a special issue on intersexuality in the journal *Chrysalis*.

The 'classic' case that Diamond and Sigmundson are referring to is the story of the twins Bruce and Brian Reimer. In 1968, after a botched circumcision, when 22 months old, Bruce was castrated, assigned female, and renamed Brenda. At age 14, Brenda was told she had been born a boy, resumed life as a male teenager and called himself David. During the 1970s, the 'case' had been publicized by John Money as definite proof for his theory of gender development. Their 1997 follow-up of the Reimer case, Diamond and Sigmundson claimed, "completely reverses the conclusions and theory behind the original reports" ("Reassignment" n.p.). What was used by John Money as evidence for a nurture-overrules-nature approach to gender was now turned into its opposite. Diamond concluded that "normal humans are not psychosexually neutral at birth but are, in keeping with their mammalian heritage, predisposed and biased to interact with the environment, familial and social forces, in a male or female mode"

(1997 n.p.).[1] In other words, with Milton Diamond, gender was again believed to be biologically determined.

Diamond's publication, then, does indeed evoke the appearance that the theory that informed and legitimated the practice of early genital surgery on intersex newborns was now turned on its head. After all, Money's first publications on the case had indicated a sweeping success. In 1972, he reported in *Man & Woman, Boy & Girl* (with Anke Ehrhardt) the twin was a happy girl who liked to wear dresses and who behaved considerably differently from her rough-and-tumble brother. Three years later, in *Sexual Signatures: On Being a Man or a Woman* (with journalist Patricia Tucker) and in a peer reviewed article for the *Archives of Sexual Behavior*, "Ablatio Penis: Normal Male Infant Sex-Reassigned as a Girl," the second report repeated much of the first and continued the successful narrative: Brenda was very active, showed some tomboy behavior, yet identified clearly as a girl. *Time* magazine had applauded already early in 1973: "This dramatic case [...] provides strong support for a major contention of women's liberationists: that conventional patterns of masculine and feminine behavior can be altered. It also casts doubt on the theory that major sex differences, psychological as well as anatomical, are immutably set by the genes at conception" ("The Sexes" n.p.). *Sexual Signatures* was also hailed by the *Times Literary Supplement* as "such an intelligent, such a sane, such an enlightened book" (Banks 1117). While the Baltimore protocols for managing intersex in newborns were in fact widely established by the 1960s, there had always remained some critical voices doubting the theory. The twin case was understood as the perfect experiment in human psychosexual development and almost silenced that critique.[2]

---

1 In his early writings, Diamond sometimes evokes heteronormative patterns to define gender identity, e.g. sexual desire for men signals a female gender identity. These arguments are more refined in later publications. Moreover, the reference to "mammalian heritage" bears a rhetorical similarity to Money's use of Konrad Lorenz' imprinting. Both invoke 'nature' or 'animal biology' to support their respective claims for gender development in humans.

2 Klöppel critically analyzes the instrumentalization of 'John/Joan' and intersex in general as 'experiments in nature' (cf. "Formierung" and *XXOXY* 525-31, 535-38).

Diamond's criticism of Money's theory did not go unnoticed: public attention was secured by a dozen media reports and interviews.[3] The biggest splash made the article "The True Story of John/Joan" by John Colapinto for *Rolling Stone*. Colapinto had contacted Reimer and gained "exclusive access" ("True" 56) and "more than 20 hours of candid interviews" (56); never before, explains Colapinto, had Reimer "told his story in full" (56). On the one hand, the article stages Reimer's story against the backdrop of a "30-year rivalry between eminent sex researchers" (56), i.e. Milton Diamond and John Money, as the touchstone between medical "triumph" and "failure" (56). On the other, Colapinto relates Reimer's "purely private catastrophe" (56) to intersex activism by introducing ISNA activists Cheryl Chase (including a picture), Kiira Triea, Heidi Walcutt and Martha Coventry in the same article.

The *Rolling Stone* feature won Colapinto a national magazine award (ASME Award Reporting 1998) and he continued to collaborate with Reimer and published the book length biography *As Nature Made Him: The Boy Who Was Raised as a Girl* in 2000. The book became a *New York Times* bestseller and media attention was again high. Reimer allowed Colapinto to use his full name in the 2000 publication and the following interviews and TV documentaries often used both the pseudonyms "John/Joan" that were introduced by Diamond and Sigmundson, and the full name David Reimer. According to Colapinto, Peter Jackson, director of *Lord of the Rings*, bought the movie rights to the story (cf. "Gender Gap" n.p.). Reimer's story as related by Colapinto provoked a flood of coverage in newspapers, magazines, and TV, and Cheryl Chase later remembers:

---

3 Preves notes print media coverage in the spring of 1997 in the *New York Times*, *Newsweek*, *Rolling Stone*, *Time*, *On the Issues*, *Out* and *Mademoiselle*. TV features for *NBC Dateline*, *Inside Edition*, or *Prime Time Live* included interviews with Reimer, various intersex activists, Milton Diamond and Anne Fausto-Sterling (cf. Preves *Identity* 97). For other summaries and analyses of the Reimer debate see also Karkazis *Fixing* 69-77; Morland "Plastic Man;" Goldie *Man* 174-93. Early reports usually end on positive notes and describe the married man and adoptive father as "forward looking" (Diamond "Reassignment" n.p.). Yet David Reimer committed suicide in 2004; his twin brother Brian had died of an overdose of antidepressants in 2002 (cf. Colapinto "Gender Gap").

We took advantage of the press's attention to the John/Joan story, making them aware that intersex children are treated every day with the sorts of medical arrogance, mutilating surgery, and willful deception that were imposed on John. The recent media coverage in *Newsweek*, the *New York Times*, and others has been very successful for us precisely because it presents the story as one of struggle and social justice (a story about us, our culture), rather than about *them* (intersexuals as freaks). ("Portrait" 92f)

In the winter of 1997/1998, another intersex related publication went into print: ISNA published its first collection of "writings about the lived experience and the history of intersexuality" (3) in *Chrysalis*, a transgender-themed journal with a circulation of about 1.500. Chase had already announced in 1993 that part of ISNA's mission was to "document[...] our lives" ("Letter" n.p.) and with the ISNA newsletter *Hermaphrodites with Attitude* (*HWA*, published since 1994[4]) and the organization's website "www.isna.org" (online since 1996[5]) they had already begun to put the plan into action. In general, the journal *Chrysalis*, whose name refers to the cocoon stage of insects, welcomed "stories, articles, letters, editorials, news clippings, position statements, research reports, press releases, and artwork" (*Chrysalis* 2). The special issue edited by Martha Coventry and Cheryl Chase contains 26 contributions ranging

---

4   *Hermaphrodites with Attitude* (*HWA*) was first published in winter 1994 and continued to be published in irregular intervals until issue 7 in 1999. ISNA resumed to produce a newsletter called *ISNA News* between 2001 and 2005 (six issues in total). In the first *HWA* issue, readers were invited to contribute "short articles, stories, poetry, and illustrations" (HWA 1, Winter 1994: 1) and the following issues of the newsletter prove a potpourri of various pieces and forms of writing.

5   In the beginning, the ISNA website "www.isna.org" was accompanied by a website called "Intersex Voices" maintained by activist Kiira Triea. Next to a section called "Real People" containing autobiographical writings of intersex people, the site had a section called "Other Voices" which collected prose and poetry. In 2000, www.isna.org had an average of 1000 visitors per day, in 2004 an average of 1800 visitors per day (cf. Morland "Critique" 193). The website is not online anymore, but can be found through "the wayback machine" on www.archive.org.

from poetry, fiction, and first person account to reprints of medical documents and leaflets, pictures, mock interviews, caricatures, a list of peer support groups and scholarly writing. What it does not mention is the story of David Reimer.

1997, as I postulated in the beginning, was a decisive year in intersex history. The stories of David Reimer, his life and treatment, were told and retold by various actors in the medical, scholarly and public field and they took on very different shapes: from supporting evidence for Money's theories to the exact opposite. And while both Money and Diamond used Reimer's case to justify and explain their respective medical theories on intersex and transsexuality, David Reimer was neither one nor the other. Following literary scholar Julia Epstein's reading, these opposing narratives may be seen as offering two different "explanatory structures" (*Altered* 19) for the same bodily experience. Reimer's body, in that sense, is used as "a cultural surface onto which have been mapped social expectations and ideological meanings" (*Altered* 21). Intersex scholar Iain Morland argues in a similar direction when he evokes the mid-twentieth century notion of "plasticity as a quintessential human attribute" ("Plastic" 81) and positions both Money's Baltimore protocols *and* Diamond's concept in this discourse. Money argued that gender plasticity was innate, and therefore 'natural,' and Diamond opposed the plasticity of gender and enforced the biological limits of such plasticity (cf. 91). So, while the two researchers seem to hold opposing opinions, Morland concludes that both of them remain within the discourse of human plasticity.

English scholar Bernice Hausman explores the narrative potential of Reimer's experience and shows that the different positions in the nature-nurture debate, biological determinism versus social constructivism, are effects of different readings of a gendered narrative. With Butler, she maintains, "becoming a man or a woman is a process of learning how to represent that identity publicly; in Judith Butler's terms, it means producing that identity through the repeated iterations of representing it as if it already existed" ("Boys" 125). In Colapinto's account, Reimer's use of narrative creates a coherent and stable male gender identity and thereby makes him a man. Diamond and Sigmundson, Hausman argues, accept Reimer's narrative "*as fact*" ("Boys" 127) and interpret his conviction as an effect of his chromosomal status and prenatal hormone dosages. She points out that Diamond and Sigmundson ignore possible effects of an "enforced and exhibitionistic femininity" on Reimer – a femininity that may be problematic for any individual regardless of their chromosomal set up (cf. 126f). Butler develops Hausman's arguments and points out that "[John's] body becomes a point of reference for a narrative that is not about this body but that seizes on the body, as it were, to inaugurate a narrative that interrogates the limits of the conceivably human" ("Justice" 627).

John Money and Milton Diamond were often cast as the major opponents in the intersex debate of 1997; however, I suggest, they may not be as opposed as previously believed. After all, as I explained above, they both participated in the nature-nurture debate (albeit from opposing positions, cf. Hausman "Justice"); they both evoked the notion of plasticity (cf. Morland "Plastic") and they both provided a medical explanatory narrative for a specific experience (cf. Epstein *Altered*). Moreover, I suggest, they both engaged in a scholarly mode of speaking: their original contributions to the debate are positioned in medico-scientific journals, they were spoken with the authority and professional distance of the academic researcher and their arguments are based on findings that they present as evidence, as facts that prove a particular claim. Both their opinions were echoed in public media and they presented their arguments in numerous interviews, newspapers and magazines.[6] Colapinto's article, from this

---

6   Diamond's first critique on Money's twin case was already published in 1982: the BBC had interviewed him for a 1980 documentary on the twins (Williams and Smith) that was screened only in Great Britain. Diamond quotes in length from the script of the documentary, culminating in the statement of one psychiatrist: "This teenager 'is having considerable difficulty in adjusting as a female. ... At the present time [1979, M.K.] she does display certain features which make me suspicious that she will ever make the adjustment as a woman'" ("Monozygotic" 184). The BBC team, explains Diamond, informed Money about their findings who then refused to participate in any interview, and he concludes, "[i]t is clear, however, that the present evidence does not support a thesis of sexual identity primarily dependent on social learning" (184). Despite Diamond's harsh critique and supposedly convincing evidence for a 'failed' gender assignment of the reassigned twin, the paper did not lead to a reevaluation of the case. At the time, Money had already stopped publishing updates on the twins and ignored Diamond's critique. Yet Money tells a different version of the story in his 2002 autobiography: in a chapter called

perspective, does not add a new layer to the discursive representation of intersex when it styles Reimer's experience as a professional rivalry between two researchers. ISNA's publications in *Chrysalis*, however, participate in the discourse from a completely different angle: they reject and devalue the medico-scientific mode of speaking and elevate the personal narrative, the testimony, to the appropriate mode of speaking about intersex.

Research in this area has so far often stressed the differences between the doctors' position and the activists' position, e.g. medical anthropologist and intersex activist Morgan Holmes has analyzed the "medical approach to intersexuality [that] is structured and contained by a form of storytelling. The narrative begins with diagnosis, hits a crisis in dealing with parents and families, and is resolved with surgical sex assignments and professional guarantees for a sunny future" (*Perilous* 154f). She opposes the medical narrative to "the narrative proposing that one take pride in one's intersexuality to reclaim it as a subject-identity as legitimate as typical maleness and femaleness in contemporary society (the Intersex Society story)" (123). With this approach, Holmes focuses on differences and contrasts between stories told by doctors and stories told by activists. While the medical story, the story told by doctors, seems clearly invested in producing intersex *as a medical condition*, the activist story seems to oppose the former and to treat intersex *as an identity*. Yet, Iain Morland already asked whether this simple "relation between medicine and activism" should not be questioned in 2009 ("Critique" 209). Neither story is opposed to the other: "Clinicians and reformists are not so different after

---

"David and Goliath" he renarrates Diamond's account of the 1980 BBC documentary along with a critique on the biographical accounts by John Colapinto. Contrary to the BBC claims, Money explained, he had not agreed to be interviewed on the twins because "[t]here was too great a risk of their being traumatized if the BBC program was traded overseas from Britain and broadcast in the twins' home city" (*First Person* 74). However, he had suggested reporting on another of his patients with a similar history of sex reassignment who had been on national television before. Against Money's advice, the BBC team had nevertheless contacted the Reimer family and done the interviews with local doctors. Money felt "deceived" (74) and refused any further contact with the team.

all [...] with regard to the ethics of their own position (206). In his critical analysis of intersex activism and politics he finds that both activists and doctors have a common goal, i.e. "to avert 'emotional trauma'" (206). It is necessary to clarify here, I believe, that causes of and remedies against "trauma" may be evaluated very differently in the different camps of the debate, but the overall goal may be shared.[7] Moreover, in my view, medicine and activism also share a similar investment in rhetoric, the "art of persuasion" (Culler 69): they both aim to convince their respective audiences, to make them believe in their arguments. Yet they differ tremendously in their respective rhetorical techniques or practices. Thus, the question in the following analysis centers on the *how* of the medical and activist contributions. *How* does John Money, as the major medical contributor to the intersex discourse, argue his points? *How* does he validate his statements? And, *how* do activists such as Cheryl Chase aim to persuade their readers? Both, I argue, rely strongly on techniques that produce effects that render their contributions 'true' while other contributions are rhetorically discredited.

THE DOCTOR KNOWS BEST:
THE CASE OF JOHN MONEY

John Money was probably the most influential and most controversial intersex researcher in the 20th century and the Reimer case figures largely in his memory. In 2014, two monographs on the work of John Money appeared and both contain chapters on Reimer (cf. Downing/ Morland/ Sullivan *Fuckology* and Goldie *The Man Who Invented Gender*). Moreover, in an obituary in the *New York Times* after Money's death in 2006, the

---

7   Katrina Karkazis also asks for a more refined analysis of the relation between doctors and intersex activists: "Although I am deeply sympathetic to intersex adults' criticisms of their medical care, Khan's comments [Surina Khan, at the time executive director of the International Gay and Lesbian Human Rights Commission; M.K.] paint a disturbing image of half-crazed doctors running down hospital corridors wielding knives – one that clashes with my knowledge of clinicians working in the field of intersexuality, whose intentions are more benevolent" (*Fixing* 2).

controversy around the case was reported and a former colleague comments that Money was right "[g]iven what the field knew at the time" (Carey n.p.). With this Solomonic judgment, the colleague simultaneously justifies Money's decision in the 1960s but also challenges its current legitimacy. Even after his death, it seems, John Money and his writings on David Reimer still serve as the backdrop for the debate about the necessary and appropriate treatment of intersex individuals. In the following analysis, I use Money's publications on the twin case from before Diamond's 1997 critique, but also his positions in the debate after Diamond's publication and his own reflections on scholarly ethics and science. Thereby, I turn away from the Reimer 'case' and focus on the 'case' John Money.

Throughout his career, the psychologist had published continuously, and did not limit his publications to scholarly discourse, but also flooded the popular market with his writings.[8] He participated in numerous TV shows, gave interviews and seemed eager to distribute his findings, and not only among his colleagues. Moreover, he wrote one novel[9] and not less than three autobiographical pieces that track his career: in 1986, Money prefixed a more than 600 pages long collection of his earlier works, *Venuses Penuses* (1986), with an autobiographical prologue called "Professional Biography." Four years later, he presented a paper on his personal and professional life at a conference in Amsterdam[10] and in 2002 the book-length *A First Person History of Pediatric Psychoendocrinology* appeared. As a motivation for his autobiographical writing, Money refers to his role at Johns Hopkins University in the 1950s: "I came to Johns Hopkins as the first psychologist to be a specialist in pediatric psycho-

---

8 For example, *Sexual Signatures* (1975), co-written with a journalist, Money explains, is a "popularized trade book adaptation of the academic book, *Man and Woman, Boy and Girl*" (*First Person* 76).

9 The novel is called *The Impresario* (1959). A reviewer referred to it as "a stimulating psychological study of a *ménage à trois*, or even *quatre*" (Pryce-Jones "Review" 664).

10 The paper "Serendipities on the Sexological Pathway to Research in Gender Identity and Sex Reassignment" was published in the *Journal of Psychology and Human Sexuality* 4.1 (1991): 101-13 and slightly altered for the 1997 collected volume *How I Got Into Sex*. Among the over forty contributors to *How I Got Into Sex* is also Money's 'rival' Milton Diamond.

endocrinology," and he continues, "that, in turn, is how I came to write this book, for much of the early history of the field is also my personalized scholarly and research history" (*First Person* 1).[11] These publications link the individual John Money to his scholarly work, and connect both almost inseparably.[12] With Money, one might say, the personal is professional.

Narrative Conventions

Although Money sometimes wrote popular books, he did not understand himself as anything but a scientist and was skeptical towards other modes of writing. In 1998, sixteen years after Milton Diamond's first follow-up report on the David Reimer case ("Monozygotic" 1982), but only one year after Diamond's second report and Colapinto's subsequent report in *Rolling Stone* magazine, Money comments on the development in the Reimer case. The essay "Ablatio Penis: Nature/Nurture Redux" was first published in his collected volume *Sin, Science, and the Sex Police* (1998) and is one of only two publications of John Money on Reimer after 1997; the other one is the chapter "David and Goliath" in his 2002 autobiography. "Redux" is interesting for an array of reasons: on the one hand, Money employs a perspective in the essay that is rather unusual for his late publications, i.e. the extra- and heterodiegetic voice in the text remains unnamed and the narrator refers to "John Money" in the third person. In various other publiccations Money does not shy away from using the first person pronoun to

---

11 Both, Money himself and the editor Richard Green, one of Money's former mentees at Johns Hopkins between 1957 and 1961, stress the significance of the text not as a scholarly text, but for its autobiographical content: "When John [Money] told me that this book had been rejected by an editor because it was 'too autobiographical' it was clear to me that that misguided soul had dismissed its unique value. While some of John's studies are summarized here – that is backdrop – it is the autobiographical dimension that delivers a document not elsewhere available" (Preface *First Person* vii).

12 Anecdotal evidence for the close connection between persona and research is also suggested by the cover design of five of his scholarly monographs: they all show a portrait of the researcher. See the covers of *Lovemap Guidebook* (1999), *Principles of Developmental Sexology* (1997), *Reinterpreting the Unspeakable* (1994), *Gendermaps* (1995), *Sin, Science, and the Sex Police* (1998).

signal identity between author and narrator.[13] Furthermore, he includes long quotes from his earlier publications such as his unpublished 1952 dissertation, but at the same time rhetorically minimizes his responsibility in the treatment of Reimer, e.g. he reports on the decision making process of the Reimer parents: "By coincidence the parents saw a male-to-female transsexual on a network television program. Her appearance and demeanor helped them to opt for sex reassignment" ("Redux" 315). The parents recall the same TV show, and Colapinto reports that a "suavely charismatic and handsome individual in his late 40s, bespectacled and with sleekly brushed-back hair, Dr. Money" ("True Story" 58) was also part of this show. So, while Money's description of the TV program and the effect of the trans woman on the parents may not be wrong, it is certainly incomplete.

These strategies, the use of third person pronouns and a reduction of his personal involvement in the Reimer case, create distance and seem to diminish the responsibility of the sexologist who was once celebrated for his treatment of the twins. In addition, Money uses another strategy to counter the critique and to legitimize his treatment. He openly discredits Colapinto's report by calling it "factually inaccurate in many places" ("Redux" 321) and points to different narrative conventions between journalism and medical science: while science is bound by "medical ethics [...] with respect to confidentiality and a patient's right to privacy. [...]

---

13 An example for Money's use of the first person pronoun can be found in the chapter "Case Consultation, Ablatio Penis" which is published as the preceding chapter to "Nature/Nurture Redux" in the same volume. It reads: "In response to the request for a written consultation, I wrote that I would not be in a position to make a specific recommendation, but that I would be able to list the pros and cons of sex reassignment that need to be weighed by an advisory board in charge of any case of infantile ablatio penis" (286f). "Case Consultation" was already written in 1996, one year before the publications of Diamond and Colapinto. The text is noteworthy because Money seems rather cautious about recommending surgery. He explains that "it is a case in which you're damned if you do undertake sex reassignment, and damned if you don't. Neither procedure is wholly satisfactory on all counts" (287). So, while he claims ignorance about the development of the Reimer case after 1979 (cf. *First Person* 73), he nevertheless changed his mind about the required treatment in case of ablatio penis.

journalism is dedicated to adversarial exposure, and the melodramatic exposé, even to the extent of insinuation, exaggeration, or downright falsification in order to make a story" (*First Person* 75). Money opposes medical ethics to journalistic ethics and argues that these differences produce his negative role in the case: "David and Goliath is one of the prototypic myths of our heritage. [...] John Colapinto found his David, and he invented me, with the help of Milton Diamond and Keith Sigmundson, to be his Goliath in a print and television drama promoting his new book, to his own financial gain" (*First Person* 75).[14] My point in this episode is Money's rhetorical strategy: instead of exchanging arguments about the new development in the case, he resolves to discredit the critics and their writing on behalf of narrative conventions. Journalism, it seems, was a mode of writing that Money believed to be grounded in cheap sensationalism. His own writings, he argues, need to adhere to a completely different set of rules, conventions, and values, e.g. rules of confidentiality, privacy, and ethics. Thereby, he positions his own writings in the realm of (medical) science and opposes them to journalism, which is presented as a narrative mode of writing ("factually incorrect") and biased by the need to sell the story. By implication, then, Money aims to present scholarly writing as evidence-based, independent, and truth-bound. Yet, I suggest, Money's implication does not make scholarly writing more ethical or true than journalistic writing. Rather, he points to the different effects each mode of writing conjures. Moreover, he rejects an exchange of arguments with Colapinto on the grounds that the rules of the scholarly mode of writing would not allow him to discuss the case and hides behind these conventions. The scholarly mode of writing, then, limits and governs the narrative that Money produces.

In addition, Money's rejection and depreciation of narrative is complicated by his own investment in narratives in his suggestions for treatment: for example, the parents of the Reimer twins "were guided in how to give the child information about herself [...]; and they were helped with what to explain to friends and relatives, including their other child" ("Ablatio" 67). Money had warned them not to harbor "any lingering doubts" (*Sexual Signatures* 93) about the decision for their son, now

---

14 Colapinto explains that David Reimer had chosen his first name exactly because of the biblical connotation (cf. *Nature* xvi).

daughter. It was important that the parents were to rear the twins "consistently as a boy or a girl, respectively, avoiding ambiguity and uncertainty of gender" ("Ablatio" 66). The demand to raise the children as consistently and unambiguously as possible resulted in rearing practices that emphasized above all stereotypical gender roles: the girl was encouraged to be neat and tidy; the boy was allowed to be wild and to get dirty. Money put special emphasis on the mother's explanations of their future reproductive roles "as mother and father, but also for their other different roles, such as wife and husband or financial supporter of the family and caretaker of children and house" (*Man and Woman* 121). These explanations ("a girl does this and a boy that") and encouragements ("being neat and tidy" versus "wild and dirty") form a consistent and continuous narrative about segregated gender identities that, in the 1970s, was a reactionary stereotype challenged by the women's and civil rights movements.

Metaphor

In view of Money's various publications, the distinction between a professional, scholarly mode of writing and an autobiographical and/or popular mode of writing may seem a little blurry at times. For Money, however, the distinction is clear. He stresses the differences between "scientific causal explanation" (*First Person* 6), i.e. the scholarly or medico-scientific mode of writing, and explanations reached "without empirical data" (6), i.e. the narrative mode of writing:

Like causal explanations, biographical and historical explanations have narrative continuity, and each may have a high degree of narrative coherence. Thus it may be tempting to attribute causal continuity to them also. However, there is no known formula by which to convert narrative continuity to causal continuity without further empirical testing, although narrative continuity may suggest hypotheses for empirical testing. (*First Person* 5)

Biography, history and science may share narrative continuity and coherency, explains Money, but to find causal explanations empirical evidence was needed. This understanding of science forms the basis of his work as a psychologist. Coherency and continuity may suggest hypotheses, but causal explanations need to be proven by empirical data.

If empirical data is all-important, then data gathering is a crucial process, and Money dedicates the final chapter in *First Person* to questions of methodology. He explains his scholarly approach and compares advantages and disadvantages of a "random probability sample," i.e. a random sampling of the population, with a "convenience sample," i.e. a non-random sampling of available individuals. Random sampling was not practical for work on hermaphroditism/intersex ("There were far too few of them for that" [117]), so he favored the convenience sample. Yet convenience sample studies such as Alfred Kinsey's reports on human sexuality also had their disadvantages as they relied on volunteers, and were therefore accused of being biased.[15] An alternative besides sampling was to work with control or contrast groups, "this meant comparing two clinical groups each as a contrast group for the other" (117) and that was what Money eventually settled on. But, *how* was data "with respect to sexual and erotic imagery, ideation, and practice [or] gender orientation as male, female, or mixed" (118) retrieved? These aspects could not be weighed with a scale, be measured with a triangle ruler, or be enlarged with a microscope. The psychologist and his colleagues used interviews. They recorded and transcribed verbatim each interview they led with an intersex person and, systematically, converted the information into a large table. A "Schedule of Inquiry" (118) was devised for each study and interviewers were to ask specified questions in a certain order, and to mark each topic that was completed. Interviewing was shared by at least two people and data was not only gathered from 'patients' but also from parents, siblings, teachers, or any other person who could contribute to the respective

---

15 Kinsey conducted extensive studies of male and female sexual practices in the U.S. The participants in the studies were mostly college students and critics deemed this group as not representative. Kinsey's reports were published as *Sexual Behavior in the Human Male* (1948) and *Sexual Behavior in the Human Female* (1953). Especially his findings on the frequency of homosexual practices and extra-marital sex challenged traditional notions of sexual behavior. Instead of a binary system of homosexual and heterosexual practices, Kinsey and his colleagues developed a scale from 0, exclusively heterosexual, to 6, exclusively homosexual, to indicate the diversity of sexual practices at a given time in a person's life. The scale ratings allowed understanding sexual identity not as dichotomous, but as a continuum.

question. "Each subject's data," Money continues explaining his method, was then entered "on a ruled spread sheet of paper," before "the tabulated data [was] reduced to a number" (118f). This reduction was either binary as in perceived absence or presence of a characteristic, or a three point-rating such as strong, medium, or weak. At the end of this process, Money concludes, "the pooling of data from several individual cases into a group master chart, [allows; M.K.] for statistical comparison with a control or contrast group, if one exists" (119). From my perspective this process describes exactly what Money had ruled out earlier: the method is the formula for turning narrative into empirical data. Converting interviews into "a databank [...] ready to be rated, ranked or otherwise evaluated" (118) involves the reduction of narrative complexity into a binary or three point rating. For this method to be effective the rating must be equated with the narrative. What is more, the rating must not only be treated as *similar* to the narrative, but it needs to be treated as if it *was* the narrative. In that sense the underlying structure of the method is strictly metaphorical, i.e. one thing *is* another.

Moreover, medical case studies transform an experience into discourse, maintains Epstein:

Layers of meaning are embedded in medical records. A patient's history translates the bodily aspects of a life into a documented aggregate of symptoms and turns what might be a human story into the professional discourse of medicine by encapsulating illness into the forms and languages of a highly bureaucratized health-care system. Only by this process of converting patient into case can this system bring to bear its formidable tools of interpretation and therapeutics. (*Altered* 55)

When Money claims "objectivity" (*First Person* 118) for his data, because "the consolidated history, not the patient is the data base" (118), he is caught up in a medical discourse that structures and governs his scholarly approach and his interpretation of the interviews. The governing structure of that discursive mode, I have argued, is necessarily metaphorical because, following Epstein, it turns "a human story" into "professional discourse."

An extract from one of Money's reports on the twins illustrates this argument. Both twins were interviewed annually and asked about their gender identity and sexual desire. In "Ablatio Penis" Money reports an incident from a counseling session with Brenda that he thought to be particularly revealing: "I resorted to the standard question of which animal she'd want to be if she could change into one. She elected to be a monkey, because a monkey can climb and swing on its arms. 'Would you want to be a boy monkey or a girl monkey?' I asked. 'A girl one,' she replied, and gave as a reason for this choice, 'I'm already a girl!'" ("Ablatio" 71). The question, qualified as "standard," asks the child to identify with an animal only to then proceed to the 'real' question of the sex of that animal. Given the choice between two, girl or boy monkey, Brenda choses girl and elaborates that she was "already a girl." Money interprets this answer as an expression of the child's gender identity. This interpretation could be challenged on the grounds of interferences or biases in the interview situation, i.e. while Brenda does not know why she is being subjected to these questions she knows the procedure and might feel inclined to give an answer that may (or may not) satisfy the psychologist. Psychologists call such interferences the *social desirability bias*. But more relevant for my analysis is Money's understanding of Brenda's reply *as a fact* (and not as a metaphor). The child tells him about her female identity, in other words, Brenda produces an identity narrative about herself; Money then takes this narrative and reduces it to a rating. The rating is equated with the narrative, turned into data and later re-narrated as part of a case study. Metaphor veils the processes of interpretation and transformation in the production of the study and the case study is presented as "a discourse of facts" (Epstein *Altered* 34). With Epstein, however, the study may be criticized because it "ignores its own linguistic material, [and] presumes that it represents a pure and neutral copy of the 'real'" (*Altered* 34). Moreover, Money negates his own position as the author of the case study, i.e. as the one who turned the words of an interviewee into a number, compared that number to other numbers, evaluated and interpreted the numbers, and finally produced the study. This study is a metaphor in itself because the scholar-doctor converted or re-turned the numbers into a report-story, and Epstein suggests provocatively that doctors in that respect are akin to "storytellers" (*Altered* 25).

Synecdoche

Medicine, explains John Money, "searches for causal continuities that apply not only to one person, but to many people with the same symptoms" (*First Person* 125). In his work, then, he aims to abstract from the *individual* intersex experience and to identify the *general* in the experience. This structure resembles the rhetorical figure of synecdoche; a part is made to stand for the whole. The underlying assumption is that analyses of the experiences described by *some* intersex people will provide valuable insights into the experiences of *all* intersex people. This basic structure enables the doctor to present his findings as supra-individual. While a patient, in Money's view, can always only deliver a personal, singular account, it is the doctor who contextualizes the account and integrates it into a larger (and thereby seemingly more meaningful) picture. Thus, the single voice in a medical study appears to stand for numerous voices and the scholarly mode of speaking or writing presented by the expert-doctor is invested with validity and authority while the intersex voices are limited to sound bites and supporting quotes. However, Money takes trouble to distance himself from 'the whole' that the part represents and positions himself *apart* rather than as *a part*: according to his practice of treatment, it is the doctor who advises the parents what to tell the child. And it is also the doctor who interprets the interviews, who deduces or assigns a meaning and reports his findings in a study. In this way, Money presents himself as an intersex expert. The synecdochical structure and the reduction of authoritative voices is a paternalistic and patronizing practice that is characteristic not only of the medico-scientific mode of writing, but for Money's theoretical framework in particular: gender identity, he argued, may be steered in any direction if it begins early enough, i.e. before the child begins to talk. Therefore, he advised carrying out any surgical intervention *before* a child began to acquire language. The child then is, literally and purposefully, left without a voice; unable to speak, to either give or deny consent to an operation and it is the parent or the doctor who speaks *for* the child.

Using the example of John Money, the above analysis has focused on the medico-scientific mode of writing. The production of authority via the rhetorical figure of the synecdoche, I have argued, follows from the elevation of the voice of the expert-doctor and a depreciation of other voices. Paradoxically, it leads to the effect that the story seems to radiate supra-individual validity. Moreover, the use of metaphor to turn interviews into data and evidence enforces the validity of the arguments and renders them 'true.' Thus, the medico-scientific mode of writing produces the effect of scientific objectivity. With Epstein, however, the medico-scientific mode of writing also needs to be read as governed by generic conventions and thereby as restricted in its 'objectivity.' Nevertheless, the well-defined limits of the scholarly mode of writing distinguished the writing from other kinds of writing, and, until the 1990s, meaningful contributions to the intersex discourse had to be phrased in this mode. The scholarly mode of writing, I conclude, functioned as a gatekeeper to the intersex discourse and blocked contributions formulated in other modes of writing. Intersex activists challenge the dominance of the medical mode of writing and I analyze their rhetorical modes of writing in the following section of this chapter.

MORE THAN THE TRUTH: ISNA'S TESTIMONIES

With the founding of ISNA in 1993 and the subsequent increase in publications of what scholars later referred to as "personal stories" (Turner 462), "first-person stories" (Hester "Rhetorics" 49), "intersex body narratives" (Nahman 1), "autobiographical narratives" (Morland "Postmodern" 319; similar Koch-Rein 240), "autobiographies" (Dreger *Hermaphrodites* 168), and "testimonials" (Nahman 15) or "testimony" (e.g. Morland "Intimate" 425, "Critique" 197; Carroll 188) the gatekeeping function of the medico-scientific or scholarly mode of writing began to be undermined. Alice Dreger had attested intersex autobiographies a "significant value" in 1998 because "in intersexuals' stories we can hear first-hand what it is like to live on one of the great cultural divides" (*Hermaphrodites* 168).[16] The range of scholarly labels attributed to this kind of writing conveys the notion that the narrator of the text is someone who experienced intersex "first-hand," who lived with or as intersex and can therefore bear witness. The witness, now, is related to the Greek

---

16 Morland ("Postmodern") introduces a critical perspective on the value of first-person accounts.

martus: in the biblical context, *martus* 'martyr' refers to early Christians who bore witness, who bore testimony to their faith in defiance of life-threatening situations (cf. Assmann 37f; Brunner 95f). The martyr is a witness to a cause who is ready to die for that cause. The death of the martyr is evidence of the ultimate truth of their dedication to the cause.

In the following, I argue that the witness function of these texts marks them as a distinct mode of writing. Testimony, in that sense, will not be read as a narrowly defined genre, but as a mode of writing that is characterized by a specific relation to the witness function and thereby to a specific form of 'truth' telling. In contrast to the medico-scientific mode of writing that uses mostly logos, the appeal to reason, to convince the audience, the testimonial mode of writing centers on appeals to character (ethos) and emotion (pathos). The persuasive power of empirical evidence, as in the medico-scientific mode of writing, is used rarely, because testimony does not aim to document or to prove something that has happened. Rather, testimony aims to bear witness to events that have "not been truly witnessed yet," explains psychoanalyst Dori Laub ("Bearing" 57). Therefore, the character of the speaker, their credibility, is much more decisive for the rhetorical success of the text. Moreover, the rejection of data produced via research emphasizes the need to appeal to the emotions of the audience rather than to their reason. Testimony, explains literary scholar Shoshana Felman, bears witness to events that exceed substantialized significance (cf. "Education" 5). They are what literary scholar Cathy Caruth calls "unclaimed experience," or "trauma" (cf. *Unclaimed* 10). *Trauma* is a term frequently used in both intersex testimonies (cf. Chase "Portrait" 89 and "Hermaphrodites" 304, Holmes and Moreno in *Chrysalis* 8, 12) and in scholarship on these testimonies (cf. Hester "Rhetorics" 51ff, Preves *Identity* 149 and Morland "Critique" 206). Therefore, a connection between trauma, intersex and testimony is suggested, but so far not explored and rarely made explicit.[17]

---

17 Iain Morland explicitly discusses medical intersex treatment as traumatizing "by design" because "nondisclosure of surgery in infancy generates a key characteristic of trauma: the unrecognized persistence in the presence of an incomprehensible past event [...] To be gendered by surgery is, by design, to be gendered without knowing that surgery is the cause" ("Intersex Treatment and Trauma" 160).

Medical discourse distinguishes between very different kinds of *trauma*, 'wounds,' among them 'penetrating trauma' (an object pierces the skin), 'blunt or non-penetrating trauma' (an object hits the body, but does not enter it), or 'psychological trauma.' The latter, Caruth has pointed out, can be traced to Freud's *Beyond the Pleasure Principle* (1920), where he introduces the notion of trauma as a "wound inflicted not upon the body but upon the mind" (*Unclaimed* 3).[18] Following Vietnam veterans' difficulties in returning to their civilian lives, the American Psychiatric Association formed an entry for "post-traumatic stress disorder" (PTSD) in their 3rd edition of the *Diagnostic and Statistical Manual of Mental Disorders* for the first time in 1980 and the entry has since been revised in each edition (cf. Cvetkovich *Archive* 17f). While trauma and PTSD were understood as belonging to medical discourse, Caruth opened the discourse on trauma for other disciplines as well. In 1991, she edited two issues of *American Imago* (1 and 4, published as the collected volume *Trauma: Explorations in Memory* in 1995) and in 1996 she published *Unclaimed Experience: Trauma, Narrative, and History*. Caruth understands trauma as "the inability fully to witness the event as it occurs, or the ability to witness the event *fully* only at the cost of witnessing oneself" (*Trauma* 7). Trauma, for Caruth, is therefore related to a crisis in witnessing. The traumatic event is per definition inaccessible, incomprehensible. It follows that talking or writing about the event transforms it into "narrative memory" and that the event is "integrated into one's own [...] knowledge of the past" (153). But the integration of the event in memory leads to a "dilemma" that Caruth describes in the words of Holocaust survivor Sonia Schreiber Weitz: "To speak is impossible, and not to speak is impossible" (154).

Testimony, then, is the act of reclaiming the traumatic event, of finding words for what cannot be said because it was never understood, or, rather because it was never 'understandable'. Yet testimony may have a considerable effect on the witness-narrator. Felman notes, for example, personally liberating experiences, "a liberation which allows [the witness after years of silence M.K.] for the first time to experience feelings both of mourning and hope" ("Education" 46). And literary scholar Talí Kal adds: "Such writing serves both as a validation and cathartic vehicle for the

---

18 For extensive discussions of notions of trauma and its genealogy see for example Young *Harmony* and Leys *Trauma*.

traumatized author" (*Worlds* 21). This function of testimony may recall the basic principle of psychoanalysis: talking (or writing) heals. Felman calls this the *clinical dimension* of testimony, which she also refers to as a "medium of healing" (9). The clinical dimension interacts with the *historical dimension* and the *poetical dimension* of testimony. The historical dimension refers to testimonies' capacity to "record events and to report the facts of a historical occurrence" (8) that go "beyond what is available, that is, as a truth transparent to itself and entirely known (15f). Felman identifies maybe the least palpable dimension in testimony, the poetical dimension, in its struggle with language itself: testimony may show itself to "reclaim and repossess the very language in which *testimony* must – and cannot simply and uncritically – be given" (28). With Felman, these three dimensions of testimony are not separate but coexistent and mutually interactive (cf. 41).

Tal identifies another dimension in testimony and explains that such writing always "advances a larger political agenda" (*Worlds* 173) and she challenges psychoanalysis for its reductive focus on the individual effects of testimony. With respect to sexual abuse testimonies she writes: "We bear witness not simply to individual crimes of abuse and brutality, but to an entire system of oppression [...] – a system in which maleness and violence are closely linked. Our testimony challenges that system" (197f). For Tal, testimony is always both personal and political. Queer studies scholar Ann Cvetkovich elaborates Tal's thinking and focuses on "cultural responses to trauma" (*Archive* 4). She aims to employ "ways of thinking about trauma that do not pathologize it, that seize control over it from the medical experts" (3). She refuses any "quick-fix solution to trauma, such as telling the story as a mode of declaring an identity or seeking legal redress" (17). Moreover, her approach embraces and values the diversity of these texts when she explains that "Trauma puts pressure on conventional forms of documentation, representation, and commemoration, giving rise to new genres of expression, such as testimony, and new forms of monuments, rituals, and performances that can call into being collective witness and publics" (7). For Cvetkovich, testimony is one possible reaction to trauma. It can be written, publicly performed, recorded, filmed or converted to a number of cultural practices.[19] Also, her understanding of trauma is much broader than e.g. Felman's. Cvetkovich is interested in "trauma as everyday and not just catastrophic" (29). This perspective allows Cvetkovich to understand trauma as "ongoing" in contrast to the understanding of trauma as a "discrete event" (33) and she argues: "Once the causes of trauma become more diffuse, so too do the cures, opening up the need to change social structures more broadly rather than just fix individual people" (33). Similar to Tal, Cvetkovich emphasizes trauma as "a collective experience that generates collective responses" (19). These collective responses to trauma may "offer alternative modes of knowledge" (8) and may be "in opposition to official histories" (8) or fill in gaps of "institutionalized documentation" (8). They form what she calls the "archive" of trauma (cf. 7). Following Cvetkovich, the activists' writings form the archive of living (with) intersex. They are writings that testify, that bear witness to intersex as a first-hand experience. While each testimony represents an individual experience, they should also be read as a collective response to "the way U.S. medicine and culture deal[s] with intersexuality" (Dreger *Hermaphrodites* 168). The intersex archive, the material that testifies to intersex life in the 1990s is diffuse: the writing is in prose and poetry; it is printed in anthologies, journals and newspapers as well as published on private websites; pictures, videos and other visual material augment it. Some testimonies are recorded as interviews, written as letters or take the form of more conventional autobiographical writing. The archive is complemented by collective actions such as public protests and conferences.[20]

---

19 These various representational forms of testimony make it difficult to subsume them under a common label and are one reason for referring to testimony as a mode of writing rather than as a genre.

20 An exhaustive list of intersex testimonies is impossible to achieve, but ISNA's actions are comparatively well-documented. See ISNA's website which preserves an extensive bibliography on intersex that covers medical, legal, activist and journalistic publications on intersex between 1876 and 2007. Other contributions can be found in trans* activist Leslie Feinberg's anthologies *Transgender Warriors* (1996, portrait Morgan Holmes), and *TransLiberation: Beyond Pink or Blue* (1998, Cheryl Chase), and Dawn Atkins, *Looking Queer: Body Image in Lesbian, Bisexual, Gay, and Transgender Communities* (1998, Raven Kaldera, Holmes, and Chase). Alice Dreger edited a special issue of the

Writings from the archive have been the object of numerous studies in philosophy, sociology and the history and ethics of medicine over the last couple of years. Scholars have looked at aspects of (individual and group) identity production (cf. Preves *Identity*, Turner, Nahman, Zehnder, Eckert), scrutinized bodily experiences (cf. Roen "Clinical," Seer, van Heesch, Gregor), and explored the role of medical intervention (cf. Hester "Healing" and "Management"). Thereby, scholars have predominantly ad-

Journal of Clinical Ethics that collects both a number of intersex testimonies and doctors' writings in 1998. The special issue marks the first combined publication of medical doctors and intersex activists in a medical journal and shows how intersex testimony writes itself into medical discourse. In 1999, another collection containing first person testimonies was published: Alice Dreger compiled material from the *Chrysalis* special issue and the *Clinical Ethics* special issue to form *Intersex in the Age of Ethics*. Probably the first video documentary on intersex life *Hermaphrodites Speak!* was produced by Chase and ISNA in 1997. Between 1994 and 1997, Chase and ISNA also wrote at least six letters (to editors, to doctors, to professional organizations, to journals and magazines) as a means to publicize their critique and to make their voices heard (cf. isna.org/bibliographies/author). In May 1996, ISNA members suggested to organize a "patient's panel" at a plastic surgeon conference in New York. The offer was declined, but activists nevertheless presented their stories "in a room adjacent to the surgeon's symposium" (*Chrysalis* 7). In October 1996, ISNA organized a public protest at a convention of the *American Academy of Pediatrics* in Baltimore challenging their early surgery policy (cf. *Chrysalis* 45ff). In 2000, Chase was invited to present the patient's perspective on intersex to the largest organization in the United States for pediatric endocrinology, the Lawson Wilkins Pediatric Endocrine Society (today: Pediatric Endocrine Society). The talk is a benchmark in intersex activism as patient's politics did no longer have to be sneaked in through the backdoor via letters to editors or via non-intersex academics such as Fausto-Sterling, Dreger, or Kessler. Rather, Chase took center stage and was received "with respect" (Fausto-Sterling "Revisited" 19). Her voice, her story, her politics were now unequivocally part of the medical intersex discourse. A similar opportunity was provided in 2002 when Chase presented ISNA's perspective on intersex medical care at the "First World Congress: Hormonal and Genetic Basis of Sexual Differentiation Disorders" in Arizona (cf. Chase "Agenda").

dressed what Felman calls the historical and the clinical dimension of testimony. They analyzed the testimonies as documents that bear witness to specific experiences and events and as part of a healing process. Another focus was on the political dimension of these testimonies, as part of an individual identity production and as part of a communal identity in the intersex movement (cf. Preves *Identity*). In the following section, I summarize some major aspects of two previous studies by philosopher J. David Hester to sketch the state of research on intersex testimony. The studies serve as examples for the intersections of the clinical, historical, and political dimension of testimony. Felman's notion of the poetic dimension of testimony, however, is mostly ignored. Thus, I focus in my subsequent analysis of two contributions to the intersex archive, Chase's 1993 letter to *the Sciences* and the 1997/8 special issue of *Chrysalis*, on this dimension.

Lessons from the Archive

In "Intersex and the Rhetorics of Healing" (2006), philosopher J. David Hester analyzes over a hundred first person accounts of intersex individuals[21] and compares their "unique rhetorical worlds, values, experiences and group dynamics" ("Healing" 64). The approach produces results that are on the one hand diagnosis specific, e.g. accounts by individuals with one diagnosis differ from accounts by individuals with another diagnosis in a specific respect. While surgery on some individuals typically involves the removal of undescended testes, surgery on other individuals is aimed at the size of the phallus. In the latter narratives, explains Hester, the "trauma of the procedure and its aftermath figures much larger" (58). On the other hand, Hester also shows similarities between the different groups and he identifies "common themes" such as relief from a sense of isolation, community building through the sharing of stories and experiences, outreach to others, and the development of non-pathologized identities (64). Hester's focus on rhetorics of healing leads

---

21 As sources, Hester lists more than 25 German and English language websites and online forums. His systematic analysis involves accounts by parents and individuals diagnosed with Congenital Adrenal Hyperplasia CAH, Androgen Insensitivity Syndrome AIS, Klinefelter's syndrome, Hypospadias, and Turner's syndrome.

him to even more specific results: he finds that individuals who have not been subjected to early surgical intervention employ a very different rhetoric of healing than individuals treated under the current medical paradigm. For individuals who have been raised in a "rhetorical space of 'acceptance' [...] for who and what they are" healing means "living comfortably and healthily with oneself as intersex" (48). He refers to this group of individuals as non-pathologized and quotes a number of studies and first person accounts before concluding that the "lack of surgical intervention upon the genitals does not seem to have the negative social effects anticipated by and justifying the modern medical paradigm adopted in the West" (51).[22] In contrast, intersex individuals with experiences of early and repeated medicalization develop an "anti-pathological identity" (49) and their rhetorics of healing center on healing from "the practice of medical intervention itself" (66). Hereby, Hester shows that "medical intervention does *not* entail healing. Rather, it creates and exacerbates 'illness'" (65).[23] Hester underlines this argument in his analysis of the

---

22 One of the studies Hester quotes is by John and Joan Hampson, John Money's colleagues in Baltimore. Reviewing data on over 250 postadolescent intersex individuals they note in 1961, "The surprise is that so many ambiguous-looking patients were able, *appearance notwithstanding*, to grow up and achieve a rating of psychologically healthy, or perhaps only mildly non-healthy" (qtd. in Hester 51, emphasis added).

23 See Hester 2003 for a close analysis of the rhetoric in medical management of intersex children where he develops this argument. One of the questions addressed there is "How does a physician first come to 'recognize' the genitalia as 'ambiguous'?" (n.p.) Hester finds subjective phrases such as "appears small" or "expected size" and follows that "expectations on the part of physicians have a profound effect on their judgment" (n.p.) and Fausto-Sterling quotes a surgeon who deemed measurement irrelevant because for him "'overall appearance' counts rather than size" (*Sexing* 60). While some studies on phallus size in infants determine an average size for infant clitoris and infant penis, others show phallus size within a range and describe a continuum. In cooperation with Lawson Wilkins, Baltimore, pediatric endocrinologist Andrea Prader has developed the *Prader scale* to measure the degree of 'virilization' in genetic females and the *orchidometer* to measure the size of testicles. ISNA developed their own scale, the *phall-o-meter*, to illustrate "medically acceptable" and

"Rhetoric of the Medical Management of Intersexed Children" (2003) and proposes that "current medical guidelines make use of rhetorical dynamics that create a state where practices of the diagnosis of the 'disease' and the procedures used in 'curing' lead the patient to a state of 'illness' wherein no 'healing' can ever be achieved" (n.p.).[24] On the one hand, Hester explains this with an ongoing medicalization and pathologization of the children.[25] On the other hand, he shows that the "current medical management [...] blurs the distinction between the 'natural' and the 'constructed'" (n.p.) and explains:

It proceeds first by taking the 'natural' gender indicators on the body of the newborn and turning them into a problem. [...] the body has been rejected in its typical role of 'natural' foundation for gender identity. [...] The solution? To 'construct' a body through surgical techniques and hormone replacement. But it is this 'constructed' body that reflects the 'true' gender. It is this 'constructed' body that is described as 'natural'. ("Management" n.p.)

"medically unacceptable" phallus size (cf. Fausto-Sterling *Sexing* 59). While these scales and numbers purport objectivity, they also demonstrate its decisive character in 20th century sex assignment. It seems that 'phallus size' (or rather 'expected phallus size') has taken the place of the gonads as the sex decisive characteristic.

24 A 2013 explorative study underlines the power of medicalization: according to Streuli et al., 66% of participants acting as "parents" are willing to submit their intersex child to early genital surgery when the counseling is done by a supposed endocrinologist using pathologizing terminology. If counseling is done by a supposed psychologist and involves depathologizing language, only 23% of "parents" decide to have an operation (cf. "Shaping Parents").

25 "Between the declaration of 'ambiguous' genitals, the authoritative assignment of gender, the rhetoric of tragedy surrounding the condition of the child, the 'necessity' of surgical intervention, the frequency of secondary surgical procedures, and the commitment of the protocol to force the child into culturally, not medically grounded concepts of gender, medical management places and keeps the intersexed child in a state of continued medical management. 'Curing' creates and maintains a state of 'illness'." ("Management" n.p.)

Hester's analyses offer useful and strong arguments against infant surgery and support non-invasive models of treatment such as counseling for both intersex individuals and their parents. He shows that trauma is not an effect of intersex. Rather, trauma needs to be understood as related to experiences of medical intervention.

In short, Hester shows that testimonies produce intersex as an identity and relate that identity to a social movement that is aimed at changing a medical practice presented as harmful. In my reading, I will emphasize Felman's poetic dimension of these testimonies, their struggle with and for language and representation. This dimension – not separate from the political, the historical, and the clinical dimension, but always interacting with them – offers an insight into what Cvetkvich calls "the emotional archive" (23) of trauma. Morland has warned that activists' stories should avoid "sentimental determinism – the assumption that a standpoint on the ethics of intersex could be fully and finally determined by how narratives of intersex make *us* feel" ("Critique" 208, emphasis added). Intersex narratives, Hester and others have demonstrated convincingly, bear witness to intersex individuals who 'feel bad' due to the medical treatment they received. Yet Morland argues that this "feeling bad" (192) should not be understood as determining the reading experience or the ethical demand for a change of medical practice. Rather, it needs to be taken into account that some people could experience these narratives differently, e.g. doctors may reject these testimonies on professional grounds as they are not the result of clinical studies (cf. 197f) and, I might add, not presented in a medico-scientific mode of writing. Thus, my focus in the following readings of intersex testimony is less on the proposed 'feeling' that may or may not be evoked in these texts but on the narrative strategies that are employed.

"As an Intersexual": Expert Writing

The first public document that describes life as an intersex person is Cheryl Chase's reply to Anne Fausto-Sterling's article "The Five Sexes" (1993). In *The Sciences* Fausto-Sterling had declared that "the nuances of socialization among intersexuals cry out for more sophisticated analysis" (n.p.) and Chase answers this cry in her letter to the editor published in the subsequent edition of the journal. "As an intersexual I found Anne Fausto-Sterling's article […] of intense personal interest" (Chase "Letter" n.p.), explains Chase and opens a discursive position that had so far been negated in intersex discourse: the intersex-identified subject. While in medical discourse the term 'intersexual' was often used as an adjective or as a diagnostic category, Chase employs the term as a noun, as an identity category and refers to herself as "*an* intersexual" (emphasis added). Rhetorically, 'intersexual' is turned from a medical condition that affects individuals to a self-proclaimed subject position. The letter produces what it names, the intersex subject, and is, in that sense, performative. Chase also claims the ability to "provide some perspective on the experience" and positions the text, a letter, in the realm of testimony; she promises to bear witness to intersex as a lived experience. Nevertheless, her letter is far from simply giving an insight into an individual's experience. Rather, Chase employs a professional style and presents a summarized story of different intersex experiences, e.g. she refers to other intersex people and reports their experiences. Using referents such as "many" and "some," or by referring to a group of intersex people, "the ones I have located", Chase also begins to speak *for* this group. In contrast to John Money, however, she positions herself firmly as a part of the whole. Yet, the effect of the synecdochical structure is similar to Money's use of it: Chase is more than an individual speaking for herself; she installs herself as a reporter of 'the' intersex experience. This impression is supported by Chase's use of the indicative mood throughout her letter, "surgery *is* immensely destructive" [emphasis added], or "the child's body [...] *is* again and again subjected" [emphasis added]. In this way, the letter is put forward as a declarative statement, as something that is supposedly clear and non-controversial. This rhetorical strategy signals confidence, turns Chase into an expert and invests her statements with authority. Closing the letter with an appeal to "intersexuals and people close to them to write to *us* at the Intersex Society of North America" [emphasis added], Chase positions herself as the legitimate representative of an institution.

The letter is the founding document of ISNA, it marks the beginning of political intersex activism and it is an extremely influential testimony to intersex life and as such the first document in the intersex activist archive. Tal has noted with respect to sexual abuse survivor testimonies in the early 1980s that "the decision of a few brave survivors to speak out was indeed revolutionary, [but] it was at the same time exclusionary: a double-edged sword" (*Worlds* 160f). This may be true for Chase's letter and intersex activism as well. Turner and Holmes have also pointed out that ISNA activists form a rather coherent group: "Most ISNA members are white, educated, and between the ages of 30 and 45" (Turner 461, cf. Holmes *Perilous* 119). Dreger and Herndon ignore this aspect and rather emphasize shared experiences when they note:

[People] tended to share a common experience: they were born with noted sexual ambiguity, surgically 'corrected' as young children, subjected to continued medicalization and stigma inside and outside the clinic, and they eventually developed a queer political consciousness that allowed them to understand their plight as unjust. ("Progress" 209)

Shared experiences coupled with similar social background lead, in the words of Preves, to "stories of medical trauma and attempts to erase sexual ambiguity [as] standard in intersex narratives" (*Identity* 149). This supposedly "standard" intersex experience is reflected in Preves five-step coming out model where she describes the process of developing an intersex identity from stigma to pride. Nahman opposes a standardization of 'the' intersex experience, pointing out that "ISNA is not representative of all intersexuals" (87), and criticizes the scholarly and journalistic focus on ISNA. This focus, Nahman argues, results in a homogenized representation of the multiple experiences of intersex living (cf. 87f). Trauma scholars address the problem of a possibly homogenized representation in testimony from a different angle: they emphasize the difficulty and fear attached to writing one's own story without turning it into "a clichéd case history from a self help book" (Cvetkovich *Archive* 2). Both Caruth and Tal make clear that it is the central task of the critic "to deconstruct the process by which the dominant culture codifies their [the witness'] traumatic experience" (*Worlds* 18) and to respond "to traumatic stories in a way that does not lose their impact, that does not reduce them to clichés or turn them all into versions of the same story" (*Trauma* vii).

From this perspective, the work of the academic critic, my work in this case, lies in scrutinizing and valuing each text on its own and in its respective discursive context. So, when Cheryl Chase talks *for* intersex people and claims to represent this heterogeneous group, she does, in a way, assume a patronizing stance. She presents her experience and the experience of a small group of individuals as representative for *the* intersex experience.[26] However, I argue, such a reading would ignore the discursive context of Chase's testimony. At the time of writing, in 1993, there was no intersex activism. Intersex discourse was dominated by the medico-scientific mode of writing and limited to doctors telling intersex people and parents what to do and, first and foremost, telling them not to tell. In this context, I suggest, Chase's positioning as a representative of a group of people needs to be read as strategic on two levels. First, she breaches the medical paradigm of silence: instead of the hushed confession of a shamed patient, she embraces the label *intersexual* proudly in a public letter and invites other intersex people to follow her example. Working against shame and secrecy will soon after become one of the major goals of ISNA and each testimony needs to be read as part of this strategy. Scholars have often emphasized the aspect of identity production through these testimonies and I agree with them. But, as Turner has already noted, these identities need to be read as *strategically essentialist* in the sense of Gayatri Spivak (cf. Turner 458, see also my analysis of the *Chrysalis* editorial below). Postcolonial critic Spivak introduced strategic essentialism as "a *strategic* use of positivist essentialism in a scrupulously visible political interest" ("Subaltern" 13). In the mode of testimony, I suggest, intersex people aim to produce a political subject position from where to speak and act. Moreover, I want to point out that each testimony is an act of resistance against the medical paradigm of silence; each testimony bears witness to an intersex individual crossing the line from mere 'patient' to mature 'person'. In this context, telling one's story is necessarily a performative and a political act. Secondly, by assuming the position of representative, Chase marks the intersex experience as a collective experience and not just as an individual one. English scholar Susan Sniader Lanser suggested the term *communal voice* to describe the "practice in which narrative authority is invested in a definable community and textually inscribed either through multiple, mutually authorizing voices or through the voice of a single

---

26 Morland also criticizes activists for an underlying paternalistic structure when he explains: activists try "to initiate treatment reform by setting up the activist account as morally superior to the conventional medical story" ("Critique" 198) and "Despite its progressive agenda, advice dispensed didactically by intersex activists remains paternalistic […]. For arguable it hampers the patient authority and autonomy that activists wish to foster" (204).

individual who is manifestly authorized by a community" (*Fictions* 21). The voice in the letter is therefore not only Chase's voice but stands for the voice of the community. Preves explains that "[...] through involvement in a social movement, one begins to shift the social location of her/his identity from an individual notion of self to a group identification. That is, the problem that was formerly individualized is now recognized as a social problem that others experience as well" (*Identity* 128). While Chase, at the time of writing, could not yet rely on a social movement, her rhetoric envisions this movement and her personal story is produced as 'testimonial evidence' not just for an individual, singular experience but for a collective experience.

Transforming Truth: Testimony in Chrysalis (1997/8)

Following Chase's first letter, more and more intersex people began to write their stories and ISNA collected 26 pieces in a special issue of the journal *Chrysalis* in the winter of 1997/8, in the year Diamond and Colapinto had published their accounts of the Reimer case. The variety of the contributions – poetry, fiction, and first person accounts, photographs, caricatures, and scholarly writing – serves as an analogy to the variety of voices and experiences. There is not one intersex experience, the multiple contributions suggest, but a range of experiences and I have selected four contributions, the editorial, a series of photos, a document section and a short prose text, to show the variety in the testimonial representation.

Guest editors Martha Coventry and Cheryl Chase introduce their editorial article with the claim: "Intersexuality [...] is a matter of being different. There are dozens of reasons why a person may be born intersexed, but its major import is the same for each of us. We are different" (*Chrysalis* 3). Intersex is presented as neither a chosen attribute nor an acquired trait. A person *is* intersex and therefore assumed *to be* essentially different. Yet Coventry and Chase link this essentializing terminology to the category "difference." This is a difficult claim, one could state provocatively; in what way might intersex people be "different"? And whom would intersex people differ from? From trans* people, from people whose bodies are deemed 'able,' or from cis-gendered people, i.e. people assigned one sex at birth and who identify with this sex throughout their lives? In my opinion, Coventry and Chase use this diffuse category for two reasons: they aim to be inclusive, i.e. they want to address as many intersex people as possible. Moreover, they are looking for non-medicalizing terminology. The editorial continues: "Although difference is not an illness or a medical condition, *sexual* difference has been treated as an illness since the middle part of the nineteenth century" (3). The seemingly essentializing phrase "We are different" is both a statement that enhances community building, bonding, and an opposition to individualizing medical discourse and pathologizing terminology. Despite its essentialist tone, however, Chase and Coventry are far from advocating separatist politics. Rather, the publication in a trans*-operated journal signals alliance and cooperation with other marginalized groups. While the majority of contributions are written by intersex people, female-to-male transgender Brynn Craffey was also invited to share his experiences in men's locker rooms. Therefore, I argue that the essentializing rhetoric, again, needs to be read as strategically essentialist: on the one hand, the envisioned intersex community is addressed using the plural pronoun "we" and marked as inherently different. On the other hand, "difference" is a reaction to medicalizing terminology and the intersex subject created in this editorial is a political subject, not a patient.

The aim of medical and surgical intervention on intersex bodies, claim Coventry and Chase, is "to transform 'different' into 'normal'" (4) and the consequences of these interventions may be both physical and psychological. Psychological healing was inhibited or delayed by "rendering [...] intersexuality unspeakable" (4) and they deem talking or writing about one's experiences as an empowering act, an act of healing: "The first step was ... to tell our stories, to overcome our shame" (4). Rhetorically, writing in the mode of testimony, to testify to one's own experience, is to reclaim one's own voice and to refuse the authority of the medical expert. While the expert in the medico-scientific mode of writing is invested with abstract, general knowledge or supra-individual 'truth,' expert knowledge is devalued in testimony and the value of the individual voice (and experience) is emphasized. Chase and Coventry repeatedly draw attention to the act of storytelling ("we have heard the same stories over and over again," "Hearing these common histories has given us the determination to speak out publicly," "The stories you will read" 4). The writers/speakers are intersex people themselves; they are witnesses to the intersex experience and not medical 'experts' and this position increases their credibility and reliability.

In addition to aspects of expert voices, credibility, and the requirement of non-pathologizing terminology, the editors note the need to intervene on the level of visual representation:

> Until we found each other through support groups, the only images we had of intersexuality were horrible photos in medical books [...] all with the eyes blacked out. [...] Now, we are finding our pride and finding the strength to show our faces. [...] These pictures are our gift to ourselves and to our intersexual brothers/sisters and their parents [...]. And to the world, to declare that we exist, we are human, we are everywhere among you. (4)

The pictures that Coventry and Chase are referring to frame the journal by adorning the cover and final page of the issue.[27] The cover is a group shot of the first intersex demonstration in 1996 and shows protesters rallying behind a large banner that reads "Hermaphrodites with Attitude." The final page shows nine individual portraits and a group shot of ten people sitting in a sunny garden spread over the bottom of the page. The photos are presented without captions or any written explanation. So, without words, they show intersex as an individual identity in the portraits, as a collective experience in the garden scene and as a politically active group at the demonstration. As Coventry and Chase have made clear, these pictures need to be read as a discursive intervention: dehumanizing medical shots are replaced with pictures of people who "exist, [... and ...] are everywhere among" us.

The photos stand in stark contrast to images that are reproduced as part of Alice Dreger's article "Doctors Containing Hermaphrodites. The Victorian Legacy" (15-22) in the same issue. From the perspective of a social historian of science and medicine, Dreger asks "how 'sex' [...] came to be thought of the way it is today" (16). Her article begins with examples from her own research, i.e. 19th century medical discourse on hermaph-

---

27 Three additional shots are inserted on page 50 (at the demonstration, with caption), and 54 and 56 (groups of people at a restaurant, no captions). The demonstration shot shows activist Max Beck holding a sign that reads "Silence = Death," a slogan borrowed from early HIV/AIDS activism.

roditism and, via popular culture (TV drama series *Chicago Hope*), and the sex testing procedures of the Olympic Committee, spans all the way to 1990s scholarship by Fausto-Sterling and Suzanne Kessler. Dreger draws a line from the 19th century to contemporary discourse and finds that simple answers are still not available, rather, contemporary science seems to have made sex assignment more complex than ever. Eight 19th century images are inserted within her article. One is a study of five drawings of an Italian peasant woman who was suspected to be a man (cf. 18). The others are photographs that show naked adults: one has hir face veiled (cf.17), another lies on hir back with legs spread and a hand (presumably the doctor's hand) reaching into the frame, holding the phallus (cf. 17). The third person poses next to flowers and looks directly into the camera (cf. 22).[28] The images are accompanied by explanatory captions that sum up the medical case history of these individuals and provide the reader with details about their lives, e.g. Dreger includes their names (if known), and dates and places. A large caption that is spread at the bottom of the last page of her article is not assigned to a specific image, but explains the rationale behind these images and captions:

Historians – since we care about dates – have a habit of putting the birth dates and the death dates of various important figures after the first introduction of their names. [...] One day I realized I should do the same thing for the particularly famous hermaphrodites whom I was introducing [...]. Suddenly they came to life as people who had been born and who had died [...]. Now they were real. (22)

Thus, Dreger tries to turn these objects of medical studies into subjects by placing them in history and as historical figures. The strategy mirrors the strategy behind the photos of the intersex individuals: Chase and Coventry want to make clear that "we exist" (4) and Dreger shows that "they were real" (22). Thus, these images and photos form a critique on medical objectification and openly challenge the practice of medical photography.[29]

---

28 For an analysis of medical photography and sex assignment around 1900 see Kathrin Peters *Rätselbilder des Geschlechts* (2010).

29 For a critique on the practice of medical photography from the perspective of doctors and psychologists see Creighton et al. "Photography."

Intersex people turn themselves into subjects and the pictures are part of a process of identity production.

I want to draw attention to two other examples from the *Chrysalis* issue that illustrate the complex poetical dimension of testimonial writings: on page 38, in between two longer articles, there is a one page interlude that is neither listed in the table of contents nor referred to in the editorial or at any other point in the issue. The page shows photocopies of two medical and one legal document. Like a collage, the documents are cut out from larger documents; they overlap and cannot be read completely. The medical documents are surgery reports: a "partial clitorectomy" (38) was performed on a "little girl" due to a pre-operative diagnosis of "clitoromegaly" and an "exploratory laparotomy, biopsy of gonads, clitorectomy" was given to a "child" with the pre-operative diagnosis "female pseudohermaphrodite." The legal document is part of a birth certificate that indicates a name change "from Brian to Bonnie Grace." It is left unclear whose documents these are; they lack captions and nothing explains them. I read these documents as complex testimonies: on the one hand, they document, they report, they serve as evidence for the medical treatment that these children received. The documents name the clinical diagnosis, the technical name of the surgery according to the standard nomenclature and the reports describe the procedures in technical terms, e.g. a "midline vertical suprapubic incision was made." This shows the historical dimension of testimony. On the other hand, these documents also bear witness to the emancipation and possibly healing process of the adults who were subjected to the treatment as children. First of all, the former patients obviously did get hold of the documents. Numerous testimonies show that this cannot be taken for granted and for several intersex people the search for their medical documents proved futile. The former patients who obtained their records then decided to go public with these confidential and personal documents and put the feminist motto "the personal is political" into practice. This demonstrates the political dimension of testimony as well as the clinical dimension of testimony (speaking as part of a healing process). With respect to the poetical dimension of testimony, these documents function very differently from narrative testimonies: the presentation of these documents completely lacks any narrative mediation. While narrative necessarily explains, arranges events, describes and comments, this form of testimony refuses any contextualization and explanation. The traumatizing events are not safely contained within a story and made conveniently accessible. The only mediation is the context of the journal: a special issue full of intersex testimonies. The documents were clearly not made for this context. They belong to the medical and the legal strand of intersex discourse, but in this special issue they are made a part of, they are incorporated into or even captured and taken over by activist discourse. In this new context the documents stand out. They are no longer reports of a medical procedure. "The patient tolerated the procedure well and returned to the R.R. in satisfactory condition," states one of the medical reports. In the context of this journal, this statement automatically activates all the written narratives and interviews where intersex people talk about the suffering and pain that these procedures brought to them and their families. Without words or written explanations, these decontextualized documents again breach the silence dogma, show how activists reclaim their histories, and the original story of the documents is completely turned around. The medical story, i.e. intersex is a condition to be treated by early genital surgery, is re-told as an activist testimony via the practice of decontextualization.

My final example in this analysis, Annie Green's "My Beautiful Clitoris" (*Chrysalis* 12), also engages with medical reports and the long-term effects of genital surgery. The story is told in three short paragraphs plus an indented quote that follows the first paragraph. The quote is set in a different font, courier new, a style that resembles a manual type writer. In the first paragraph, Green grieves the loss of her clitoris due to an operation 32 years ago. She explains: "I have only one connection to the clitoris that I was born with: a pathologist's report on the bit of tissue the surgeons sent him for analysis" (12). The following quote, then, is from the pathologist's report. It refers to the clitoris as "the specimen," gives its exact size (length 2.8 cm and 1 cm in average outside diameter) and continues a detailed description. The quoted report consists of three sentences and shows some aspects of "report style," e.g. an article is omitted in the beginning of a sentence as in "Section shows [...]" opposed to "[The] section shows [...]." It uses anatomical terms such as "prepuce," which denotes the clitoral hood, the skin that surrounds and protects the outer clitoris. In contrast to this technical description stands the rest of the report: "a soft pinkish piece of tissue," "covered with wrinkled, pinkish tissue," "soft, pinkish-white, somewhat shiny, half cylinders, each outlined by a thin rim of shiny whitish tissue," "covered by a thin rim of soft, shiny, pink tissue" (12). Set apart from the rest of the text in font and by indentation and introduced as a pathologist's report, the technical part of the quote lives up to all narrative requirements of the genre. The descriptive part, however, comes as a surprise: adjectives like "shiny," "soft," "wrinkled," "pinkish" and "whitish" are said to "cover" and "outline" the specimen. This description does not evoke the image of a dangerous or malignant object that needed to be feared and removed from the body of the patient. The quote ends here and Green asks: "It sounds beautiful, doesn't it?" She emphasizes the poetical aspect of the report and continues, "I imagine it, my clitoris, [...] such an alive, vascular, beautiful, sensitive organ." Green's description, I suggest, is not in opposition to the medical report. The contrast between the medical report and the rest of the story that is evoked on the visual level (indentation and font) is less a contrast than a new frame: Green's story, literally, integrates the report into her own writing, and puts the clitoris back into her body, the body of her story. The effect of the medical report is once again turned up-side-down and made a part of the activist's testimony.

In activist writings of the 1997/8 issue of *Chrysalis*, subjectivity is emphasized and the 'truth' of the personal experience is valued higher than the 'truth' produced by empirical research. A need for 'scientific objectivity' is rejected and medico-scientific practices (paternalistic language use, medical photography, genital surgery and pathologization) are criticized. The exemplary analyses of the contributions by Annie Green and the documents page revealed a strategy to use the mode of testimonial writing to capture medical narratives and to transform them into their opposites.

NOTHING BUT THE TRUTH

My exemplary analysis of John Money's contributions to the intersex discourse revealed these texts to be put forward in a medico-scientific mode of writing: the voice in the text was reduced to the medical expert who spoke about intersex individuals; texts relied strongly on statistical data presented as facts; the author's own investment in practices of interpretation and narration was ignored or downplayed; findings were portrayed as evidence-based and supra-individual. Moreover, individual, non-scientific, subjective contributions were generally devalued. One effect of this mode of writing is the production of scientific objectivity. In this fashion, Money and other scholars dominated the intersex discourse with their contributions until the early 1990s. With Chase's 1993 letter the situation began to change; writing about intersex spread to other strands of discourse and the modes of writing diversified. Activists such as Chase challenged the dominance and unequivocal authority of the doctors' voices and began to speak out in their own voices. In the mode of testimony, experience was set against evidence and the personal and subjective brought up against the seemingly supra-individual. Testimony was claimed as an authoritative mode of speaking and medico-scientific generalizations were questioned. While intersex individuals in medico-scientific writing were reduced to informants and patients, they turned themselves into people and experts in testimonial writings.

Yet both modes of writing, I argue, share an investment in truth claims; one being based on scientific objectivity and the other on its exact opposite, i.e. individual, subjective experience. While the possibilities to make a meaningful contribution to the intersex discourse have multiplied, due to the pluralization of legitimate modes of writing (medico-scientific *and* testimonial) in the 1990s, the need to make a 'true' contribution to the discourse seems still intact and strong. The following analyses will scrutinize the discourse for meaningful fictional, i.e. neither experience-based nor evidence-based contributions to intersex discourse.

Hermaphroditus ♥ *Middlesex*:
Novel Interpretations of Old Myth

Lo(o)sing Plenty: Intersex in Fiction and Myth

Intersex, a term that was coined in 1916, was used in medical and psychological discourses throughout the 20th century. From the 1990s onwards, the term was appropriated by intersex activists and became known to a wider audience by their awareness-raising work. LGBT audiences, especially, grew more familiar with the term and the politics surrounding the concept by the late 1990s, and a number of inclusive gay and trans* rights organizations expanded their scope and added an *I* for *intersex* to their acronym. In addition to medical and political-activist discourses, academic gender and queer studies used intersex in the development of theory and it became a prime example for the construction of not only gender, but sex. After all, medical intersex management meant that numerous babies with bodies that looked different than other babies were literally cut into shape to fit the visual norms of sexually dimorphic girls or boys – drastic evidence for the 'man-madeness,' for the construction of sex. Nevertheless by 2000, intersex was hardly a topic for dinner table conversation. The debate was limited to specialized groups such as endocrinologists, pediatric surgeons, activists, scholars and gender studies students. In literary and cultural discourse, intersex was neither debated as a lived reality nor as a specific discursive position. Rather, literary and cultural scholars limited their analyses to the figure of the hermaphrodite as a mythical or metaphorical figure. With the publication of Jeffrey Eugenides' novel *Middlesex* in 2002, this situation appears to have changed. The novel's narrator Cal is an intersex character born in 1960 and analyses have repeatedly drawn comparisons to medical and activist discourses: from John Money and the Baltimore protocols to Cheryl Chase and ISNA. The novel was awarded the Pulitzer Prize for Fiction in 2003, sold more than 3 million copies and was translated into more than 35 languages.

While the preceding analyses have dealt predominantly with forms of autobiographical writings, I focus on fictional representations of intersex in the present chapter. Owing to the history in literary and cultural studies that often focused on the mythical hermaphrodite, I discuss the literary representation of intersex as entangled with the mythical tradition. Before turning to the fictional representations of intersex, I outline the mythical basis and some current readings of the mythical representation. The following analysis postulates three overlapping periods in the literary history of intersex: representation, I argue, begins in the 1960s, mostly in science fiction, historical adventure stories, and erotica ("Sexy Feminism"). In 2002, the publication of *Middlesex* marks a turning point in the representation of intersex figures and the debate in literary and cultural studies ("All in the Family"). The commercial success of *Middlesex* adds to the popularization of the topic and the number of publications with intersex characters increases during the following years ("Murder, Mystery, and Medical Drama"). As *Middlesex* seems to have triggered a scholarly and literary debate on intersex, my analysis then focusses on this debate and positions the novel within the context of the scholarly debate on the mythical hermaphrodite and the intersex figure ("Pooling with Hermaphroditus: *Middlesex* and the *Metamorphoses*").

In a 1990 reading of Ovid's story of Salmacis and Hermaphroditus, classicist S. Georgia Nugent reflects on the literary traditions of the hermaphrodite and reports two major lines of analysis. She claims that Marie Delcourt had constructed "a two-stage development of the myth: an original (mainly Greek) phase which valued, even revered, the completeness and potency of such a figure and a later phase (with Ovid as its avatar) which devalued the figure, viewed it as monstrous and introduced the principle bisexual=asexual" (Nugent "Not One" 179). Delcourt's reading of the hermaphrodite in Classical Antiquity had "become standard in philological sources" (179) and set the tone for imagining the hermaphrodite either as a metaphor for excess and plenitude, or for loss and deficit (cf. Nugent 163; 179). *Plenitude* refers to the hermaphrodite's double sex as both male and female and is related to the tradition of the androgynous myth in Plato's *Symposium*.¹ In consequence, the hermaphrodite could be read as a hypersexual or over-sexed figure. This line of representation may also be connected to a pre-Ovidian tradition that connects Hermaphroditus to Aphroditos, a male Aphrodite who wore female garments and a beard. Aphroditos was connected to sexuality and fertility. S/he was worshipped mostly in Cypria, where stone pillars adorned with a phallus and the deities' head marked the roads. Greek *herme* stands for 'pillar' and Hermaphroditos is then said to be a compound word designating the statue-pillar of Aphroditos, i.e. the herme of Aphroditos. Brisson explains that such statue-pillars could also be adorned with other deities and refers to Cicero, who mentioned a "Hermathena", and Pliny, who "refers several times to Hermeros pillars" (*Ambivalence* 54).²

The representation of the hermaphrodite as loss, deficiency or deficit stands in the tradition of the myth of Salmacis and Hermaphroditus laid down by Ovid in the *Metamorphoses* in 8 A. D., suggests Nugent (cf. 163ff). The Latin poet Ovid had explained the dual sex of Hermaphroditus as the result of a violent embrace of the innocent son of Hermes and Aphrodite, Hermaphroditus, by the nymph Salmacis. Traveling across the country the youth comes across a pool of clear water. The nymph Salmacis falls instantly in love with the beautiful boy and, when he dives naked into the water, she follows and embraces him. While he struggles to free him-

---

1 Silberman reports various traditions of the androgyne and the hermaphrodite in English literature from the Middle Ages and the Renaissance. Linda Woodbridge, explains Silberman, distinguishes a tradition "partly deriving authority from Plato's *Symposium*, of honoring the Hermaphrodite as the symbol of oneness from an abhorrence of physical androgyny associated with the Ovidian figure of Hermaphroditus" (Silberman "Transformations" 643). For the hermaphrodite in Classical Antiquity see Delcourt *Hermaphrodite*.

2 See Brisson *Ambivalence* for an extensive discussion of the different traditions of the myth. For the pre-Ovidian tradition see especially Brisson 53-5; handbooks on mythology by Seyffert 1894, William Smith 1880, and Roscher 1930 all list this tradition, but Romano calls the evidence "too slim" ("Invention" 553) and questions the validity of the argument. Ajootian dates the earliest mention of the name Hermaphroditos to 319 B.C. and notes that other compound names occurred "considerably later" ("Hermaphroditus" 269).

self, she prays to the Gods to never let them part again. The Gods then fuse the bodies of nymph and boy and Hermaphroditus emerges the pool with both male and female characteristics. Hermaphroditus then asks his[3] parents to drug the water of the pool so that every man who swims in it will experience the same effect. There is an ongoing debate on how to understand (and translate) this metamorphosis.[4] Both Miller 1984 and Melville 2008 [1986][5] translate Ovid's Latin *nec femina dici / ne puer ut possit; neutrumquue et utrumque uidetur* (*Metamorphoses* IV. 378f) to the effect that Hermaphroditus seemed 'neither sex and both.'[6] While *both* alludes to the hermaphrodite as excess, as over-sexed, *neither* implies sterility and therefore deficit and loss. Brisson explains: "The fusion of Salmacis and Hermaphroditos establishes a state of indifferentiation that blocks all activity, hence all generation, and arrests everything in a union that is permanent and so, perforce, sterile. The very notion of sex disappears, for to have both sexes is to have neither" (58).

This traditional reading of Ovid's story has been challenged repeatedly, as can be seen in the readings of Canadian philosopher Luc Brisson *Ambivalence*, German philosopher Michael Groneberg ("Mythen"), and US classical scholar Allen Romano ("Invention"). Brisson interprets the myth as an explanation for "the origin of passive homosexuality" (42), while Groneberg reads the transformation of the boy as post-coital relaxation and the scene as a heterosexual sex act and the perfect union of male and female (cf. esp. 89-103). Romano sees Ovid's story as a tongue-in-cheek adaptation of a Greek inscription dating back to the second century B. C. The inscription found in 1995 near the spring of Salmacis at Halicarnassus is the earliest narrative of Hermaphroditus to date (cf. 552) and introduces

---

3   Ovid and his translators continue to use male pronouns for the transformed Hermaphroditus.
4   See Stone "Mirror" for a discussion of some Early Modern English translations and adaptations of the myth.
5   Following English citations of the *Metamorphoses* refer to Melville's translation.
6   Compare Miller, "they were no longer two, nor such as to be called one, woman, and one, man. They seemed neither, and yet both" (qtd. in Brisson 48), and Melville, "They two were two no more, nor man, nor woman - / One body then that neither seemed and both" (85).

Hermaphroditus as the founder of marriage and Salmacis as the nymph who raised him. The waters of the spring, then, do not transform men into hermaphrodites, but are said to tame and heal savage minds.[7] Romano reads the waters as a powerful magic love potion that tames wild men (or civilizes barbarians, as Vitruvius put it) and makes them fit for marriage with women (or for Greek society, in Vitruvius). Salmacis, the spring, and Hermaphroditus, then, work hand in hand for the institution of marriage (and civilization). According to Romano, Ovid describes Hermaphroditus as experiencing an overdose of this love potion (he almost drowned in the pool) and, as a consequence, as permanently weakened, i.e. unfit for marriage due to his softened limbs. Romano also explains that Hermaphroditus' transformation from boy to hermaphrodite in Ovid may be his addition as "most sources make no reference to a transformation in the manner of Ovid and we are left with the impression that Hermaphroditus is a god who is a union of male and female from birth" (553).[8] The debate I have sketched here shows the myth of "Salmacis and Hermaphroditus" to have been and to be open to various interpretations. While it seems disputed whether the spring's water provokes civilization, homosexuality, effeminacy, heterosexuality or something else it seems agreed that Hermaphroditus' dual sexual nature serves as a metaphor, i.e. the hermaphrodite represents an idea rather than a real human being.[9]

---

7   This explanation of the powers of the spring is confirmed by one of Ovid's contemporaries, Vitruvius, who explicitly rejects Ovid's version of the story ("This fountain, however, by a mistaken opinion, is thought to afflict with a sexual disease those who drink of it") and instead praises the "virtue of the spring," its "clearness" and its "excellent flavor." Vitruvius explains that the effect of the spring was to attract "barbarians", who drank from the water, consequently began to interact with Greek society and slowly changed their "rough and wild habits to Greek customs and affability" (qtd. in Brisson 52f). See also Nugent 179f.
8   Nugent also stresses Hermaphroditus' ambiguity from the start, "both in appearance and in name he already unites masculine and feminine aspects, *before* he even encounters Salmacis" (163, emphasis added).
9   Ajootian notes that the "distinction between H[ermaphroditos] the divinity and humans with both male and female genitals" ("Hermaphroditos" 284) was

German philosopher Hans Blumenberg emphasizes the significance of Ovid's renderings of myths for Western literature and art and claims that the "European imagination is a network of reference that centers, to a large extent, on Ovid" (*Myth* 351). Given this influence, representations of hermaphrodites in literary and cultural history since Antiquity need to be read in the context of this text.[10] With respect to the connection between 'real' intersex experiences and mythical hermaphroditism, literary scholar Anson Koch-Rein explains that the "mythic, metaphoric, monstrous hermaphrodite [...] seems to have eclipsed the existence of intersexual bodies, and silenced their realities" ("Norm" 242f). Scholar and activist Morgan Holmes adds that "One reason why the canonical hermaphrodite texts – Plato's *Symposium,* Foucault's introduction to Alexina Barbin's autobiography as the memoirs of a 'nineteenth-century *hermaphrodite,*' Ovid's poems, and so on – offend some intersexuals is that they mythologize and eroticize hermaphroditism" (*Perilous* 98). Ovid's Hermaphroditus has provided a name (or a body) to metaphorical figures of duality, androgyny, ambiguity, or neutrality.[11] But as Holmes and Koch-Rein have pointed out, the figure cannot be read as a representation of intersex experiences.

Before I explore Eugenides' *Middlesex* in the context of Ovid's hermaphrodite, I tentatively outline the development of fictional representations of intersex or representations that have been discussed in

---

already recorded by Greek historian Diodorus Siculus in his Bibliotheca Historica dated to 60 to 30 B.C.

10 The *Cambridge Companion to Ovid* (2002) contains six papers in a section titled "Reception" which cover a time span from "Ovid in the Middle Ages" to "Recent Receptions" and which span topics from "Ovid and Art" to "Aesthetics of Place."

11 See Jenny Mann for Early Modern English translations of the myth. Mann finds that English Ovidian poetry presents "the hermaphrodite as a veiled figure of corporeal ambiguity, capable of being all things to all readers" ("Look" 68) and positions the poetic tradition in contrast to contemporary anatomical writings that "unveil and anatomize the secret parts of the hermaphrodite" (74). Karen Pinkus reads the hermaphrodite in some Early Modern writings and describes the hermaphrodite "as a trope" and a "mode of writing" ("Poetics" 94) that makes use of alchemy's notion of ambivalence.

relation to intersex in three sections. These three sections, "Sexy Feminism," "All in the Family," and "Murder, Mystery and Medical Drama," do not represent a completely continuous and coherent development from one section to the next. Rather, the sections overlap; some publications resist a seemingly fixed arrangement in sections, and confound the suggested chronology. My presentation rests on a number of exemplary publications and should be read as a dynamic structure, not as a rigid grid. A comprehensive list of fictional representations is provided in the appendix "Bodies beyond the Binary in Books and Movies."

Sexy Feminism

The figure of the hermaphrodite as either androgynous, a sexual neuter, or both male and female, has remained prevalent in Western cultural memory throughout the century. Numerous fictional accounts in science fiction, fantasy and adventure stories, and erotica evoke images of alternative sexes with bi- or omnipotent features, simultaneous or consecutive hermaphroditism. Some better-known examples are grouped under the label *feminist science fiction* and their authors, such as Theodore Sturgeon,[12] Ursula K. Le Guin,[13] and Octavia E. Butler, are connected to second-wave feminism.[14] These novels often depict alternative societies with a single-sex species such as *Venus Plus X* and *The Left Hand of Darkness* or more than two

---

12 Sturgeon's *Venus Plus X* (1960) depicts a technically advanced, peaceful society whose inhabitants possess both male and female genitalia. The novel was a Hugo award nominee in 1961.

13 Le Guin published *The Left Hand of Darkness* (1969), introducing the inhabitants of Gethen, who develop either male or female sexual characteristics for a monthly coupling period depending on pheromonal negotiation with a partner. Any Gethenian can get pregnant and father children. The novel won both the Nebula and the Hugo Award in 1970.

14 Octavia Butler's *Xenogenesis* trilogy consists of *Dawn* (1987), *Adulthood Rites* (1988), and *Imago* (1989) (published in an omnibus edition as *Lilith's Brood* [2000]). The Oankali, an alien race that come to rescue the human survivors of a nuclear war on earth, know three sexes. All three are needed for reproduction.

sexes e.g. *Lilith's Brood* and Melissa Scott's *Shadow Man* (1995).[15] These "what if…?"-scenarios function as thought experiments and offer alternatives to 20th century Western societies that have been criticized as structured by patriarchy and androcentrism.[16] Some of the species are indeed called hermaphroditic or intersex, but apart from Scott's *Shadow Man*, the novels have not been acknowledged within activist and/or medical intersex discourses. Moreover, within scholarly debates, the novels have not been read as representations of the mythical hermaphrodite or as intersex characters, but their connection to feminist politics has been emphasized.

In the 1990s, Gary Jennings exploits hermaphroditism as a trope of sexual omnipotence in his historical erotic-adventure novel *Raptor* (1992) with its protagonist Thorn, a hermaphrodite enjoying sex with both men and women in active and passive roles. Mary Flanagan's *Adèle* (1997) is set in the 1990s. It features a journalist's search for a famous 1930s Parisian prostitute, the 'wild child' and 'hermaphrodite' Adèle who has been exploited sexually, economically and medically by a ruthless gynecologist. The novel interweaves diverse erotic encounters with a historical crime story and some 1930s medical perspectives on hermaphroditism. Both novels clearly over-sexualize their hermaphrodite protagonists and stand in line with the metaphoric use of the hermaphrodite as plenitude and excess. Neither novel has been discussed in literary and cultural studies so far.

Before the millennium, two novels form notable exceptions to the outlined formation of the literary discourse on hermaphroditism and intersexuality: Israeli writer Batya Gur published *Lo Kach Tearti Li* ('I Didn't Imagine It Would Be This Way') in Hebrew in 1994 and German author Robert Schneider published *Die Luftgängerin* ('The Air Walker') in 1998. While Gur's crime novels are all translated into English, her novel on a gynecologist's first encounter with an intersex child of ultraorthodox

---

15 Melissa Scot modeled *Shadow Man* on Anne Fausto-Sterling's 1993 article "The Five Sexes," and Fausto-Sterling acknowledged the text in her 2000 revision of the article (cf. *Sexing* 295, note 5).

16 For a scholarly introduction to feminist science fiction see Attebery *Decoding*; Garber and Paleo *Uranian*; James *Companion*; Larbalestier *Battle*; Melzer *Alien*.

Jewish parents is not available in English.[17] The story centers on the gynecologist's struggle to understand the child's parents, who follow their rabbi's advice and do not consent to surgery. Schneider's second novel *Die Luftgängerin* was not as well received as his debut *Schlafes Bruder* (1992). While the latter was translated into 36 languages, adopted as a movie, a play and an opera, *Die Luftgängerin* has so far not been translated. The protagonist Maudi is a young AIS-girl, i.e. a girl with XY chromosomes and androgen insensitivity, full of love and compassion for misfits, outcasts and the lonely. Despite her angelic features and altruistic behavior, she is the object of repeated acts of (physical) violence and is finally killed by an aggressor. While intersex activists reviewed the book and the depiction of the protagonist favorably,[18] feuilleton and scholarly criticism acted reservedly.[19]

It can be attested that a fictional literary discourse on intersexuality was not established in the Anglosphere in the 20th century. The trope of sexual variation was used in (feminist) science fiction to reflect on the binary gender system and hermaphrodites were sexualized or fetishized in erotica and adventure stories. The only two novels with intersex protagonists engaging with 20th century intersex discourses, *Die Luftgängerin* and *Lo Kach Tearti Li*, lacked public and scholarly responses and have not been translated into English.

All in the Family

This situation began to change in 2002 when three novels[20] that center on intersex protagonists and their families were published: French author

---

17 The novel is available in German, *So habe ich es mir nicht vorgestellt* (1996).
18 Lucie Veith, chair of the German support group "XY-Frauen" recommended the novel to the audience of a public lecture in Hamburg, March 29, 2011. See also the review on the British AIS Support Group's website www.aissg.org
19 A BDSL search (International Bibliography of German Literature and Literary Studies) for both texts showed 47 entries for *Schlafes Bruder* and one for *Die Luftgängerin* (accessed August 14, 2014).
20 A fourth novel, *The Book of Shadows* by James Reese, was also published in 2002. The protagonist in this erotic-gothic tale is called Herculine and the beginning of the story is modeled on the memoirs of Herculine Barbin (i.e.

Noëlle Châtelet published *La Tête en Bas*[21], German author Ulrike Draesner *Mitgift*, and American author Jeffrey Eugenides *Middlesex*. *La Tête en Bas* was adapted for the theatre and played in France and Belgium. The novel tells the story of an intersex person who was assigned female at birth, grew up as a tomboy called Denise and later transitioned to the male gender, calling himself Paul. The story alternates between Denise's and Paul's voices and shows the protagonist's struggle to form a coherent gender identity from the warring parts in hir body and mind. After a mental breakdown and hospitalization, Denise_Paul transcends the binary and unites hirself in music. The novel is dedicated to someone who has told the author about hir life[22] and Châtelet thereby acknowledges the influence of an intersex individual's life on the fictional text. Having been written by a well-known writer and actress, Châtelet's novel has received positive reviews in France and Germany, but no scholarly attention so far.

Draesner's *Mitgift* tells the story of Aloe, an art historian who is struggling with a family secret and the cooling of her relationship with her boyfriend Lukas. Aloe's sister Anita is intersex and the family guards this secret from everyone despite repeated visits to the hospital, including genital operations, and ongoing hormone treatment. Not knowing or not understanding what is going on, Aloe feels left out and while the sisters grow up the alienation between them increases. Years later, Aloe is still haunted by feelings of inadequacy and estrangement and enters a dramatic downward spiral to keep control over her life by controlling the weight of her body. Aloe's anorexia is the major topic of the novel, but Anita's

---

Herculine grows up in a Catholic convent, excels in school, but feels isolated due to a perceived physical difference). But soon the story diverts from its historical source material and Herculine is caught up in a plot of mystery, desire, and witchcraft. Author Reese also explained that he used Herculine's hermaphroditism to portray her as the "ultimate outsider" and adds that the novel "is about a hermaphrodite to the same extent *The Old Man and The Sea* is about a fish" (jamesreesebooks.com). Owing to its erotic content the novel may be counted among the tradition that over-sexualizes the hermaphrodite.

21 Available in German as *Mit dem Kopf Zuerst* (2004).
22 The dedication in the German edition reads: "Zur Erinnerung an den, der mir ein wenig aus seinem Leben erzählt hat, das so ausgesehen haben könnte" (*Mit dem Kopf zuerst* 7).

intersexuality forms the background to this story. Draesner is a well-known poet and her language reflects this. Nevertheless, she also uses a rather crude gender transition to describe the dramatic long-term effects of Anita's treatment. The beautiful girl had married, pursued a successful career and given birth to a baby, before she collapsed and shed the layers of heteronormativity she felt trapped in. Anita breaks with her parents, takes masculinizing hormones, and starts living as a man. Her sister Aloe feels left out again, but the two somehow manage to reconcile shortly before Anita is killed by her husband and Aloe becomes the foster mother of her nephew. In interviews, Draesner points out that she did extensive research on intersex before writing the novel that she believes to be about the ultimate indeterminacy of the body – be it intersex as in the case of Anita, anorexic as Aloe's or presumably unmarked.[23]

While Draesner's and Châtelet's publications provoked some journalistic responses – interviews and reviews – and also some scholarly attention, both novels have been surpassed by far by the publicity that Eugenides' *Middlesex* created: the author was already well-known after his debut novel *The Virgin Suicides* (1993), which was adapted for the screen by director Sofia Coppola and released in 1999. Published in North America in September 2002 by Farrar, Straus and Giroux and a month later by Bloomsbury Publishing in the United Kingdom, *Middlesex* was awarded its first major prize, the Pulitzer Prize for Fiction, in May 2003. The audiobook was released in 2002, a Book-Club-in-a-Box companion to *Middlesex* was published in 2005 and US talk show host Oprah Winfrey featured the novel in her TV book club in 2007.

With its international success *Middlesex* introduced intersex to a wide audience and the assumption of *Middlesex*'s narrator and protagonist Calliope_Cal[24] may well have become true: "When this story goes out into the world, I may become the most famous hermaphrodite in history" (*Middlesex* 19). Narrator Cal explicitly refers to himself as a *hermaphrodite*

---

23 Cf. Küchemann 2002 for an interview with the author. Baier "Beyond" and Catani "Hybrid" discuss the representation of intersex in the novel from a scholarly perspective.

24 *Middlesex*'s protagonist and narrator transitions from female-identified Calliope to male-identified Cal. See below for an analysis of narration and focalization techniques in the novel.

– not as intersex. This choice of terminology aligns the Greek-American with the mythical Hermaphroditus rather than with 20th century intersex discourses and the novel's relevance in a chapter on intersex in fiction may be disputed. Yet the novel should not be discarded too easily as a look at the introduction shows. Eugenides had explained that the beginnings of his novels usually serve as "blueprints" (van Moorhem 2003 n.p.) for the rest of the novel and this is certainly true for *Middlesex*: "I was born twice: first, as a baby girl, on a remarkably smogless Detroit day in January of 1960; and then again, as a teenage boy, in an emergency room near Petoskey, Michigan, in August 1974" (*Middlesex* 3), reads the first sentence of the novel. While the sentence somehow mirrors the beginning of N.O. Body's *Maiden Years* ("I was born a boy, raised as a girl." *Maiden Years* 7), the reference to the emergency room places the gender transition in medical discourse and Cal continues, "Specialized readers may have come across me in Dr. Peter Luce's study, 'Gender Identity in 5-Alpha-Reductase Pseudohermaphrodites,' published in the *Journal of Pediatric Endocrinology* in 1975" (*Middlesex* 3). Cal's transition is therefore not related to transsexuality but to the medical diagnosis of 5-alpha-reductase deficiency (5-ARD), a diagnosis implying a genetic variation in XY-individuals that influences the synthesis of testosterone to dihydrotestosterone; both androgens are effective in the development of male genitalia. In *Middlesex*, the condition serves as a background to explain Calliope_Cal's transition in puberty: born with male internal reproductive structures and so-called female-looking external genitalia, Calliope_Cal virilizes during puberty due to an enhanced production of testosterone. The 19th century term *pseudohermaphrodite* in combination with a 20th century intersex diagnosis, 5-ARD, reflects the language use of endocrinologist Julianne Imperato-McGinley and her medical research team. Eugenides lists a 1979 study by Imperato-McGinley et al. as one of his sources for the novel on the copyright page. In the study Imperato-McGinley et al. found that "exposure of the brain to normal levels of testosterone in utero, neonatally and at puberty appears to contribute substantially to the formation of male-gender identity […] [and that […] the effect of testosterone predominates, over-riding the effect of rearing as girls" ("Androgens" 1233). Within the nature-nurture debate, Imperato-McGinley et al. side with the opponents of John Money's sex-of-rearing approach and argue for a biologically determined male or female gender identity. Their use of the term *pseudo-*

hermaphrodite underlines their belief in a binary gender (and sex) system: a person may either *be* male or female. A third option, hermaphrodite, is discursively negated by qualifying it as *pseudo*. Ironically, *Middlesex* attributes the publication to Dr. Luce, Calliope's doctor, who represents the theory and approach of John Money. The opposing theories of Money and Imperato-McGinley are then combined in the figure of the fictional Dr. Luce, whose name – a short form of Lucifer – already marks the doctor as an evil character.[25]

While the first paragraph in the novel introduces the medical discourse on intersex and offers opportunities to read the text as a contribution to the nature-nurture debate, the second paragraph contains references to Greek mythology, such as Tiresias, the seer who was transformed into a woman for seven years ("Like Tiresias, I was first one thing, and then the other" [*Middlesex* 3]), or Hermaphroditus ("a swimming pool turned me into myth" [3]). These repeated citations of and allusions to Greek myths of transition at the beginning of and throughout the novel connect it to literary and mythical discourses on hermaphroditism.

The third paragraph claims the genre memoir or autobiography for the novel when Cal explains: "But now, at the age of forty-one, [...] I find myself thinking about departed great-aunts and -uncles, long-lost grandfathers, unknown fifth cousins, or, in the case of an inbred family like mine, all those things in one. And so before it's too late I want to get it down for good" (4). The story of his life that Cal wants to relate spans three generations and he hands over to the "Muse" (4) who should "Sing now, O Muse, of the recessive mutation on my fifth chromosome! Sing how it bloomed two and a half centuries ago on the slopes of Mount Olympus [...]. Sing how it passed down through nine generations, gathering invisibly within the polluted pool of the Stephanides family" (4). The muse addressed here may well be Calliope, the Greek muse of epic poetry, who served as a namesake for the narrator's girl self. With the address to the muse and the reference to genetic variation, the third paragraph in this introduction intertwines discourses of hermaphroditism and intersex. Both had been treated as distinct and separate by science, medicine, mythology, and history throughout the 20th century. In 2002, *Middlesex* sets out to

---

25 See Saglimbeni "Cal(lie)", who identified Dr. Peter Luce as a representation of John Money and the novel as a contribution to the nature-nurture debate.

combine and entangle them and presents itself as an amalgam of diverse ingredients. Judged by the pure amount of scholarly and journalistic attention, *Middlesex* surpasses every other novel with an intersex character by far and I focus on the novel's discursive entanglement below.

Murder, Mystery, and Medical Drama

In the following year, fictional representations of intersex spread to yet another fictional genre: with *Bare Bones* (2003) by Kathy Reichs and *Monkeewrench* (2003) by P. J. Tracy, two crime novels engage intersex characters. Both novels combine the search for an XY chromosomal suspect, presumably a man, with a character living as a woman. Here, intersex is used as a simple plot twist. Two 2005 German novels continue this element, Renate Kampmann's *Fremdkörper* and Ralf Isau's *Die Galerie der Lügen*, and contribute to a further popularization of intersex in literature. Similar to fictional representation in literature, intersex characters' involvement in TV series increases: before *Middlesex* only the medical dramas *Chicago Hope* (1996) and *ER* (1998) had each aired one episode with an intersex patient. Since 2005, crime drama *Law & Order: Special Victims Unit* (2005) and medical(-comedy) dramas *Nip/Tuck* (2005), *Grey's Anatomy* (2006), and *House, M.D.* (2006; 2009) have featured intersex characters.[26] Each airing has provoked responses by intersex activists and in some cases a flood of letters of complaint about the

---

26 List of episodes from popular TV series with intersex characters in chronological order: "The Parent Rap" *Chicago Hope* (April 29, 1996). "Masquerade" *ER* (October 29, 1998). "The Little Things" *Freaks and Geeks* (July 8, 2000). "The One with the Rumor" *Friends* (November 22, 2001). "Identity" *Law & Order: Special Victims Unit* (January 18, 2005). "Quentin Costa" *Nip/Tuck* (December 20, 2005). "Begin the Begin" *Grey's Anatomy* (January 15, 2006). "Skin Deep" *House, M.D.* (February 20, 2006). "The Softer Side" *House, M.D.* (February 23, 2009). 2011 and 2012 longstanding German crime series *Tatort* aired two episodes with intersex characters, "Zwischen den Ohren" (September 18, 2011) and "Skalpell" (May 28, 2012). Canadian medical drama series *Saving Hope* included an intersex character in "Vamonos" (Aug. 20, 2013). See Amato *Intersex Narratives* for a critical analysis of intersex in medical drama series.

representation of the intersex character has led the broadcasting company or the producers to include additional information on intersex on their websites or to show an address of a support group in the following show. Activists have often been torn between the positive aspect of heightened awareness for the topic and the negative depiction of the characters as outsiders or murderers.[27]

In addition to further contributions in science fiction, bizarro fiction,[28] and historical adventure stories,[29] one notable fictional representation of intersex was Canadian Kathleen Winter's *Annabel* (2010). The coming-of-age story of an intersex character in the Canadian wilderness won the Thomas Head Raddall Award (2011), was shortlisted for three Canadian literary awards in 2010 and made it to the shortlist of the 2011 Orange Prize for Fiction (now Bailey's Women's Prize for Fiction).[30] Coming-of-age stories have also featured in two major motion pictures with intersex characters: Argentine Lucía Puenzo's *XXY* (2007) was an international success and was followed by fellow Argentine filmmaker Julia Solomonoff's *El último Verano de la Boyita* (2009). Preceding these movies, Peruvian-American Lisset Barcellos' *Both* (2005) was the first motion picture with an intersex character. Although the story of the adult stunt woman Rebecca Duarte received standing ovations at international queer film festivals and with intersex audiences, the movie was not widely distributed. *Both* is fiction, but the filmmaker is open about her own intersexuality and Cheryl Chase is said to have worked as a consultant for the project.[31] The adult character in *Both* does receive genital surgery and struggles with desensitization and the non-disclosure of her history.

---

27 For activists' reactions see aissg.org, intersexinitiative.org, isna.org.
28 See for example r. muir's *Skin* (2009), or Gina Ranalli's *Sky Tongues* (2009).
29 See for example Canadian Lydia Kwa's *The Walking Boy* (2005), the coming-of-age of an intersex boy in 8th century China and Australian Amanda Curtin's *The Sinkings* (2008). The latter features a historical 19th century murder case of a presumed intersex person and a late 20th century mother-daughter relationship. The daughter is intersex and was subjected to early genital surgeries.
30 See Neuhaus "Inventions" for a discussion of the text and my suggestions for further analyses in the conclusion of the present study.
31 See the discussion on www.bodieslikeours.org (accessed August 25, 2014).

Puenzo's and Solomonoff's heroes_heroines have not been subjected to genital surgery and are purely fictional. While representations of intersex in movies and novels have significantly increased since around 2002, 'successful' stories (i.e. wide distribution, prizes, reviews, and sales figures) have tended to depict a teenage hero_heroine on a quest for their gender identity. Moreover, none of the heroes_heroines have been surgically mutilated. Here, these fictional accounts stand in contrast to the testimonial writings from the 1990s that often focused on the lasting negative effects of early genital surgery and to ISNA's mission statement claiming intersex was "primarily a problem of stigma and trauma, not gender" (isna.org). Intersex activists have voiced this critique since the publication of Eugenides' *Middlesex* and it was Thea Hillman who explored activists' double bind between an increase in public awareness and misrepresentation in fictional accounts such as *Middlesex*. Her *Intersex (for Lack of a Better Word)* (2008) is a collection of 47 pieces of short prose and poetry that won the LAMBDA literary award in 2009. *Better Word* is categorized as 'memoir' and marked as autobiographical. Yet its structure of diverse prose and poetry pieces, non-chronological order and numerous gaps and overlaps stretch the formal characteristics of the genre. As a writer and performer, as an activist and intersex person, Hillman reflects critically on (fictional) representations of intersex and hermaphroditism.[32]

So far, I have outlined the development of fictional representations of intersex, especially during the first decade of the 21st century. The publication of *Middlesex* in 2002 marks the beginning of a general popularization of the topic and the fictional account will shape the public understanding of intersex for years to come. The history of fictional intersex representations, critique by intersex activists, and *Middlesex*'s references to hermaphroditism, all suggest an entanglement with classical myth. Thus, I explore *Middlesex*'s connection to Ovid's *Metamorphoses* in the following.

---

32 See the following chapter, "Intersex in Pieces," for an analysis of Hillman's *Better Word*.

POOLING WITH HERMAPHRODITUS: *MIDDLESEX* AND THE *METAMORPHOSES*

Following the publication of *Middlesex*, Jeffrey Eugenides was sometimes asked whether he was intersex himself.[33] The author rejects these autobiographical approaches to his second novel and explains that he set out to write "the fictional memoir of a hermaphrodite," and continues, "in contrast to the way hermaphrodites have appeared in literature – miserable creatures like Tiresias for instance – I wanted to write about a real person with a real condition. I did a lot of research on the details, but in terms of figuring out what hermaphrodites psychologically went through, I did that from my own imagination" (van Moorhem 2003 n.p.).[34] The Greek-American author who had "Latin as [a] major" and who lists "Virgil and Ovid" (van Moorhem 2003) as literary influences seems familiar with the literary tradition that represents hermaphrodites only as myth and metaphor. Yet, he names another source for his novel, Foucault's edition of Herculine Barbin's memoirs:

Originally I worked from the Memoirs of Herculine Barbin, published by Michel Foucault in the late seventies. The book is obviously interesting from a historical point of view. […] But as an expression of what it is like to be a hermaphrodite, from the inside, Herculine Barbin's memoir is quite disappointing. She just tends to go into this moaning, talking about how misfortunate she is and… it's sad. You can go and read it, but she didn't have enough self-awareness to be able to understand what was going on. In a way she was pre-psychological in her knowledge of her self. And when I read that book I didn't get any information about someone with such a condition. (van Moorhem 2003)

---

33 Only some insignificant family details in the story may indeed be called autobiographical, the author explains, for example, he lived in Detroit and grew up on a street called Middlesex Boulevard. Furthermore, Eugenides lived in Berlin while writing the book, the once divided city where the adult Cal lives (cf. Van Moorhem 2003 and Bedell 2002).

34 Eugenides repeated these explanations in different interviews (see, for example, Bedell 2002, Miller 2002, Weich 2006).

Eugenides claims that he had set out to produce a story that provided insight into the psychological processes of a hermaphrodite, but ignores the fact that 'hermaphrodites' did not exist in the 20th century outside of myth and metaphor. Medical discourse had long since taken over and 'hermaphrodites' had been redefined as 'pseudo-hermaphrodites' and, since the 1920s, increasingly referred to as 'intersex' (cf. my chapters "At a Glance I: Hermaphrodite History" and "At a Glance II: Intersex History"). Moreover, Eugenides' disappointment with Barbin's memoirs reveals his own, late 20th century expectations and assumptions about living "with such a condition," but says little about Barbin's 19th century experience (cf. my chapter "Truth or Dare"). Referring to 20th century Calliope_Cal as a 'hermaphrodite' is anachronistic, and brought him a lot of criticism from intersex activists (cf. "Q&A with Jeffrey Eugenides" Oprah.com, Hillman *Better Word* 24-26; 27-9). Yet it also shows Eugenides' commitment to the mythological tradition that portrays hermaphrodites as metaphor. Although he claims that he wanted to write about "a real person with a real condition," the term *hermaphrodite* necessarily places Calliope_Cal in the realm of myth. At this point, it becomes obvious that *Middlesex* is not just about a 20th century intersex character, but that it grew "out of Greek mythology," as Eugenides explains in his answer to the intersex critique on his choice of terminology ("Q&A with Jeffrey Eugenides"). Furthermore, he explains that he used the term *intersex* for talking about 'real people,' while *hermaphrodite* was reserved for literary characters (cf. "A Conversation with Jeffrey Eugenides"). For Eugenides, it may be said, Calliope_Cal embodies both a mythical hermaphrodite and a 20th century intersex character.

Given Eugenides' choice of terminology, it is surprising that the influence of Classical Greek and Roman mythology on the novel has been mostly ignored so far. Scholars dutifully note quotations of the story of the nymph Salmacis and the young boy Hermaphroditus as evidence for *Middlesex*'s strong use of intertextuality,[35] but the traces of the myth have

---

35 Despite long years of theorizing since Julia Kristeva's coinage of the term in 1966 ("Any text is constructed as a mosaic of quotations; any text is the absorption and transformation of another. The notion of *intertextuality* replaces that of intersubjectivity […]" ["Word" 66]), *intertextuality* has remained "one of the most commonly used and misused terms in contemporary critical

not been fully explored yet. I contend that the influence of the *Metamorphoses* as an epic poem and the story of "Salmacis and Hermaphroditus" on *Middlesex* surpasses that of mere reference. Rather, the *Metamorphoses* as a whole and the story of "Salmacis and Hermaphroditus" in particular resonate and are explored in *Middlesex* in various ways.

The following analysis then ties in with what Philip Hardie, editor of the 2002 *Cambridge Companion to Ovid*, called a "recent flood of scholarly criticism" (2) on Ovid's works. In his 'Introduction' he maintains that "Ovid's star shone brightly in the sky" (1) at the end of the twentieth century and generally attests to a "current revival of interest" (10) in the Latin poet. While the text had enjoyed unbroken popularity from the Middle Ages through the Renaissance, interest had subsided between the 18th and the early 20th centuries. Hardie explains Ovid's comeback with a reassessment of what "formerly was seen as superficial wit and an irredeemable lack of seriousness [...]. 'Parody,'" he explains, "has moved to the theoretical centre of studies of allusion and intertextuality" (4). Ovid is obviously not a postmodern author, but what Hardie emphasizes is the

---

vocabulary" (Graham *Intertextuality* 2). The least common denominator among scholars such as Roland Barthes, Harold Bloom or Michael Riffaterre seems to be that *intertextuality* focuses on "textual relations" (1), suggests Allen Graham in the introduction to Routledge's New Critical Idiom Series *Intertextuality*. Genette, *Palimpsests*, offers a systematic description of various relations between texts that he refers to as *transtextuality* and distinguishes five major categories: intertextuality (including practices of citation, plagiarism and allusion), paratextuality (e.g. title and foreword, publishers' announcements or blurbs), metatextuality (commentary, especially scholarly criticism), architextuality (a (possibly unmarked) relation between a text and poetic traditions etc.), and hypertextuality (the relation between the text that is the object of analysis and its source texts) (cf. Genette 1-7). Genette's systematic approach is helpful for categorizing different forms of intertextuality, but the terminology he suggests has not been widely accepted (cf. Allen 101ff). I use the term *intertextuality* in the sense of the least common denominator and to point to relations *between* texts.

text's adaptability to postmodern criticism.[36] "The *Metamorphoses*," argues classicist Vanda Zajko in 2009, "has functioned as a mythological handbook for postmodernity" ("Listening" 183), and, I would like to add, to Jeffrey Eugenides as well. Zajko, then, prefaces her reading of Ovid's myth by a quote from Eugenides' *Middlesex* (cf. 175) and links the two texts. Anecdotal evidence for a connection is also suggested by advertising endorsements on the cover of both texts: the blurbs on Melville's translation of the *Metamorphoses* announce the "wittiest poem of the wittiest poet of classical antiquity" while the blurbs on *Middlesex* echo "a rich comedy," "wildly funny" and "witty phrasing." But these reverberations are by far not the only links between the two texts, as I will show in the following.

Thereby Hangs a Tale: Genre

The *Metamorphoses* have often triggered genre debates and Andrew Feldherr asks provocatively whether the poem may be called an "anti-epic" or even a "Hellenistic assemblage of separate tales" ("Metamorphosis" 169). Stephen Harrison comments dryly that "scholars have rightly assumed that it meets epic criteria (being long, in hexameters, and treating mythological material)" and suggests focussing "on the more fruitful question of precisely how the *Metamorphoses* negotiates its own complex position within the tradition of hexameter epic" ("Genre" 87). He stresses the poem's "generically multifarious character" and identifies "elegy and Hellenistic/neoteric narrative, tragedy" as some genre traditions outside of epic that are treated in the *Metamorphoses*. Harrison adds "literary hymns" and "pastoral scenes" to the list and explains that "the sheer range of other genres which are included in some sense in the *Metamorphoses* [...] suggests that generic multiplicity within a formally epic framework is

---

36 The *Postmodern Reader* (1993) edited by Joseph Natoli and Linda Hutcheon collects a number of seminal texts on postmodernism, among them Ihab Hassan's "Toward a Concept of Postmodernism" [1987]. Hassan attempts to distinguish postmodernism from modernism and lists a number of characteristics for each. Among the postmodern characteristics are play, intertext, irony, and indeterminacy (cf. Hassan in Natoli/Hutcheon 80f). All of these terms are discussed by scholars in reference to both texts, *Middlesex* and the *Metamorphoses* (see also Hutcheon *Poetics*; Hutcheon *Politics*).

particularly fundamental to the poem" (89). From this perspective, the *Metamorphoses* contain a programmatic metapoetic dimension and metamorphosis, or transformation, is reflected not only on the level of content, but also on the level of form and genre. Harrison concludes: "literary *forms* are transformed into new *bodies* of poetic work" (89).

The genre debate about *Middlesex* shows similarities to the debate about the *Metamorphoses*. While *Middlesex* is surely not an epic poem, it has been described as a "transatlantic epic" (Turrentine n.p.), a "comic epic of Greek-American identity" (Carroll "Retrospective" 187), an "'elegiac romance'" (Saglimbeni "Outsider" 182), as a "bildungsroman" (Sifuentes "Strange" 146), as an example of "historiographic metafiction" (Collado-Rodriguez "Self" 74), a work of "hysterical realism" (Hsu "Ethnicity" 92), or as an "immigrant epic [which] rubs shoulders with the sexual memoir" (Shostak "Hybridity" 386), and Eugenides is said to have "courted the label of the 'hybrid' for the formal structure of his novel" (Shostak 384).[37] The blending of elements from different genres in *Middlesex* may, on the one hand, mark the novel as postmodern. On the other hand, it links the form of the novel – a blend, a mix of some kind, something in-between, or in the middle – to its content, the story of a character depicted as being in the middle between two sexes. *Middlesex* and the *Metamorphoses* may be said to combine a programmatic title with a genre structure that ties in with the respective topics of the texts.

Causing a Good Life: Aetiological Epic

In a study on Ovid's use of myth, classicist Fritz Graf elaborates that "among the most elementary and most widespread functions of myth is aetiology – to explain and, by the very explanation, to organize natural and social phenomena by giving accounts of how they came into being in events of the distant past" ("Myth" 115). Graf embeds the *Metamorphoses* in a tradition of Greek aetiological stories of metamorphoses by Callimachus (*Aitia*), Nicander of Colophon (*Heteroioumena*), and Boios

---

37 See Foer 2002 for the full interview with Eugenides that Shostak refers to. Other interviews where Eugenides discusses the novel as a hybrid include Miller 2002, van Moorhem 2003, Weich 2006. For a review see Mendelsohn 2002 or Bedell 2002.

(*Ornithogenia*). Ovid's story of Salmacis and Hermaphroditus is a good example for the aetiological function of myth.[38] A short introduction announces the riddle that the story sets out to solve: "Hear how the magic pool of Salmacis / Found its ill fame, and why its strengthless waters / Soften and enervate the limbs they touch. / All know its famous powers but few the cause" (*Met.* IV. 285-9). In addition to the explanation of the softening effects of the water, the story also gives the cause for the sexual duality of Hermaphroditus. Brisson explains that stories of the spring Salmacis and about Hermaphroditus had existed independently, but that Ovid was the one who merged the two into one: "This story kills two birds with one stone, explaining the origin of Hermaphroditus as the result of metamorphosis and providing an *aition* for the reputation of the spring" (398).

Callie's three-generation family history in *Middlesex*, I believe, serves a similar purpose. Like the *Metamorphoses*, *Middlesex* is divided into different parts, called books. I have analyzed the introductory paragraphs of Book One above and explained how 20th century intersex discourse and mythical hermaphroditism are entangled. But the introduction does more than to prepare the ground for a story about intersex and hermaphroditism. Rather, narrator Cal announces the reason for the following story when he states that he was first born as Calliope and later becomes the teenage Cal. Looking back at his life story, he finally wants to "get it down for good" and explain "this roller-coaster ride of a single gene through time. [...] how it bloomed two and a half centuries ago on the slopes of Mount Olympus [...] how it passed down through nine generations, gathering invisibly within the polluted pool of the Stephanides family" (*Middlesex* 4). The "polluted pool of the Stephanides family" meant here, is, of course, the gene pool, but the term may allude to Salmacis' mythical pool near Halicarnassus as well. In other words, Cal states a 'fact', his transition from girl to boy or to young man, and then prepares to explain this circumstance. His explanation, the *aition*, for his story is a recessive genetic mutation that gets passed down through incestuous relationships until Callie's parents are both carriers of the mutation and pass it on to Cal, where it finally becomes effective. The first three books of the novel deal mostly with the family

---

38 See also Ajootian who refers to the story as "Ovid's lengthy aetiological tale" ("Hermaphroditos" 269) and Zajko 187ff.

history and the reader follows the gene from the generation of Callie's grandparents to Callie's parents and finally to Callie her-, later himself. It is only when she is fourteen that her body lives up to "the narrative requirements" (396) and the story of Callie's transformation to Cal is reported in Book Four. So, while three books deal with the causes for Cal's intersexuality, it is only in the last book that Cal actually deals with the effects of being called intersex.

In the novel, incest works as a causal explanation for 5-ARD, Callie's intersex diagnosis. Although 5-ARD may occur more often in smaller gene pools, incestuous relationships are not a prerequisite for the occurrence of 5-ARD or any other intersex diagnosis. In classic mythology incest occurs rather frequently. Hercules, the namesake of Milton Stephanides' fast food chain, is the son of Zeus, who was the child of the siblings Rhea and Kronos, and who was married to his sister Hera. Hercules' mother Alcmene is also Zeus' great-granddaughter and Hercules himself later marries his half-sister Hebe. Relationships between family members took place in all imaginable combinations, between siblings,[39] among fathers and daughters,[40] or mothers and sons.[41] Though the relationships usually end unhappily, the offspring of such relations do not seem to suffer any negative consequences. In the context of Greek myth then, the incestuous relationship between Lefty and Desdemona may be condemnable and in a way it is punished in the course of the novel: Lefty loses all their savings in gambling and the couple has to move in with their children. He suffers his first in a series of strokes that render him speechless on the day Calliope is born. Desdemona always feels guilty for marrying her brother and spends her last years bedridden and increasingly senile. She believes that Cal's intersexuality is the result of their relationship, but when the senile Desdemona, who never spoke English fluently, apologizes to Cal, "'I'm sorry, honey. I'm sorry this happen [sic] to you.'" Cal replies, "'I like my life [...]. I'm going to have a good life'" (528). And indeed, Cal later works

---

39 Ovid mentions the story of Byblis who falls passionately in love with her twin brother Caunus, cf. *Met* IX.
40 Myrrha is said to have tricked her father Cinyras into sleeping with her; she is turned into a myrrh tree and later gives birth to Adonis, cf. *Met* X.
41 Famous King Oedipus unknowingly kills his father and marries his mother Jocasta, cf. Sophokles *Oedipus*.

as a diplomat for the U.S. government in Berlin and begins a promising romantic relationship with the Japanese-American Julie Kikuchi. *Middlesex* reintroduces the mythical incest discourse and combines it with modern genetics to provide a cause, an *aition*, for Callie's condition; yet in the context of myth, incest is neither a criminal nor an immoral act and Cal's intersexuality does not need to be read as a punishment for his parents' actions.[42]

Hermaphroditus in America: Intertextuality

While Ovid's *Metamorphoses* is clearly related to the tradition of aetiological stories of transformation, he "tended to treat his material with some freedom" (xxiii), opines E.J. Kenney in his 'Introduction' to Melville's translation. Rather than making things up, argues Kenney, Ovid's mastery lay in finding the material: "the art of discovering and combining the materials from which an argument could most effectively be constructed" (xiii). In classical rhetoric *inventio*, he claims, was less about inventing than about "combining, varying, and embellishing the available materials" (xxii). Similarly Graf points out that Ovid "is in full command of his mythological tradition" ("Myth" 119), but often chooses to focus on stories that have not been told in detail before. An example is the fight between Ajax and Ulysses over Achilles' armor (*Met* XIII.1-306) that takes place *after* the part of the Trojan War that Homer's *Iliad* covers (cf. "Myth" 119). Kenney calls this technique of variation "refinement" (xxiii) and adds "combination" as the "most characteristic and successful technique" (xxiii) to Ovid's repertoire. The story of "Salmacis and Hermaphroditus" is a case in point when Ovid combines accounts of the spring Salmacis and accounts of Hermaphroditus.[43] While only a few of Ovid's sources survived, scholars agree that, as a "learned poet" (Kenney xxi), Ovid made ample use of his literary predecessors and rhetoric traditions while he, nevertheless, changed and developed his sources and explored or mocked conventions.

---

42 For a critique on the incest topic from an activist perspective see www.isna.org.
43 Translator Melville also notes the semblance between Salmacis and Hermaphroditus and Narcissus and Echo in Ovid (cf. 398). See also Zajko 186 and 191; and Nugent 161.

The *Metamorphoses* consist of more than 250 myths that are roughly chronologically ordered from the creation of the world to the advent of Julius Caesar. They are held together by various framing devices such as the "dinner-table as a setting for story-telling" (Kenney xxii), but the stories within stories within stories sometimes leave readers uncertain of their bearings, remarks Kenney (cf. xxvii). And Alessandro Barchiesi attests the poem to be "mostly *about* narrative" ("Narratology" 181) and explains that repeated use of prolepses (e.g. prophecies) and analepses (e.g. recollecttions), extensive use of reported speech, various internal (intra- and hypodiegetic) narrators, constant shifts between hetero- and homodiegetic narration, and the blurring between authorial voice and mimesis of speech draw attention to "an overarching presence of textuality" (184).[44] The "multitude of narrative voices" (195) serves to make narrative conventions visible and show the *Metamorphoses* to be heavily involved in questions of "representation" (199), concludes Barchiesi. These questions show the *Metamorphoses* to be a meta-poetical, self-reflexive, and intertextually engaged text.

The story of Salmacis and Hermaphroditus is narrated by one of the three daughters of Minyas, Alcithoe, explains Allen Romano. In the *Metamorphoses* the daughters are young maidens and tell each other stories while they work inside and reject the worship of Dionysus/Bacchus.[45] Romano connects the divergence between the story set down in the inscription near the spring at Halicarnassus and the story told by the young

---

[44] Barchiesi analyzes a passage from the *Metamorphoses* and identifies five levels of narration: "Ovid narrates (to the reader) that a muse narrates (to Pallas) that Calliope narrates (to the referees) that Arethusa narrates (to Ceres) that [...] '''I heard an indistinct noise under the middle of the water; terrified I stood on the nearer bank of the river. 'Where are you rushing to, Arethusa?' said Alpheus from his waves, 'Where are you rushing to?' he said again with his raucous voice...'''" (188f, cf. *Metamorphoses* V 597-600)

[45] Nugent reads the stories that the daughters share as narratives of "erotic tragedy" (160) in which a "woman asserts her desire and is punished" ("Not One" 161). The Minyeides' metamorphosis into bats transforms their voices "into meaningless screeches" (161). See also Zajko 186ff for an elaboration on the Minyeides and their refusal to participate in the celebration of Bacchus/-Dionysus.

Alcithoe in Ovid, and he argues that Alcithoe's account was marked by her "ignorance" ("Invention" 559): "Alcithoe shows little knowledge of love or the effective use of love magic. As an overwhelming demonstration of this point, Ovid puts into the voice of Alcithoe a careful misreading of the myth found in the Halicarnassus inscription" (559). On the one hand, the innocent Alcithoe turns a story of marriage into a story of rape (including a marked role reversal with the nymph as aggressor), while, at the same time, her lack of experience leads to Hermaphroditus' overdose of love potion with lasting consequences. As a narrator Alcithoe is thereby rendered highly unreliable and in the following story she and her sisters are transformed into bats (cf. *Met* IV 389-ff). Romano calls the comic effect of this double transformation "Ovid's punchline" (559) and this instance seems to me to be another example of Ovid's playful approach to narratological devices.

Eugenides' *Middlesex* mirrors a number of the devices employed by Ovid. The author shows himself to be familiar with the literary tradition and refers to, alludes to and quotes numerous myths and stories that are associated with hermaphroditism and intersexuality. Already on the copyright page, Eugenides lists and explicitly acknowledges different historical, medical and intersex activists' works such as *The Smyrna Affair* by Marjorie Housepian Dobkin, *Venuses Penuses* by John Money and the ISNA newsletter *Hermaphrodites with Attitude*. Furthermore, the fictional family saga brims with historical dates and events such as the Great Fire of Smyrna in 1922 and the Detroit race riots in 1967. References throughout the course of the novel are made in the form of pastiche when Cal's narrative is interrupted by an insertion of Dr. Luce's medical report (cf. *Middlesex* 435ff) or en passant when Callie reads Homer's *Iliad* at school (cf. 322). Intertextual references include the historical cases of so-called hermaphrodites such as Gottlieb Göttlich and Herculine Barbin (cf. 19), medical history such as Lord Coke's "the sexe that prevaileth" and Klebs' taxonomy (cf. 410), international cultural history such as Indian hijras or the guevedoche of the Dominican Republic (cf. 495), activism such as ISNA (cf. 488)[46] or biblical Tiresis (cf. 338). These various explicit

---

46 See Hsu "Ethnicity" for a contextualization of the novel within the emergence of US intersex activism and ISNA's development from strategically essentialist

references to seemingly *all things intersex or hermaphrodite* show the author to have done extensive research on his topic and to be 'in full command of his mythological tradition' (and everything that has been discussed since then). Although the listing of names, historical facts and issues mentioned in *Middlesex* adds up to little more than name dropping, it helps to project an image of debates on intersex and hermaphroditism as far-reaching and long-ranging, contested and polyphonic.

In addition to explicit references to intersex and hermaphrodite history and myth, *Middlesex* frequently alludes to other forms of intersex representation. Anson Koch-Rein identifies 1990s intersex testimonies as a model for Calliope_Cal's experience:

> Calliope/Cal also deals with some more or less familiar features of an 'unthinkable intersexual's' narrative – including painful, humiliating and dehumanizing medical examinations [...], hate violence [...], self-discovery [...] and struggle for information [...], being reduced to a myth in a sexualized freak show [...], befriending an early intersex activist [...]. ("Norm" 247)

While I agree with Koch-Rein's argument, the narrative also contains aspects that are rather uncommon for intersex testimonies, such as Calliope_Cal's gender transition. The female-to-male transition begins with Calliope buying a men's suit and getting a haircut. While Calliope, calling herself Cal by now, hitchhikes her way across the continent from New York to San Francisco, she practices her masculine performance and explains at some point that *she* now identifies as the *he* she has been performing for a while: "And it is right then that it happens. At some moment on Route 80 something clicks in my head and suddenly I feel I am getting the hang of it. [...] I become male-identified" (*Middlesex* 450).[47] The metaphor of crossing a country or going on a journey while

---

identity politics to cooperation with the medical establishment and the recognition of DSD guidelines.

47 "Like a convert to a new religion, I overdid it at first. Somewhere near Gary, Indiana, I adopted a swagger. I rarely smiled. My expression throughout Illinois was the Clint Eastwood squint. It was all a bluff, but so it was on most men. [...] Its very falseness made it credible" (449). For other examples of Cal's doing masculinity see 441, 451.

transitioning from one gender to another is, of course, a stock element in transgender narratives and relates Calliope_Cal's transition to trans*-experiences.[48]

Moreover, I suggest, Cal's narrative comments ironically on the truth claims in both activist testimony and medico-scientific case studies. In a passage set in Dr. Luce's office[49] in New York, Cal remembers having to write what Luce calls a psychological narrative: "Half the time I wrote like bad George Eliot, the other half like bad Salinger. […] [O]n that Smith Corona I quickly discovered that telling the truth wasn't nearly as much fun as making things up. I also knew that I was writing for an audience – Dr. Luce – and that if I seemed normal enough, he might send me back home" (418). Similar to this fictionalized narrative, Callie also fashions her answers in interviews with Luce to match her image of "the all-American daughter" (418) and renders Luce's, i.e. Money's scholarly methods pointless and absurd. The testimonial truth claim is countered by Calliope_Cal's emphasis on his_her own unreliability: "Of course, a narrator in my position (prefetal at the time) can't be entirely sure about any of this" (9). Narrator Cal also reflects on the process of writing and on literary predecessors: "Her [Herculine Barbin's M.K.] memoirs […] make unsatisfactory reading, and it was after finishing them years ago that I first got the idea to write my own" (19). While Cal denounces Barbin's memoir here, he mischievously confesses to having entertained "the dream of

---

48 Jack Halberstam notes: "Metaphors of travel and border crossings are inevitable within a discourse of transsexuality" (*Female Masculinity* 165. See also Kilian *GeschlechtSverkehrt*, esp. 132-9).

49 The character of Dr. Luce mirrors not only Money's opinions on sexual development, but seems modeled in detail on John Colapinto's description of Money in his 1997 article "The True Story of John/Joan," e.g. Luce is described as "a famous sexologist, a guest on Dick Cavett, a regular contributor to Playboy […]. He was a brilliant, charming, work-obsessed man" (*Middlesex* 408); his office is full of erotica, "The restful doctor's office was churning with activity. The paperweight on his desk, for instance, was not a simple inert rock but a tiny Priapus carved from stone" (407); he is "in favor of orgies wherever they happen" (409) and uses "the diagnostic tool of pornography" (418). While Callie's and David Reimer's story develop very differently, their experiences with Luce/Money at the clinic show some similarities.

writing a [...] Great Book with another long Greek name on the cover," inviting the double entendre of the author's long Greek name, Eugenides, and the narrator's, Stephanides. In a cynical-ironic remark Cal claims to have "given up any hope of lasting fame or literary perfection. I don't care if I write a great book anymore, but just one which, whatever its flaws, will leave a record of my impossible life" (302).[50] Cal, here, reflects on the narrative construction of memoir and aligns it to fiction. Consequently, argues Francisco Collado-Rodríguez, Cal's "playful unreliability" ("Self" 76), the "metafictional asides" (76), the use of intertextuality, and multiple genres all link the novel to postmodern literature and refuse insights into a singular and lasting truth.

Intertextual references also take the form of parody as in the episode about the Minotaur: one night Callie's maternal and paternal grandparents all four, Desdemona and Lefty Stephanides, and Sourmelina and Jimmy Zizmo, are aroused by watching a play of the Minotaur. The offspring of an overly beautiful white bull and a wife who has tricked the bull into mating with her by climbing into a wooden cow, the Minotaur had an insatiable appetite for men and had to be kept in a labyrinth on Crete. The grandparents' babies, Tessie and Milton, Callie's parents, were both conceived on this same night and therefore aligned to twins. This is one of many examples for the use of playful intertextuality in *Middlesex*: Cal identifies the "play about a hybrid monster" as "the direct cause" (109) for the respective copulations and also points out that both babies receive "One mutation apiece" (125). Yet the Minotaur episode does not stop here: Cal vividly remembers his father's attempts "to instill in me a sense of my heritage" and takes young Callie "to dubbed Italian versions of the ancient Greek myths. And so, every week, we saw Hercules slaying the Nemean lion [...]. But our favorite was the Minotaur"(123). Between the child and her second generation Greek-American father, who was conceived after his parents watched the Minotaur play and who himself is barely literate in Greek, classic mythology is reduced to cheap movies consumed with

---

50 While Cal had dismissed Barbin's memoirs earlier, this passage shows their plights to be similar: with the memoirs, Barbin wants to leave a record of things that go "beyond the limits of what is possible" (Barbin *Memoirs* 15). Moreover, Barbin also broods over the status of her writings between a "novel" and a "personal story" (35).

"butterscotch candy" and shivers of "fear and delight" (123). Of course, the lesson that Callie learns from these movies is not an understanding of "betrayal" or "a thing of shame hidden away" (123) but the realization that the "monster always approaches from the direction you least expect" (124). The play and the movies turn the Greek myth into an erotically charged action story. Similar comic references to myth include "Hercules Hot Dogs^{TM}," Milton's fast-food chain with its "distinctive 'Pillars of Hercules' out front" (201) that Callie's brother Chapter Eleven ruins later, and Sophie Sassoon's beauty parlor "Golden Fleece" that Callie visits regularly for a facial wax , but not to cut her "unbelievably abundant, thirteen-year-old hair" that "could turn the Medusa to stone, hair snakier than all the snake pits in a minotaur movie" (305). These references import the classic myths into 20th century America and Greek-American everyday life. Like Desdemona and Lefty, the myths have been transformed not only by age or time, but also by traveling from the old continent to the U.S.

Middlesex is full of these and other references to texts and discourses that deal with intersexuality or hermaphroditism. One text that is repeatedly referred to is Ovid's account of "Salmacis and Hermaphroditus." The story's first reenactment is by seven year old Calliope and her neighbor-friend Clementine Stark. Calliope considers Clementine "worldly" (263) because she has already been to Krakow, and "highly educated" (264) because she is already eight years old. On their first afternoon Clementine begins to give Callie kissing lessons and while Clementine "swiveled her head back and forth the way actresses did in the movies" (265) she instructs Callie to be "the man" (265). A week later the two girls play in the bathhouse and soon "silk robes fall to the floor" (265) and they dive into the hot water. Narrator Cal looks back at his seven-year old self and remembers:

I see Clementine breasting through the water to me. Her face appears out of the steam. I think we're going to kiss again, but instead she wraps her legs around my waist. She's laughing hysterically […] I fall between her legs, I fall on top of her, we sink … and then we're twirling, spinning in the water, me on top, then her, then me, and giggling, and making bird cries. Steam envelopes us, cloaks us; and we keep spinning, so that at some point I'm not sure which hands are mine, which legs. We aren't kissing […] but we're gripping each other, trying not to let the other's slippery body go, and our knees bump, our tummies slap, our hips slide back and forth. (266)

The image of the innocent Calliope being embraced by the experienced Clementine and the two spinning, indistinguishable bodies clearly recalls Salmacis' embrace of Hermaphroditus. The analogy between Clementine-Salmacis and Calliope-Hermaphroditus is continued when Cal sums up the following events: Clementine's father dies of a heart attack; her mother sells the house within three weeks, moves away and Cal remarks, "I never saw Clementine again ..." (267). As in Ovid, Clementine-Salmacis disappears and it is Calliope-Hermaphroditus who is left behind. Yet while Ovid's story is set in a remote location with no visitors and, I would like to add, no witnesses that could report the events to narrator Alcithoe, Clementine-Salmacis and Calliope-Hermaphroditus are observed by Callie's grandfather Lefty, who sits as a "dark shape in the corner" (265) of the bathhouse. But Lefty has already suffered a couple of strokes, and is speechless and unconscious during the pool episode. His witness function is thereby rendered obsolete; however, Calliope-Hermaphroditus prays for forgiveness "because it was clear to me [Calliope M.K.] that I was responsible. It was what I did ..." (267). She promises "never to do anything like that again" (267) and strays a little from the part that is ascribed to the innocent Hermaphroditus in Ovid by taking some of the blame. In Eugenides' revision of Ovid's myth, the fusion with Clementine-Salmacis is a pleasant experience for Calliope-Hermaphroditus that she knows to be somehow "improper" (265), but that she will not be able to "understand until years later" (266). The erotic attraction between the two is, I contend, not the only thing to "understand" here. It is the episode with Clementine Stark that aligns the seven-year old girl for the first time with mythical Hermaphroditus.

The second time that Cal embodies Hermaphroditus takes place in a less innocent environment: 15 year-old Cal, recently transitioned, is the attraction of the Sixty-Niners, Bob Presto's sex club in San Francisco. Together with his co-workers Zora, an AIS woman performing as "Melanie the MerMaid" (481), and Carmen, a pre-op transwoman announced as "Ellie and her Electrifying Eeeel," Cal is part of a pool show called "Octopussy's Garden." His stage name is "**The God HER**maph**ROD**itus" (481) and his job is to exhibit himself in the pool while customers pay to watch through little peepholes. In a chapter titled "Hermaphroditus," three of Cal's performances are retold. The first introduces Mr. Go, a regular customer of the sex club who is visiting Octopussy's Garden for the first time. A seemingly extra- and heterodiegetic narrator describes how the elderly man is about to leave when the myth's opening is announced via speakers, "'Once upon a time in ancient Greece, there was an enchanted pool. This pool was sacred to Salmacis the water nymph. And one day Hermaphroditus, a beautiful boy, went swimming there.'" (482). On his cue, "Ladies and Gentleman, behold the god Hermaphroditus," Cal lowers himself into the water and Mr. Go "presses his face right up to the porthole. He has never seen anything like what he is seeing now. [...] He isn't sure he likes what he sees. But the sight makes him feel strange, light-headed, weightless, and somehow younger" (482). The passage is externally focalized and provides an image of the voyeur watching Cal, not an image of the performer. The exploiting male gaze of Mr. Go is thereby denied.[51]

The second instance is narrated by the intra- and homodiegetic adult Cal, who reports his experience of the performance: "'Once upon a time in ancient Greece, there was an enchanted pool. This pool was sacred to Salmacis the water nymph. And one day Hermaphroditus, a beautiful boy, went swimming there.' Here I lowered my feet into the pool. I lolled them back and forth as the narration continued" (490). The narration that continues is similar to the Ovidian account of the myth that culminates in the forced fusion of Salmacis and Hermaphroditus: "Their bodies fused, male into female, female into male" (491) and when Cal plunges into the pool and the peepholes slide shut "No one ever left a booth [...] Underwater I could hear the tokens clinking into the change boxes" (491).

---

51 Throughout the novel, Cal's genitalia are described in vague metaphors such as the "crocus" (cf. 330). One exemption is Luce's report, which uses medical terminology (cf. 435ff). The distinction between the medical gaze (and genre) that "demands visual exploration" of the hermaphrodite body and the literary presentations of the hermaphrodite that "resist picturing the hybrid parts that make up the hermaphroditic body [...]. And that present the hermaphrodite as a veiled figure of corporeal ambiguity, capable of being all things to all readers" ("Look" 68) was already noted by Jenny Mann in her study on representations of hermaphrodites in Early Modern England. See Carroll "Retrospective" for an analysis of the floral metaphors and genitalia in *Middlesex*.

The sound of the tokens reminds Cal of the clinking pipes while he was bathing in a bathtub on Middlesex and he pretends to be at home (cf. 491). Three other things make the sex work endurable for Cal: For one, he does not have to show his face and always keeps his eyes closed when underwater. Otherwise, he fears, the voyeur's "gaze would have sucked my soul out of me" (484). Two, he feels "prepared" for this work after the experiences at Dr. Luce's clinic with repeated examinations by various doctors that had benumbed his "sense of shame" (483). And three, he and his colleagues are always stoned (and drunk) for work. In this episode, the gaze is directed by the adult narrator Cal, who looks back at his younger self and at the "faces [that] filled the portholes, gazing with amazement, curiosity, disgust, desire" (491). The teenage performer Cal is reported as being the object of the voyeur's gaze and his necessary coping strategies (drugs, mental dissociation, and physical detachment) show the abusive character of the situation, but, again, the gaze of the voyeur on Cal's body is denied.[52]

The third performance that is described shows the teenage Cal turning the tables:

When it was time for my act, I plunged into the pool. I was high, drunk, and so that night did something I didn't normally do. I opened my eyes underwater. I saw the faces looking back at me and I saw that they were not appalled. I had fun in the tank that night. It was all beneficial in some way. It was therapeutic. Inside Hermaphroditus old tensions were roiling, trying to work themselves out. Traumas of the locker room were being released. Shame over having a body unlike other bodies was passing away. The monster feeling was fading. (494)

While the teenage Cal is still focalized by his adult self, he manages to meet the gaze of the voyeurs and to reclaim his body by identifying with "Hermaphroditus." Dissociation and detachment due to traumas he has acquired during puberty, at Luce's clinic and during the performances begin to fade. Cal also remembers that "Hermaphroditus was beginning to forget about the Obscure Object" (494), his teenage love affair. The identity

---

52 The exhibition of Cal's naked body in a peep show recalls the 18th century practice of exhibiting 'hermaphrodites' in fairgrounds (see Senelick "Enlightened").

between Cal and Hermaphroditus is clear and Cal begins to own his body once again. In the following weeks, Cal educates himself by reading everything about hermaphrodites that Zora gives him and he familiarizes himself with all varieties "we hermaphrodites came in" (494).

Zora, as Cal has explained earlier, "was using the term 'intersexual'" (488) already in 1974, so almost twenty years before the founding of the Intersex Society of North America in 1993 (cf. 488), and identifies as "a hermaphrodite." She is the first intersex person he meets and identifies with: "She was the first one I met. The first person like me" (488). Cal lives with her during his time at the sex club and describes his life "during those months [...] as divided as my body" (491); nightly stoned performances of Hermaphroditus in the pool alternate with sober days and learning. It is only when the club is raided a few weeks later and Cal ends up at the police station that he decides to return home. The club is closed. Cal leaves mythical Hermaphroditus behind, but carries with him the intersex education by Zora and the experiences that he has gathered during his flight from New York to San Francisco. Back home at Middlesex his father has died and, following a Greek tradition, Cal blocks the door to prevent Milton's spirit from entering the house. "Middlesex," remembers Cal almost sentimentally, was "a place designed for a new type of human being, who would inhabit a new world" (529). His "Byzantine face," he notes, shows traces of his "grandfather" and of the "American girl" he had once been (529). At Middlesex then, Cal finally reunites with his male and female features, feels "happy to be home" (529), and seems to embody a certain androgyny. According to Ovid, the story ends with the fusion, the mingling of a male and a female body, and "Hermaphroditus [who] cried, / His voice unmanned" (*Met* IV. 80f.) seems to have acquired a form of androgyny – at least his voice and his "weak and soft" limbs (*Met* IV. 79) imply effeminacy in the male-addressed youth, the "son" (*Met* IV. 87) of Hermes and Aphrodite. The image of the teenage Cal as androgynous complies with Ovid's Hermaphroditus. Both are 15 years old, have travelled alone and have gone through a metamorphosis.[53] Yet Ajootian

---

53 Eugenides explained that Cal's transformation from girl to man functions as a metaphor for adolescence: "What Calliope goes through is what we all go through, in the maelstrom of puberty. Her experience of the process, physically and psychologically, is merely more dramatic than our own. Callie's life differs

maintains that antique images on vases, paintings and sculptures of Hermaphroditus do not show the half-god as an androgynous figure, but with "female breasts and male genitals" and names as the main criterion for identifying images of Hermaphroditus "the unambiguous rendering of dual sexual features" ("Hermaphroditos" 283). Here again the teenage Cal is shown to stand in the tradition of the Ovidian myth that depicts the hermaphrodite in terms of loss or deficit.

The adult Cal, on the other hand, points out that he is "not androgynous in the least" (*Middlesex* 41) and describes himself as "a forty-one-year-old man with longish, wavy hair, a thin mustache, and a goatee. A kind of modern Musketeer" (42) and the narrator tries to sum up the effects of his transformation:

> My change from girl to boy was far less dramatic than the distance anybody travels from infancy to adulthood. In most ways I remained the person I'd always been. Even now, as I live as a man, I remain in essential ways Tessie's daughter. I'm still the one who remembers to call her every Sunday. I'm the one she recounts her growing list of ailments to. Like any good daughter, I'll be the one to nurse her in old age. We still discuss what's wrong with men; we still, on visits back home, have our hair done together. (520f)

Cal stresses here the long-term effects of socialization; nurture, and recounts a number of characteristics and stereotypical behavior that are associated with femininity or womanhood. Luce might have argued that nurture could not be subdued by nature, or, in other words, gender identity

---

from ours in degree but not in kind" ("Q&A with Jeffrey Eugenides"). In large parts, *Middlesex* is another coming-of-age story, a story about a teenager's quest for their gendered identity, complete with reflections on sexual desire. Rachel Carroll "Retrospective" has analyzed this strand of the narrative and points to the reproduction of heterosexual norms in the novel. Flirting with lesbianism while female-identified, the transition leads Cal to a strongly reinforced heterosexual identity. Similarly, N. O. Body uses the transition to re-write his sexual experiences with women when he was still female-identified as heterosexual (cf. my chapter "N.O. Body and the Making of a True Man" and Zachary Sifuentes' "Strange", who criticizes the conflation of sexuality and anatomy in *Middlesex*).

was constructed via socialization and not (only) genetically determined. Nevertheless, I argue, Calliope has essentially vanished from Cal's life and his body. Similar to Ovid's account, where Salmacis practically disappears and a weakened Hermaphroditus shows only mild traces of the fusion,[54] the adult Cal has left his girl self behind and asks, "Did Calliope have to die in order to make room for Cal?" (520). He is the undisputed, albeit unreliable narrator of the story and he is also the dominant focalizer of the account. The adult Cal looks back at his former life as Calliope and at his androgynous teenage self. Calliope's and teenage Cal's perspectives are missing completely from the account. But there is one instance when this patronizing stance is broken: sometimes, explains Cal, "Callie rises up inside me, wearing my skin like a loose robe. She sticks her little hands into the baggy sleeves of my arms. She inserts her chimp's feet through the trousers of my legs" (41f). In these situations Calliope takes over Cal's body. She "surfaces" inside him and the male, non-androgynous Cal is seen "doing a hair flip, or checking her nails" (41). Cal describes these situations as "like being possessed" (41). Calliope's spirit that makes use of Cal's body from time to time is likened to the water nymph, the spirit of the pool, Salmacis, who "rises up," "surfaces," and takes over, or "possesses." The relation between the adult Cal and his girl self may then be said to mirror the post-fusion relation between Salmacis and Hermaphroditus.

THE METAMORPHOSIS OF *MIDDLESEX*

Zajko has suggested that Ovid's account of Salmacis and Hermaphroditus "holds significance both for ancient models of sexuality and for those emergent in the twentieth and twentieth-first centuries" ("Listening" 181). My analysis has shown that the *Metamorphoses* holds a special significance for the supposedly quintessential intersex novel of the early 21st century. The scholarly debate around form and narrative structure shows striking resemblances between *Middlesex* and Ovid's *Metamorphoses*. Cal, I have

---

54 Salmacis' significance after the fusion is still the subject of scholarly debate (see Zajko 193). Groneberg argues that Salmacis disappears only seemingly as a person with a name and material body, but reappears in Hermaphroditus' voice (cf. "Mythen" 98f).

argued, may be considered a postmodern Hermaphroditus, sometimes possessed by his girl self Calliope as Salmacis. Ovid has transformed and adapted his sources to his own needs and exemplified the telling of myth not as a static but as a highly dynamic process. Similarly, Eugenides used his sources freely and has transformed the classic hermaphrodite myth into a 21st century intersex novel. Reading *Middlesex* in the context of myth suggests that the novel is better understood as a postmodern adaptation and re-narration of Ovid's account than as a story about 'real' intersex people or 'first-hand' intersex experiences. With its international success and discursive presence, *Middlesex* forms a meaningful contribution to the intersex discourse. Its form and mode of writing differs strongly from earlier contributions by activists and doctors. Moreover, *Middlesex* shows a different relationship to truth claims: while truth claims were characteristic of both activists' testimonial writings and doctors' scholarly writings, *Middlesex* and other fictional intersex representations do not insist on the truth of their accounts. Quite in contrast, *Middlesex* borrows material from activist and medical discourses and mixes it deliberately with myth, popular culture, and unreliable narration. In the 21st century, intersex discourse has again multiplied and the modes of speaking and writing about intersex seem to have differentiated even further. However, I argue, the novel's international success in terms of sales figures and prizes, and its omnipresence in the media and scholarly debate, automatically push other contributions to the margins of the discourse. Thus, at the beginning of the 21st century, intersex discourse is dominated by a seemingly postmodern story about a hermaphrodite that was written by a white heterosexual man who is neither intersex nor a medical doctor. While *Middlesex* does not claim to tell the truth about intersex, its dominant discursive position silences other stories and reduces the voice in the discourse to the voice of the fictional Cal.

Intersex in Pieces
Thea Hillman Refuses to Know Better

INTERSEX AT THE END OF GRAND NARRATIVES

Jean François Lyotard already proposed the end of the grand narratives, metanarratives, in 1979, and announced *The Postmodern Condition*. From a postmodern perspective, grand narratives – ones that aim to explain the world and its workings in large pictures – are to be regarded with incredulity and substituted by local, small narratives. John Money succeeded in establishing a medico-scientific intersex metanarrative in the second half of the 20th century, yet the narrative has been challenged by intersex activists, especially Cheryl Chase and ISNA, since the 1990s. While Money claimed that intersex was a medical condition that needed early treatment, Chase countered the pathologizing notion and turned the condition into an identity. Characteristic of both stories is their claim to be telling the only legitimate or 'true' intersex story. Jeffrey Eugenides' *Middlesex*, with its unreliable and part-time omniscient narrative voice, has repeatedly been called a postmodern tale and Eugenides' reworking of the classical myth of Salmacis and Hermaphroditus fulfills a number of characteristics of what is called postmodern literature. Yet, at the beginning of the 21st century, *Middlesex* tells a story about a single intersex character and her_his coming of age. The "exhilarating reinvention of the American epic" (blurb *Middlesex*) is another grand story, another intersex metanarrative, and anything but a small, local narrative. In 2005, however, the grand intersex stories were unsettled by the results of the Chicago Consensus Conference and its terminological move from *intersex* to *DSD*. By then, ISNA had developed their 'politics of confrontation' into a 'politics of cooperation' and signed the DSD consensus. The shift in terminology led to great turmoil among intersex activists and a number of new groups with varying politics formed. Finally, in 2008, ISNA, the world's largest intersex organization, officially shut its doors and transferred all assets to a new organization called Accord Alliance. Accord Alliance was founded in cooperation with medical doctors and focuses on the improvement of the medical standard of care for people with DSDs. Money's medical story and ISNA's identity narrative dispersed, mingled, and merged in this move. Yet smaller, local organizations stepped in and their websites still brim with stories about individual intersex experiences. The pluralization of organizations has led to a pluralization and sometimes localization of voices and stories. Moreover, fictional stories, above all Eugenides' *Middlesex*, are discussed and criticized by activists for their reductive representation of a complex experience. Thea Hillman's collection *Intersex (for Lack of a Better Word)*, which was published in the year ISNA closed down, serves as a document of and in this debate.

Hillman, former ISNA board member and spoken word artist, published her debut, *Depending on the Light*, in 2001. The collection of short stories set in San Francisco is described as showing the gaze of the female flaneur, the "lone female observing in the city" (Clement 289). *Depending* is marketed as 'fiction,' but the short prose piece "Contradiction" (50f) already introduces a first-person account of an intersex experience. Hillman's second publication, *Better Word*, contains 47 chapters of short prose and poetry, is marketed with the label "LGBT / memoir" and was awarded the Lambda Literary Award, category transgender, in 2009.[1] The book's main title boldly announces its topic, *Intersex*. In the subtitle, however, this confidence seems twisted around and in brackets it reads: *(for Lack of a Better Word)*. This spin puts the main title in a different perspective and indicates doubt about whether the term is appropriate. This technique of naming or telling something and taking it back or questioning it afterwards is characteristic of the text. Only rarely does Hillman provide definitive answers or causal explanations. Instead, the focus is on questions and effects. Moreover, the arrangement of the 47 chapters or 'pieces' as Hillman calls them, opposes the form and structure of classic autobiogra-

---

1 Eugenides' *Middlesex* was a nominee in the same category in 2003, but did not win.

phical writing with a continuous line of events that are presented in a cause-effect relation. *Better Word* rejects continuity and causality by employing a non-chronological order and by continuously shifting focalization between Thea, the child, and Thea, the adult. The pieces are not linked, but separated by gaps or silences between them; deliberate blanks, overlaps and repetitions emphasize the episodic or anecdotal structure of the text and a continuous, coherent and retrospectively fashioned life narrative is rejected. Nevertheless, the identity of the narrative voice throughout the text produces coherency and unity. Thus, the body of the text is at the same time interrupted *and* coherent.

Having been diagnosed with Congenital Adrenal Hyperplasia (CAH) when four years old, Hillman has life-long experiences with medical treatment and she witnessed and participated in intersex debates for years. As a writer, activist, and intersex person Hillman explores her topic from various angles. Structure and content, in my view, form a body of text that is both interrupted and coherent and *Better Word* ultimately provides a notion of intersex as a physical *and* performatively produced experience. Moreover, *Better Word* dismisses intersex metanarratives, stories – be they medical, activist, or fictional – that provide more answers than questions, that claim to tell the unequivocal 'truth,' or that generalize a subjective experience. *Better Word*, I argue, opposes another grand intersex narrative and develops an intimate representation of an experience that bridges the gap between body and word, between constructivism and essentialism. In the following, I use queer theorist Eve Sedgwick's analysis of the protest function, periperformatives, her deconstruction of the binary opposition between essentialism and constructivism, and her theory of shame-induced identities to analyze Hillman's struggle with fictional ("To Be or Not to Be Intersex"), medical ("Does Doctor Know Best?"), and activist ("Words Don't Come Easy") notions of intersex and to analyze her own notion of intersex ("Performing Intersex Bodies").

TO BE OR NOT TO BE INTERSEX:
THE MATTER OF REPRESENTATION

Better Word is marketed as a memoir. The label evokes Lejeune's autobiographical pact and establishes the identity of the empirical person

Thea Hillman with the name on the cover and the narrator in the text. It evokes a claim to authenticity and opposes the label 'fiction.' In the acknowledgments section of the book, Hillman thanks her family, "who have decided that it's better not to be mentioned in one of Thea's books and yet still let me" and "everyone who created these stories by living them with me" (*Better Word* 157). Moreover, Hillman reveals insider knowledge about Cheryl Chase without lifting her pseudonym by thanking both Cheryl Chase and Bo Laurent, the former being the pen name of the latter. Thanks are also given to "the ISNA board members, the activists, my intersex friends, my friends with DSDs, and those who trusted me enough to come to me with questions about the scars they know very little or nothing about" (157). Hillman's language use here marks her as being familiar with intersex discourses and the debate about the term *DSD* replacing *intersex* in medical taxonomy. Furthermore, the book is dedicated to a plural "You" and elaborates "the ones who make room in the world for each of us" and thereby addresses an activist readership ("the ones who make room") while including the author ("us"). Thus, Hillman aligns herself with activist discourse in the paratext and marks her voice as rooted in personal experience and as the voice of an 'authentic' intersex person. This claim to authenticity is continued throughout the text and Hillman struggles with non-authentic or non-activist representations. In two pieces, "Telling" (*Better Word* 24ff) and "Opinion" (27ff), Hillman discusses Eugenides' *Middlesex* and other non-autobiographical representations. She is critical of the fact that intersex people were still being used "to satisfy the interests of others: as scientific specimens, teaching models for medical students (naked, of course), literary metaphors, gags for popular sitcoms, and lastly where we at least might get a cut of the profits as circus freaks and peep show attractions" (28). Hillman's critique of the exploitation and representation of intersex people by non-intersex people, I contend, is not only a demand for 'authentic' representation, but it *is* the representation she asks for.

Queer theorist Eve Sedgwick explains that the need "to *be* representation" (*Touching* 31, emphasis added) is an effect of the denial of representation and more specifically, a denial of the "exemplary function" in representation. Intersex bodies and voices may represent *intersex people*, but they are denied the exemplary function, i.e. they are denied the ability to stand just for *people*. Non-intersex bodies and voices, on the other hand, are endowed with that function. Public protest and criticism, explains Sedgwick, is generally aimed at "shaming" the accused with the goal of provoking change. Fictional accounts like *Middlesex* may criticize the medical standards of care, present an appealing intersex character and attempt to "shame them [the institutions or individuals criticized] into compliance or negotiation" (31).[2] To shame the accused and to protest the denial of representation, however, is not to *be* representation. With her spoken word performances and her writing, Hillman goes "public as a written-upon body" (*Touching* 30) in words and deeds. She outs herself as intersex to emphasize the lack of representation (and to criticize misrepresentation), in other words "to shame." Yet she also aims to fill the gap of representation and "to smuggle" some form of that denied representation on stage or in print.

Fiction lacks the aspect of smuggling and thereby reproduces a patronizing structure that ultimately does what it claims to criticize: *Middlesex* shames when intersex protagonist Calliope_Cal is shown rebelling against Dr. Luce's treatment plans and fighting for the right to physical integrity. However, it is Jeffrey Eugenides, a heterosexual non-intersex man, who presents his views and his assumptions about the experiences of intersex people in interviews and through the experiences of his protagonist Callie. In an interview, Hillman points to this dilemma and explains the gap between fiction and activist writing:

I see *Middlesex* as totally outside the worlds of intersex and trans writing. *Middlesex* was written by a non-intersex man who never interviewed an intersex person before writing his book. He's an author who used intersex as a metaphor, but he is in no way an advocate for intersex people, nor has his work sparked any activism (except activism targeted at him). (jewcy.com n.p.)

---

2   Hillman acknowledges Eugenides' sympathetic representation of Callie in an interview: "*Middlesex* presented a very likeable intersex character that people could identify with. One of the most powerful things Eugenides did was illustrate the dilemma many intersex people face: while they might accept and enjoy their body as it is, people around them want to 'fix' their body so it matches some mythical ideal" (jewcy.com n.p.).

Better Word, however, does not only criticize and 'shame' *Middlesex*, but it also represents and 'smuggles' intersex representation into that critique. In "Telling," Hillman recounts an episode when her mother asked her to join a book club discussion of Eugenides' *Middlesex*:

> I couldn't explain why I didn't want to talk to her group. I couldn't begin to explain what it had been like when Middlesex [sic] was first published. How […], when the book came out, I spent every minute for a week trying to write the perfect op-ed about the intersex response to *Middlesex*; and how […] the piece didn't get published. I couldn't tell her that during that same week I heard Jeffrey Eugenides read from *Middlesex* at Books Inc.; couldn't tell her that he used the word 'hermaphrodite' instead of 'intersex', as if it were appropriate; […] I couldn't tell her that […] I started crying. Crying because Eugenides who'd never actually talked to an intersex person before he published that book, had access to so many millions of people, and that I couldn't get an op-ed published. [I was c]rying because I sat there while he read from his book and while he answered questions as if he were an expert, as if he knew about intersex, and I sat there, an expert, silent and fuming and hot with shame as he called me and people I love hermaphrodites. (*Better Word* 25)

Hillman feels offended by Eugenides' use of terminology and she is denied access to the public discourse about the novel. Her writing, the text itself, names and shames, it protests this denial of representation. Striking is the way Hillman phrases the critique: she repeatedly uses negative performatives, what Sedgwick calls periperformatives, such as "couldn't explain," "couldn't tell," or "didn't get published." Periperformatives "*allude* to explicit performative utterances […] they explicitly refer to explicit performatives," explains Sedgwick (*Touching* 68).[3] Negative performatives, a sub-category of periperformatives, draw attention to the performative aspect of each utterance and they "tend to have a high threshold of initiative" (70). Hillman's emphasis on *not* being able to tell, on *not* being able to explain, and on *not* being able to publish does not signal a lack of

---

3 Sedgwick introduces periperformatives in her essay "Around the Performative" and challenges Austin's distinction between constatives and explicit performatives. Periperfomatives and negative performatives represent aspects of language that perform, but may not be called explicit performatives (cf. *Touching* 67-91).

agency, but rather the opposite: the act of disinterpellation that is central to negative performatives is "less prone to becoming conventional than the positive performatives" (70), explains Sedgwick. Paraphrasing Dante she concludes: "refusal [...] [is] something 'great'" (70). Thus, Hillman's phrasing, the negative performatives, draws attention to the differences in talking about intersex for people with or without intersex experiences. Denial, rejection, and negation of representation are characteristics of an intersex experience that Eugenides as an author and *Middlesex* as a text do not share. Rather, author and text are granted an amount of public attention and exemplary representation that stands in stark contrast to intersex authors and writings. Moreover, narrator Cal tells his story from the secure position of an economically successful middle-aged white man – not as someone who struggles for representation. On the one hand, then, Hillman's critique of Eugenides and *Middlesex* points to these shortcomings of *Middlesex*'s intersex representation. On the other, the critique carries with it, it contains and smuggles some representation of the intersex experience that remains unrepresented in fictional accounts. Hidden among the periperformatives, *Better Word* represents what *Middlesex* lacks – the experience of denial of (exemplary) representation. Thereby, *Better Word* shames and smuggles; it criticizes a lack of representation and it is representation.

Moreover, *Better Word* not only shames and smuggles some form of Hillman's individual intersex representation and is thereby self-referential, but it also presents itself as an exemplary representation of memoir. The pieces recount various incidents from early childhood to adulthood and explores everyday life: from family issues (taking care of grandmother, relationship to parents) to finding a job; from being Jewish in America to falling in love and breaking up; from sexual abuse to class issues, the 'war on terror,' and art. In effect, some of the pieces do not seem to be about intersex at all. Integrated in the collection *Better Word*, however, the single pieces form a collage that shows Hillman to be a fully grown up adult, a person with various experiences and interests. Her life is as complex as anyone else's and, by showing that "intersex people are whole human beings (*Better Word* 147), she presents the memoir as exemplary – not just as a model for an intersex experience, but as a model for a human experience.

DOES DOCTOR KNOW BEST?
PATERNALISM REVISITED

Better Word does not only engage with fictional accounts of an intersex experience but also assesses the medical care that Hillman received. In the third piece of the collection, "Special," Hillman remembers how she was diagnosed with what her doctors referred to as "Congenital Adrenal Hyperplasia" (CAH) when she was four years old. Through a switch in focalization and again through the use of negative performatives, in my view, Hillman challenges the silencing in intersex treatment and reveals the pathologizing character of medical intersex discourses. When Thea's mother discovers pubic hair on her four year old daughter, she takes her to a pediatrician and to numerous endocrinologists. Various blood and other tests are run and show that Thea's "bone age is advanced" and that she has "high levels of androgens – hormones that are speeding up [her] growth and development process" (17). Doctors, it seems in the text, highlight the overall developmental functions of androgens instead of focusing on the reductive description of androgens as "male" sex hormones. Nevertheless, her mother has studied medical books from the library and is highly aware of the virilizing effects of androgens: "The pictures that scare her the most are the pictures of the girls with excess virilizing hormones, the girls that I might grow up to be like, the girls who are dwarfs, who have full beards" (17). Doctors consider Thea's case of CAH "very slight" (17) and they are optimistic that they will be able to "get [the child] back on track. With close supervision and monitoring of [her] hormone levels through regular blood tests, they can try to stave off puberty. And if it is successful, [Thea] will reach a short-to-normal height, will begin [her] puberty at a normal age, and won't have excess facial and body hair" (18). The doctors' explanation makes clear that their treatment is less about maintaining health than about achieving *normalcy*. Yet, *normalcy* is not made explicit or explained in the medical context. But characteristics of *normal* can be deduced from their claims: *normal* girls do not have excess facial and body hair; *normal* girls experience puberty at a certain age; and *normal* girls reach a certain body height. These norms openly discriminate against people with disabilities or with non-standard bodies. Furthermore, the language use veils another norm that can be challenged by effects of CAH: the norm of being unambiguously sexed. In the older medical books that Thea's mother studies, the discourse about the sex of the 'patient' is reflected more openly: "Each book is filled with pictures of naked children [...] with strange-looking genitals, their bodies vulnerable and small [...]. And then there are the words: disorder, masculinized, hermaphrodism, cliteromegaly, abnormal" (17). Here, the virilizing effect of CAH in individuals assigned female is stressed and strongly pathologized. But the young Thea's doctors do not use the same pathologizing terminology any more. In fact, the term *intersex* is not used in this piece at all. While the older medical books that Thea's mother consults focus on genital formation and pictures of "strange-looking genitals," Thea's doctors do not discuss the possibility of so-called enlarged clitorises due to CAH. Under the cover of politically correct, seemingly non-pathologizing language use, CAH is re-classified in the medical discourse from a genital formation that challenges the sexual binary to a hormonal imbalance. The term for the condition, *Congenital Adrenal Hyperplasia*, does not hint at possible effects of the imbalance, rather it locates the reason for the condition: an over-production of the adrenal glands. For laypersons and even for doctors without training in endocrinology, the connection to intersex is almost impossible to make. However, this shift in terminology and classification does not mirror a shift in the evaluation of CAH or the standards of care. The underlying, but unmentioned norm that 'requires' medical treatment is still the 'normal' sexual binary and the link between CAH and intersexuality is veiled. This practice of not naming and not telling stands in contrast to the standard of informed consent implemented in the 1970s, continues the standards of care developed by John Money in the 1950s, and discursively marginalizes intersexuality.

In "Special," however, Hillman does not leave it at that and challenges both the discursive negation of intersex and the pathologizing character of the discourse on CAH. To undermine the medical discourse where CAH is a 'condition,' an 'illness' that needs treatment, the adult narrator Hillman reevaluates the results of her diagnosis from the perspective of four-year-old Thea:

My mother tells me about the diagnosis. She tells me I have an imbalance. And that I have to wear a medic alert bracelet. I love jewelry and find this news very exciting. She tells me I have to have a lot of blood tests and that I'll have to take medication, maybe for the rest of my life. I think this makes me very grown up, because adults take pills [...]. She tells me about periods, and that I might get mine early. I can't wait. She tells me that I won't have more pubic hair than anyone else, just that I got mine earlier. I love the idea that I have something other kids don't. I decide this makes me special. (18)

The young Thea is neither terrified nor ashamed by the diagnosis or the treatment. Rather, she contextualizes the "condition" as something that makes her "special", not ill, and expresses very positive connotations. By titling the piece "Special", Hillman enforces the perspective of the four-year-old and denies the pathologizing medical discourse.

Hillman concludes the piece with a statement by the adult Thea, who tells the reader what her mother (and the doctors) did *not* tell her when she was diagnosed. As the final statement in the piece, the conclusion positions Hillman as the expert on her condition and clearly (re-)connects CAH to intersex: "What she *doesn't tell* me is that CAH is a condition that can result in hermaphrodism in girls. This usually reveals itself with an enlarged clitoris and precocious puberty, which can result in shortened stature, masculinization, and other effects including inability to get pregnant" (18, emphasis added). The quote continues with an enumeration of fears and negative connotations her mother did *not* express when Thea was a child:

She *doesn't tell* me that CAH speeds up brain maturity, or that she worries about me being socially advanced beyond my peers and the hardships that might cause. She *doesn't tell* me many of the girls with CAH end up being bisexual or lesbian, or that she's concerned about the possibility of me being very sexual because of the increased androgens running through me. (18, emphases added)

Here, the use of negative performatives emphasizes the limits of discourse and points to things that her mother deemed unspeakable. Despite the silence between mother and daughter and between mother and doctor on the subject, Hillman explains that the things unsaid "were there, between us and around me, hovering between every word and gesture" (18). Hillman's mother was silenced by her fear and Hillman uses negative performatives like Perseus' polished shield to face the petrifying gaze of Medusa, a mother's fear of hermaphrodism, sexuality and homosexuality, and negotiates a way around the silence. Through negative performatives she names what was feared and left unsaid; she pierces the silence and expands the area of what is say-able.

WORDS DON'T COME EASY: INTERSEX BY NEGOTIATION

In two pieces called "Change" and "Present," Hillman discusses notions of intersex by activists. Both pieces relate specific events; one is an account of the "Creating Change" conference in Atlanta in 2000 and the other is an account of the "Queeruption" conference in 2001 in Oakland. Both pieces are positioned in time and place; they are marked as 'local' stories. Moreover, both pieces emphasize the aspect of negotiation and *Better Word* will be shown to raise questions and to promote debate, rather than to proclaim definitive answers.

"Change", the longest piece in the collection and the 23rd out of 47, marks Hillman's first contact with the term *intersex*. The term that signifies prominently in the title of the book is only used twice before, in chapters six, "Telling," and seven, "Opinion," the two chapters on *Middlesex* and fictional representation. In these pieces the term is used to contrast or to oppose it to the often pejorative and exoticizing term *hermaphrodite*. *Intersex* as a concept is not introduced or discussed in those chapters. Positioning the piece in the middle of the book mirrors Hillman's life experience: her doctors classified CAH as a hormonal imbalance but never mentioned intersexuality in connection. It is only as an adult that, by chance, she came across the term and started to understand her condition as an intersex condition: "The first time I ever heard the 'word' intersex, it was from my friend Victoria […]. She told me there was such a thing as intersex, people born with ambiguous genitalia, and that these babies were given plastic surgery to make them look normal. […] I am blown away to hear that doctors perform surgery on babies to make them look normal" (74). At first, Hillman does not connect the term to her diagnosis as her genitalia are considered 'within standard range.' Her neighbor David is the second person who talks to her about intersex. He tells her: "'I have Klinefelter's Syndrome. […] My chromosomes are XXY, but I didn't know about my condition until my thirties'" (74). Hillman starts to investigate the connection of CAH and intersex:

My conversation with David haunts me. I wonder if I have something to tell him […]; namely, that if my condition had been worse, I could have been a hermaphrodite. My mom told me that once. I remember asking her, 'Why were you so worried when I was little, when I was getting diagnosed with Congenital Adrenal Hyperplasia?' She told me they were afraid I'd be a hermaphrodite. (75)

It becomes clear that the doctor's naming strategy effectively blurred the relation between intersex and CAH for Hillman. Yet her mother was aware of the possible challenge of sexual norms through CAH.

Hillman gets in touch with Cheryl Chase from ISNA and some other activists and remembers being surprised that the activists consider her intersex and include her in the community: "When I tell Sandy, the facilitator [of the intersex support group], that I have Congenital Adrenal Hyperplasia, she seems convinced I am intersex" (77). One activist points out that, in addition to being intersex, he would also consider her transgender: "'By taking hormones,' he tells me, 'you transitioned away from being intersex toward something else, toward a more traditional female'" (77). This opinion reflects a close connection between trans* and intersex issues and stands for the more inclusive position within the queer political arena where *queer, trans** or *transgender* are used as inclusive umbrella terms.[4] Nevertheless, Hillman reflects on the limits of this inclusive concept for the intersex movement as well: "[…] in San Francisco, for civil rights purposes, intersex appears under the umbrella category of transgender. I explain that intersex is about sex, not gender, so it should have a category all its own" (80). Although at that moment Hillman is arguing for intersex as a category independent from transgender, she "can't quite explain why this is the case, or how an intersex person's civil rights issues are different from a transgender person's" (80).[5] Among activists, the relation between intersex and transgender seems disputed. Yet,

---

4   For an introduction and thorough discussion of the concept see Stryker/Whittle; Stryker/Aizura.

5   The discussion touched here is taken up and elaborated in other pieces as well (cf. "Allies," "Testosterone," "Community"). Hillman also reflects upon the connections and draws analogies between intersex and disability (cf. "Pray"), and intersex and sexual abuse survivors (cf. "Haircut," "Telling," "Out," "Condition").

they agree on CAH as an intersex condition: "Those three words [Congenital Adrenal Hyperplasia] are like a password into a secret club. She [Sandy] calls my condition by its initials, CAH, like she's superfamiliar with it and says it all the time. It's as if CAH is how intersex people say it and Congenital Adrenal Hyperplasia is for people who think it's an enzyme imbalance" (77). The different terminology or different language use reflects the debate on CAH as an intersex condition or an enzyme balance, and Hillman leaves the debate unsolved. Moreover, she complicates the debate about terminology and meaning by pointing to the limits of Cheryl Chase's definition of *intersex*: "'I hate to bug you about this, Cheryl. [...] But your definition, that intersex is people whose genitals make them subject to surgeries or medical intervention, well, that definition doesn't include me" (81). Hillman's genitals are considered "normal" (78) and the question reveals the limiting and essentialist norm of Chase's definition. Yet neither Chase nor Hillman offers a definitive answer to this problem and Chase replies: "'You're right. I'll have to think about that'" (82).

In "Present," chapter 25, Hillman continues the debate about activists' definitions of intersex. The polysemous title of the piece can be read as *now* opposed to an earlier or later or as opposed to an *always* or eternity. Thereby, the piece is connected to a specific and deictic moment in history, the Queeruption conference in Oakland in 2001. With this title, the piece explicitly does not express an eternal truth. Rather, it captures the discussion at a specific moment in time and serves as a snap-shot of that discussion. In addition to the temporal aspects of the term, *present* may also function as a verb – either as an infinitive of *to present* as in *to demonstrate* or *to show* or as the determining part of a complex predicate in *being present* as opposed to *being absent*. The latter points to one of the major concerns of the overall text *Better Word* and the piece "Present" itself: intersex is marked as something that is *there*, something real and relevant – not just a myth, a metaphor or a medical case study. The former meaning of *to present* (to show, to demonstrate) invites connotations of agency and performativity: through the agent, Hillman, the account is localized and claims to universality or objective truth are denied. Moreover, the narrator is the *presenter* of the story, and, in Hillman's case, may even be the performer of the piece on a spoken word stage. In addition, the term *present* also functions as a noun, as a synonym for *gift*. In the context of the piece, I believe, the gift that is given to Hillman (or what she allows herself to understand as a gift) is that she learns to acknowledge her life experience as an intersex experience:

> I told my story next. I talked about being nervous because I'm still trying to figure out what parts of my experience are about maintaining health and which are about maintaining gender. I said I was thinking about going off my medication. I spoke about how my mom caught my condition early, that I always felt proud of being special, but also that I was aware that my difference or freakishness originated *from my genitals*. (91, emphasis added)

Having been medicalized since early childhood, Hillman wonders whether the medication she is prescribed is really about maintaining health or whether it is part of a normalizing discourse that serves a binary gender system. She challenges the medical discourse that constructs intersex as a 'deviation' that can and needs to be treated and points to the heteronormative functions of the discourse. Yet despite her critical view of the medical discourse she lacks a definition of intersex that does not rely on this discourse. This becomes evident when Xander, another activist, criticizes her for her use of language:

> Xander said he wasn't comfortable with the language I was using, like 'condition' to refer to CAH or 'should have' when I said my body 'should have produced one enzyme and didn't […].' While I agreed with him, I felt really embarrassed. I felt exposed, my language clearly reflecting the experience of having a body that had been pathologized and medicalized and described to me as the result of a mutation. […] I also understand the problem with words like 'condition.' Condition is a polite way of saying something unpleasant, something you're stuck with that gives you gas, dandruff, or inappropriate genitalia. It's a euphemism for freak or hermaphrodite, the person becoming conflated with the affliction. Condition is something wrong, most likely uncorrectable, with the desire for normalcy implicit. (91f)

Hillman reflects on the limitations of the vocabulary she uses but it seems difficult to agree on a definition and a language that is inclusive, yet specific and non-pathologizing. Xander's definition, "intersex [is] an identity outside of the gender binary" (91), does not necessarily include an anatomical variation of the body but expresses the need for a position outside of the gender binary. His definition largely overlaps with descriptions of transgender experiences and may be criticized for a lack of specificity. Activist Hida's definition, "'people born with anatomy which is not standardly male or female'" (90), is essentialist or materialist and rather exclusive as it does not represent individuals whose anatomy is judged standard. At the time, Hillman is not sure whether she is "intersex fully" (90) and her understanding of the term as "a set of shared experiences of sex and gender oppression" (91) emphasizes the performative aspects of intersex identity. Moreover, Xander's critique of her pathologizing language use leads her to reevaluate it and she explains: "Condition is also to train, groom, lick into shape. To habituate. And that's where the word became more accurate for me: I've become accustomed to being different, broken in" (92). Hillman's understanding of the term "condition" reaches beyond the medical discourse that Xander criticizes and she succeeds in making the term productive for her own definition and identification as intersex: "What happened that day was that I began to claim my experience as an intersex person, no matter how awkward or imperfect it might be. Soon, I'd come to know that that awkwardness, that feeling that there was some way to be that I couldn't quite attain, was one of the most intersex things about me" (92). Hillman identifies the doubts about her experience, the experience of not being able to live up to expectations and standards (both medical and activist), as a constitutive part of her intersex experience. Intersex, it may seem, was thereby reconceptualized from a physical fact to a performative experience. Yet Hillman does not negate the physical aspects of the experience when she explains that her intersexuality "originated from [her] genitals" (91). Thus, Hillman rejects Hida's, Xander's, and Chase's intersex definitions, opposes medical taxonomies, and emphasizes the limitations of fictional representations. What she offers in return, I argue in the following, is an understanding of intersex that combines the material, the physical, with the performative, the experiential.

PERFORMING INTERSEX BODIES: ESSENTIALISM REVISITED

Building on Foucault and Austin, Butler argued in 1990 that not only gender but also sex, the material body, was an effect of performative practices. Her seminal *Gender Trouble* robbed the body of its factuality and her concept of performativity demonstrated that the body was not a natural given. Hillman explores the potential of performativity for queer identities and elaborates the practices for transgender and drag experiences. In "Transition," she recounts the female to male transition of a lover. Together, the two "renamed body parts [...] breast became chest, clit became cock" (145) and the "woman became boy, born into sweaty sheets" (146). BDSM scholar Robin Bauer identifies the strategy of renaming as part of a process he calls *recognition* (cf. *Queer* 208ff) and links it to the act of seeing someone else or oneself "as differently gendered than before" (208). Hillman also refers to the act of "recognizing" to what had not been seen before, but it is the act of naming, of finding words that allow the body to be recognized: "Within weeks, you came out as trans. 'Genderqueer' fell from your lips, that week's new vocabulary word" (*Better Word* 146). *Recognition*, then, is a practice that involves reading ('seeing') as well as writing ('naming'). The piece shows the flesh to be open for interpretation and negotiation, and it shows, as Butler put it, that bodily surfaces "can become the site of a dissonant and denaturalized performance that reveals the performative status of the natural itself" (*Gender* 186).

In "Community," Hillman reflects on similarities and differences between trans* and intersex experiences and on the limitations of the process of recognition: "I hate that surgeons touch the bodies of my lovers. I hate that they hold the solution. Maybe as much as some of my lovers hate that a man can get me pregnant and that they can't, I hate that I can't give my lovers the body they want or even the gender they want, that my love of their body, our sex, our queerness doesn't enable them to have it or to realize it" (*Better Word* 135f). Hillman's ability to see in her lover's body what had not been "recognized in you yet" may seem to complicate Butler's notion of the body as a surface without original and always ready for inscription or re-inscription. Yet it is framed by Hillman's familiarity with trans* discourses and therefore re-enforces rather than challenges Butler's argument. In "Hard," Hillman explores the potential of drag practices for identity formation and switches easily between different roles – man, butch, spoken word performer – but refrains from revealing one of these roles as 'true' or 'original' identity. Rather, she emphasizes the fluidity and temporality of these identities as much as their 'realness': when in male drag, Hillman wears a strap-on dildo that she refers to as her "dick underneath my Calvin Klein boxers" (65). Kissing a woman makes her "hard" and the dildo is turned from a sex toy into what Bauer calls a *cybercock*: "As for cyborgs, for trans* people and genderqueers, these artificial extensions of their body are incorporated and become part of the self, expanding bodily integrity to a hybrid of flesh and artifact, a cyborg embodiment" (*Queer* 205). Hillman incorporates the silicone device and embodies the male drag identity, and her *cybercock* clearly answers Donna Haraway's suggestive question "Why should our bodies end at the skin [...]?" ("Cyborg Manifesto" 36). Moreover, when she meets the woman again some time later she feels the body part that the dildo manifests without actually wearing it. Bauer compares this kind of experience to the experience of "phantom limbs of people who have lost body parts, but continue to feel them as part of their body" (*Queer* 207) and proposes the term *holodick*. "Both the cybercock and the holodick," explains Bauer, "are ways of reassigning and reinventing sexed bodies that transgress the boundaries and transform the meanings of the body and bodily integrity" (208). Well-versed in BDSM practices, Hillman employs these performative strategies and demonstrates how to expand the experiences of bodies and genders. Both are intricately linked and the gendered body that Hillman inhabits is neither fixed nor does it necessarily end at the boundary that her skin suggests.

In general, Butler's concept of performativity proves very useful for analyzing processes of identity production (queer or other) and it has often been used in opposition to the supposed essentialism of the Natural Sciences. Yet Hillman insists on an essentialist, a physiological basis or material core of her intersex experience and, to me, Butler's approach does not seem apt to capture this complex experience. One of Butler's early critics is Eve Sedgwick, who explains polemically that deconstructivist approaches affiliated with Butler had at their heart the notion that "language itself can be productive of reality" (*Touching* 5). While Sedgwick does not generally question the concept of performativity, she argues that nonverbal or nonlinguistic phenomena cannot be adequately analyzed with linguistic tools and points out that "the line between words and things or between linguistic and nonlinguistic phenomena is endlessly changing, permeable, and entirely unsusceptible to any definitive articulation" (6). Moreover, she criticizes assigning a "very special value, mystique, or thingness to meaning and language" and explains that many "kinds of objects and events mean, in many heterogeneous ways and contexts, and [that she sees] some value in not reifying or mystifying the linguistic kinds of meaning unnecessarily" (6).[6] Sedgwick suggests a specific notion of *shame* to overcome the limitations of antiessentialist or deconstructivist projects and explains that "'queer performativity' is the name of a strategy for the production of meaning and being, in relation to the affect shame" (61). She borrows her concept of *shame* from the affect theory of Silvan Tomkins.[7] The American psychologist Tomkins identified nine discrete *affects* and distinguished them from Freudian *drives*. While both systems are understood as "thoroughly embodied" (*Touching* 18), in other words, as a biological universalism, as innate, Sedgwick explains that according to Tomkins, *drives* are relatively more constrained than *affects* with reference to aims (breathing will not satisfy hunger), time (breathing is necessary within a relatively short time span), and range of objects (only a specific mix of gases satisfies the need to breathe) (cf. *Touching* 18). Affects, then, enjoy relatively more freedom with reference to the three dimensions: time ("anger can evaporate in seconds but can also motivate a decades-long career of revenge" [19]), aim ("my pleasure in hearing a piece of music can make me want to hear it repeatedly, listen to other music, or study to become a composer myself" [19]), and object ("any affect may have any 'object'" [19]).

The affect that Sedgwick explores in detail is *shame* and she explains:

Shame floods into being as a moment, a disruptive moment, in a circuit of identity-constituting identificatory communication. Indeed, like a stigma, shame is itself a form of communication. Blazons of shame, the 'fallen face' with eyes down and head averted – and, to a lesser extent, the blush – are semaphores of trouble and at the same time of a desire to reconstitute the interpersonal bridge. (36)

---

6   Sedgwick's critique on the reductive binary distinction between essentialism and constructivism (or antiessentialism) and on the privileging of the constructivist approaches has also been addressed by scholars in New Materialism such as Karen Barad. For an introduction to the diverse approaches loosely labeled *New Materialism* see Alaimo/Hekman; Coole/Frost; Dolphijn/Tuin; Barrett/ Bolt.

7   See Sedgwick and Frank.

This explanation is based on observations of interaction between infants and their caregivers. Having learned to recognize the face of the caregiver, infant and caregiver enter into a circuit of mirroring expressions. When the caregiver breaks the mutual gaze, the infant inevitably experiences shame. Shame, explains psychoanalyst Michael Franz Basch, is "a reaction to the loss of feedback from others, indicating social isolation and signaling the need for relief from that condition" (qtd. in Sedgwick *Touching* 36). Thus, *shame* is not defined by either repression or prohibition (cf. *Touching* 36). Rather, it is an affect that is triggered only after interest or joy had been activated and then incompletely reduced (cf. *Touching* 134).

For Tomkins, the affect system is innate and affects are inevitably triggered by (external or internal) stimuli that may lead to increasing, stable or decreasing neural firing in the brain over time (cf. *Touching* 102ff). The affect *shame* resides specifically "in the muscles and capillaries of the face" (64): the blush, the lowered eyes, and averted head are physical responses to stimuli. While the capacity for the affect is innate, the specific stimulus or the trigger for shame in a person is indeterminate and subject to change. With this openness and layering of essentialist and performative aspects, Tomkins' affect model combines what Sedgwick calls "digital (on/off) with analog (graduated and/or multiply differentiated) representational models" (101). Tomkins' affects are rooted in the body, but Sedgwick warns theorists to withdraw to a position of "reflexive antibiologism" (101) and suggests that there "is not a choice waiting to be made [...] between essentialism and no essentialism" (114). Rather, she argues for theories that combine analog and digital models and that do not reduce complex processes of identity formation to either nature/biology/digital or nurture/culture/analog. For assessing "difference (individual, historical, and cross-cultural)", Sedgwick advocates "a complex, multilayered phyllo dough of the analog and the digital (114) and presents *shame* as such a model: while Tomkins insists on the innate structure of the affect system, this biologism does not lead to an essentialist understanding of the concept or to the assumption that *shame* would be triggered universally by the same events or circumstances. Rather, the relative freedom of affects guarantees that *shame* can be attached to anything, explains Sedwick:

Shame [...] is not a discrete intrapsychic structure, but a kind of free radical that (in different people and also in different cultures) attaches to and permanently intensifies or alters the meaning of – of almost anything: a zone of the body, a sensory system, a prohibited or indeed a permitted behavior, another affect such as anger or arousal, a named identity, a script for interpreting other people's behavior toward oneself. (62)

Thus, *shame* is both biologically determined (neural firing) and socially constructed (the trigger) and Sedgwick concludes "one of the things that anyone's character or personality is is a record of the highly individual histories by which the fleeting emotion of shame has instituted far more durable, structural changes in one's relational and interpretative strategies toward both self and others" (62). The self then negotiates his_her place in society based on experiences of shame, i.e. based on (negative) reactions towards his_her interests. Sedgwick proposes the study of *shame* to think about identities and suggests that "at least for certain ('queer') people, shame is simply the first, and remains a permanent, structuring fact of identity: one that [...] has its own powerfully productive and powerfully social metamorphic possibilities" (64.). With this understanding, the study of *shame* is a point of departure for the study of identity formation or for the study of practices and processes that lead to the notion of identity. With Sedgwick, *shame* is both enabling and limiting, and it values the material body while celebrating performance and performativity.

In "Out," I contend, Hillman demonstrates how *shame* is the affect that governs her own intersex experience between or beyond performativity and essentialism. She was never subjected to genital surgery, but when Hillman reads through transcripts of videos with people who were involved in the treatment of intersex individuals she comments: "What I read chills me" (*Better Word* 109). The transcripts she reads and that she recounts in the piece include narrations of violent, post-surgery dilation procedures such as the following:

I read a mother's account of having to dilate her six-year-old child after the child's vaginoplasty. Her daughter would scream, 'Nooo,' as her grandmother held her down while this woman attempted to do what doctors had told her she had to do so that when the child was older she could have sexual intercourse. (110)[8]

---

8 Vaginal dilation after infant genital surgery is among the measures most strongly criticized by intersex activists: a dildo-like tube is to be inserted into

The presentation in indirect speech as well as the setting of the accounts marks them as representation. Thereby, the accounts are removed from the immediacy of first person accounts, but Hillman acknowledges the violence of the medical practices and aligns herself with the critique of these practices. Yet the focus of the piece is not on the accounts as such, but on Hillman's reaction to the accounts: "I start to feel small and cold. ... And I want to cry, but I don't, I just get tight, my throat constricts" (110). The physical (feeling cold, throat constricts) and emotional aspects (feeling small, wanting to cry) of the experience are inextricably linked in the piece. As a result of a social worker's explanation that "it's not the fear that's the most harmful, but rather the profound sense of *shame* and humiliation," Hillman's "memory takes over" (110, emphasis added). She recalls her own history of repeated genital examinations and tells her story:

> I'm three, four, five, six, I don't know how old, I just know that every time I go to my endocrinologist's office, he feels my chest to see if I'm developing. This is not the part I fear before every appointment. And it's not when he tugs down my underwear to see if I have any more pubic hair, and then pulls apart my labia to see if my clitoris is growing at an abnormal rate. The part I dread is when he touches my stomach, pressing in several places. He'd touch my stomach, feeling around, and I'd giggle convulsively. It tickled so deeply and completely that I couldn't keep still. (110)

The examinations take place with her mother in the room and Hillman describes the doctor as a "nice man" (111). Nevertheless, these examinations leave their traces. Triggered by the social worker's explanation that shame was profoundly harmful, the ticklishness that she developed as a child returns to her memory. The adult narrator Hillman interprets the ticklishness, the convulsive giggling of the young girl, as a kind of defense mechanism of her body. Although she "was never scared. [...] never cried [...] never complained [...] never said no," there was a "terrified little girl" "hidden far away from everyone, and especially me" (111). Hillman relates the ticklishness to the suppressed feelings during the examinations. The

---

the surgically created vagina of the patient to prevent the neo-vagina from narrowing or closing up. The procedure is reported to be extremely painful (cf. www.isna.org).

"terrified little girl" did not muster the authority or power to refuse any of the examinations. But disguised as ticklishness the suppressed fear and lack of trust broke to the surface of the body. In "Haircut," the first piece in the collection, Hillman explains that "the ticklishness started with the doctors" (10) and describes the meaning of ticklishness as a sort of body knowledge: "I realize I haven't said 'No' very often. That I apologize for being ticklish instead of listening to what it's telling me. That I need to teach people how to touch me so my body will trust them, that my body is smarter and wiser than I am" (11). The memory of the examinations is not only stored in her mind, but also in her body.

In "Out," Hillman's lover suggests that the ticklishness may be related to experiences of sexual abuse and Hillman agrees that there may be some overlap (cf. 113). Yet she also points to differences in the experiences: "I have a friend who's an abuse survivor. He told me he started dealing with his past hurts because he got tired of floating around the ceiling during sex" (113). This can be read as an illustration of the account of the social worker who described *shame* as "the most disconnecting thing for human beings" (110). Yet Hillman's experiences did not lead to a disconnection between body and mind. Rather, she describes the connection between her body and mind as inextricable: "I'd like to float around the ceiling. A little flight would be good right now, a little release from this confusing body, this body that holds answers that will reveal themselves when my mind is finally up to hearing them" (113). Her *self*, I contend, is not provided release from her body, because the *self* is the body as much as it is the mind.

With Sedgwick and Tomkins, shame is an embodied affect and Hillman recounts her experience of this affect. After watching documentaries on intersex she explains:

> What [I] didn't really register at the time, I realize now, was that while watching the films, I would *get hot and flushed*. A *deep sense of shame, of feeling found out*, would *rise and swell and push up against my throat*. A part of me recognized myself in those films. If it wasn't in the body itself, it was in sharing the name of the condition Congenital Adrenal Hyperplasia, or seeing the clear disgust of the doctor, or watching a child being turned into a freak right in front of my eyes. Those things I shared. Maybe that's what being intersex was about. Maybe I didn't need to have had surgery. Maybe the most intersex thing about me was *my experience of how my body was treated and how I felt*, rather than whether or not I had confusing anatomy or genital surgery. (113, emphases added)

Hillman's intersex experience does not include surgery or "confusing anatomy." Nevertheless, she has been medicalized, her body closely monitored and hormonally treated for decades. These experiences reflect and manifest in a "deep sense of shame, of feeling found out" and exemplify Tomkins' notion of *shame* as biological *and* performative, or, in Sedgwick's words, as digital *and* analog (cf. *Touching* 101). With this notion of intersex, Hillman combines essentialist and constructivist approaches. Her intersex experience is both rooted and manifested in the body *and* an effect of repeated performative practices. Sedgwick suggests that shame "can be a switch point for the individuation of imaging systems, of consciousnesses, of bodies, of theories, of selves – an individuation that decides not necessarily an identity, but a figuration, distinction, or mark of punctuation" (*Touching* 116f). Hillman constructs her intersex self around this specific experience of *shame* and projects a notion of intersex that is not defined either in accordance with medical diagnoses or in opposition to these categories. Rather, intersex is described as a fully embodied but nevertheless performatively produced identity.

In the 1990s, ISNA had declared that "People who are intersex will tell you that the primary thing they've been harmed by is induced *shame* about their intersex" (isna.org, emphasis added) and the organization had devoted itself "to systemic change to end *shame*, secrecy, and unwanted genital surgeries for people born with an anatomy that someone decided is not standard for male or female" (isna.org, emphasis added). Hillman's treatment was deemed a "huge success" (*Better Word* 112) and "I had never had a body that others wanted to operate on to make it look normal. I had a determined sex that everyone agreed on, including me" (112). Nevertheless, the specific type of medicalization she had experienced throughout her life did not only envelop her body, but infused and imprinted the body and thereby her *self*. For Hillman, the shame she experiences is both individuating and harmful and a starting point for, a marker of, her intersex identity. It is the experience of *shame* that she shares with other intersex people who otherwise might have very different bodies and experiences. And it is this specific type of *shame* (or the marked lack of it[9]) that distinguishes her from non-intersex people.

A SHAMED SUBJECT:
HOW INTERSEX BODIES COME TO MATTER

I argued at the beginning of this chapter that *Better Word* documents the pluralization of voices in intersex discourses following the 2005 DSD consensus, participates in the discussion about appropriate terminology, necessary or unnecessary medical treatment, and expresses an ongoing need for exemplary, i.e. authentic intersex voices. Hillman's presentation of the debate, in form (47 single pieces form an interrupted, fragmented but nevertheless coherent body of work) and content (the representation of different, sometimes opposing voices) localizes the debate. The text points

---

9   A marked lack of shame is described in Hillman's experience of an emergency hospitalization when she is seventeen. The doctors suspect a tubal pregnancy and, "At one point, a doctor gave me a pelvic exam. 'This might feel strange,' she told me. 'This might hurt,' she told me, behaving as if this was the first time anything like this had ever happened to me. And the oddest thing was [...] that I felt like a slut when that doctor tried to reassure me. I felt dirty and too experienced for my age because I wasn't scared, because it wasn't new to me, because she had no idea, but this had been happening to me since I was a very little kid" (111). The incidence illustrates Hillman's lack of shame in a supposedly shameful situation and reveals her lifelong treatments as individuating experiences.

to variations and differences, opposes a unified or general intersex experience, and thereby argues against an intersex metanarrative. Moreover, the concept of *intersex* that Hillman's text suggests rejects both medical, diagnosis-based and thereby essentialist notions of intersex and purely constructivist notions that argue for intersex as a part of the LGBT umbrella. Instead *intersex* becomes an experience distinct from trans* (because intersex is an experience that is rooted in and that manifests through the material body) but nevertheless allied (because both intersex and trans* experiences are pathologized due to supposed 'violations' of the binary sexual order). Furthermore, the body is both the source for intersex experiences and an effect of historically contingent *practices of intersexualization*.[10] Hillman's concept then layers essentialist and constructivist notions. The intersex body is an effect of performative practices, e.g. repeated genital examinations and hormonal treatment shape Hillman's body and her experience of this body. But these practices of intersexualization (treating the body as intersex and thereby producing the intersex body) originated in a (medically) perceived variation of a gendered/sexed physical norm or standard. In line with Butler one might argue that the (inter)sexed body had been gendered all along and argue that the intersex body is an effect of processes of intersexualization. Sedgwick and proponents of New Materialism would oppose this strictly constructivist argumentation and claim the materiality of the body as being meaningful besides (and before) discursive inscription. In Hillman's case, comparatively high levels of androgens and pubic hair at four years old distinguish her *self* and her body from the bodies (and selves) of her peers; it makes her "special" (*Better Word* 18). The experience of her body as "special" is tied to both the medical attention the body receives, and to the body as a carrier and producer of meaning and knowledge. It is her body that reacts with uncontrollable ticklishness to the repeated genital

---

10 Cultural Studies scholar Lena Eckert elaborates this term in her 2010 dissertation and explains: "I will not look at what 'intersexuality' is but what the grounds and means were for initiating, manifesting, and re-articulating the processes of intersexualization time and time again during the last few decades. I attempt a historicization of the epistemic logic and discursive operations within and through which intersexualizations have been cross-culturally produced in psycho-medical and anthropological discourses" (2).

examinations. And it is her body that reacts with shame (not empathy or something else) to intersex documentaries and a marked absence of shame to genital examinations. Hillman's body and bodily experiences are marked as both individual and specific, but also as tied to a set of shared, i.e. supra-individual, experiences that she calls *intersex*. In *Better Word*, the question of which came first, the chicken or the egg, the intersex body or the practices that produce the body as intersex, proves futile. Sedgwick suggests the image of phyllo dough to solve the dilemma; the entangled layering of supposed causes and effects, sometimes causing causes to look like effects while seemingly turning effects into causes in the next fold, describing the relation between cause and effect as circular and interdependent. *Better Word* folds multiple thin layers of bodies and voices from the intersex discourse to form a local specialty, a body of text that is both sweet and savory – and always hot.

Conclusion: Teaching the Octopus

LOOKING SIDEWAYS

Discursive Intersexions, I proposed at the beginning of this study, looks at discourses invested in the formation of intersex and hermaphrodite subjects from the perspective of literary and cultural studies. Texts – autobiographical, factual, and fictional – are scrutinized in their encounters with one another. Presuming the discontinuity and specificity of discourses, the five analytical chapters provide snapshots of the discursive ensemble at a given time and place. What is said about hermaphroditism or intersex in a specific context? Who claims or rejects an assignment as hermaphrodite or intersex and on what grounds? And how do these grounds, these reasons for assigning the label, change? How do discourses such as myth, medicine, and memoir work together to shape the hermaphrodite or intersex subject? The present study, then, describes discursive intersections on hermaphroditism and intersex and contributes to the historical reconstruction of discourse formations. Foucault refers to this scholarly practice, the "analysis of local discursivities" ("Two Lectures" 85), as *archaeology* and he exemplifies the archaeological study of hermaphroditism with the republication of Herculine Barbin's memoirs. On a different but closely related level, *Discursive Intersexions* describes the intersections as struggles between different sets of knowledges, e.g. subjugated knowledges (low-ranking, local, disqualified) and scientific, prestigious knowledges (theoretical, unitary, formal) (cf. "Two" 82-6). In this sense, the present study may also be called a partial genealogy: it attempts "to emancipate historical knowledges […], to render them […] capable of opposition and of struggle against the coercion of a theoretical, unitary, formal, and scientific discourse" ("Two" 85). Again, Foucault's edition of Barbin's memoirs provides an example for this practice: while the memoirs had originally served as mere illustration to the medico-scientific case studies, Foucault reversed the position of the memoir and the case studies by making Barbin's text the center of his 1980 edition and the case studies the appendix; the dossier. This new arrangement of the texts, in my view, indicates a relationship between low-ranking, subjugated knowledge and scientific knowledge that emphasizes the aspects of opposition and emancipation. Building on Foucault's work, I have interrogated Barbin's struggle with the general demand to "speak the truth" ("Two" 93). Each text, Foucault postulates, is invested with a different form of *power /knowledge*,[1] i.e. a different authority to telling the truth. *Truth* is an effect of power and he explains: "Each society has its régime of truth, its 'general politics' of truth: that is, the types of discourse which it accepts and makes function as true" ("Truth and Power" 131). Yet, these regimes of truth are under constant negotiation and I have shown how presumably low-ranking knowledges, i.e. experience-based, local accounts such as Barbin's memoirs, challenge supposedly more prestigious or scientific accounts such as medical reports and case studies. Moreover, my close reading has revealed that Barbin's text deconstructs the autobiographical mode of truth production as normative and that the text rejects attempts to determine the truth about hir sex or hir self.

LOOKING BACK AND FORTH

In the five analytical chapters, *Discursive Intersexions* has addressed the texts primarily in the context of their historically and locally specific struggles, i.e. I have analyzed the synchronic dimension of discourses. However, the chronological order of the analyses in this study also suggests

---

1 The artificial compound "power/knowledge" is used here following Colin Gordon's edited collection of the same title. The term demonstrates the inseparable connection between power and knowledge that Foucault explains in *Discipline and Punish*: "power and knowledge directly imply one another; [...] there is no power relation without the correlative constitution of a field of knowledge, nor any knowledge that does not presuppose and constitute at the same time power relations" (Foucault *Discipline* 27).

a diachronic dimension. What, then, is the relationship between these seemingly disparate analyses? If discourses are discontinuous and specific, a coherent and continuous development or progress is ruled out from the outset. So what could a concluding diachronic perspective on hermaphrodite and intersex discourses show other than gaps, ruptures, and maybe overlaps?

The two analyses on Herculine Barbin and N.O. Body in the first part of this study explore the intersections between memoirs and medical case studies in late 19th century France and in early 20th century Germany. Despite these different historical and local contexts, the texts contain some similarities. Barbin's text, for instance, highlighted the singularity of hir experience,[2] while hir doctors positioned Barbin's case in a long tradition of medical observations on doubtful sex.[3] For them, Barbin's experience was not a singular event, but part of an ongoing professional debate. However, the doctors acknowledged the singularity of the written account as such, which is the reason why the manuscript was published in the first place (cf. *Memoirs* 123; 130). More than thirty years later, and in a different country, N.O. Body also emphasized the singularity of his experience.[4] Moreover, he chose not to align his experiences with the experiences of other people who Magnus Hirschfeld had considered sexual intermediaries or hermaphrodites, or with Barbin's experience. After all, Barbin's account had already been published in Hirschfeld's *Yearbook* in 1902 (cf. Neugebauer "Interessante Beobachtungen"). Similarly, Hirschfeld and editor Rudolf Presber ignore Barbin's account as a precursor to Body's memoirs. Hirschfeld's ignorance is especially surprising given that he, like his 19th century colleagues, positions Body's 'case' in his epilogue to the

---

2   "[T]his incredible journey, which no other living creature before me has taken!" (*Memoirs* 35)

3   Barbin's doctor Chesnet found in his report, "In its essential features, his [Barbin's] history is almost the exact reproduction of a case that is related by Marc in the article 'Hermaphrodite'" (*Memoirs* 128) and E. Goujoun confirms in his autopsy report: "science [...] has records of a rather large number of such mistakes [about the sex of an individual M.K.], some of which have the greatest analogy with the one that concerns us" (*Memoirs* 137).

4   "This book tells a true story. In it, what was probably the strangest youth ever lived shall speak with its own voice" (*Maiden Years* 7).

text in a long tradition of medical research on hermaphroditism.[5] Of course, their ignorance could have been feigned for marketing reasons or the like, but I am less interested in speculations about the reasons for their silence on Barbin's text, and more interested in its effects: both Barbin's and Body's doctors seemed eager to incorporate their case studies in an ongoing debate, as part of a – seemingly – continuous discourse. Yet both authors, Barbin and Body, insisted on the uniqueness, the singularity of their experience. In the light of contemporary narrative conventions, memoir, autobiography, or life narratives can be considered genres that were reserved for the exceptional experience – not for the everyday. The singularity of the experience sustained the uniqueness of the individual who is the subject of memoir. After all, Rousseau had announced his uniqueness above all else when he claimed, "I am not made like any [man] that I have seen" (Rousseau *Confessions* 5). Both Body and Barbin, I conclude, render themselves *unique subjects* by emphasizing the singularity of their experiences. Moreover, the genre memoir invests both accounts with authenticity and renders their respective accounts true. Though neither of the two authors claims a hermaphrodite identity, their accounts are discussed in medical discourses on hermaphroditism and underline hermaphroditism as a lived reality distinct from Ovid's myth.

The three analyses in the second part of *Discursive Intersexions* direct the gaze to 20th and early 21st century US-American publications on intersex. By the 1950s, the term *intersex* had come to replace *hermaphroditism* in some areas of medical taxonomy, yet the outdated term remained (and still remains) in common and medical usage. In 1993, John Money wrote a letter to the editor of *The Sciences* in reply to Anne Fausto-Sterling's article "The Five Sexes." His reply was printed in the same issue as Chase's letter "As an Intersexual." Money complained that Fausto-Sterling suggested the wrong percentage (too high!) of intersex individuals

---

5   Hirschfeld ignores Barbin's account when he explains: "*For the first time*, an intelligent person gives an exhaustive account [...]" (*Maiden Years* 109, emphasis added) and he positions Body's case within a medical tradition: "[...] the exact and scientific research on hermaphroditism in human beings began, research that proved beyond doubt that the above-mentioned is, with relation to every sexual characteristic, infinitely more widespread than previously thought" (*Maiden Years* 110).

in society, and deemed it "reckless to conjecture that on the campus of Brown University there are 240 students with a birth defect of the sex organs that would justify their being diagnosed as intersexuals, that is, hermaphrodites" (Money "Letter" n.p.). First of all, the letter demonstrates Money's habit of using the two terms interchangeably and illustrates his perspective on intersex genitalia as pathological. Moreover, he provokes a debate over the frequency of intersex and calls Fausto-Sterling "reckless" because, in his view, the frequency she claimed was too high. Fausto-Sterling retorted that she "had hoped my tentative language about that number would emphasize that there are really no accurate figures about the total frequency (from all causes) of intersexuality [...]. My point, however, is that intersexuals are not as rare as people may think" (Fausto-Sterling "Reply" n.p.). Regardless of the accuracy of the one or the other number, Fausto-Sterling attempted to make intersex seem more common, while Money insisted on rarefying it, to make intersex seem less common. Hirschfeld, Chesnet and Tardieu had easily positioned their case studies on Barbin and Body in a medical debate and evoked the impression that both cases were far from exceptional. With Money, intersex was not treated with such ease. After all, the Baltimore Protocols called for genital surgery for individuals with non-standard genitalia to 'correct' or to normalize the appearance of these unruly bodies. If intersex was revealed to be common, the 'standard' would have to be reconsidered and the reasons for treatment would evaporate. Ultimately, Money's treatment suggestions, gender theory, and the scholarly mode of writing centered on the figure of the medical expert, obliterate the possibility of an intersex reality and render intersex people *disowned subjects*.

With the testimonial writings, I suggest, Cheryl Chase and ISNA have reclaimed the reality of their experiences and defeated the myth that intersex is 'rare.' While Barbin and Body presented their experiences as unique, the testimonial writings in *Chrysalis* and other publications produce the appearance of a coherent, almost homogeneous group experience, despite various forms of representation. This seeming homogeneity produces a strategically essentialist position. The various voices collected in the journal *Chrysalis* complement each other. They do not erase one another, but they build upon each other and what emerges in the 1990s is a political, a *communal subject* that can no longer be reduced to a 'rarity.' Medical discourses of the time downplayed and marginalized intersex as a lived reality; the narrative mode of testimony, I contend, is especially apt at rebutting rarity-claims because it allows for polyphonic interventions (i.e. 'we are many'). Moreover, medico-scientific discourses use abstraction and theory to produce high levels of prestige. The testimonial mode of writing draws on a completely different set of power/knowledge: authority and authenticity are not produced by evidence or theory, but by experience. Scholars and scientists like Fausto-Sterling and Milton Diamond challenged the Baltimore Protocols within academic discourses, applying similar narrative strategies to Money and his colleagues. Reverting to the mode of testimony aligns intersex people with other groups of people who have suffered as a result of various injustices and crimes – from Holocaust survivors to activists in Civil Rights movements. In this mode, the local and subjective account is endowed with power/knowledge by its character as a witness report. Moreover, the testimonial mode does not only bear witness to an experience, but it also produces the witness. Via the mode of testimony, then, intersex people have not only told their stories, but they have produced themselves as politically active intersex subjects.

Middlesex, I have argued, reads in large parts like a postmodern adaptation of Ovid's *Metamorphosis*. Calliope_Cal's repeated impersonation of Hermaphroditus suggests that, in 2002, intersex is again reduced to myth. Moreover, *Middlesex* employs Calliope_Cal's intersex experience as a metaphor for the coming-of-age of an all-American teenager. If intersex is myth and metaphor then Cal's refusal to actively participate in the intersex movement is not surprising and he characterizes his experiences and his account as distinct from both Barbin's and ISNA's experiences and narrative accounts. However, Cal calls his account a memoir. Thereby, the emphasis on singularity and uniqueness may be read as fulfilling the requirements of the genre. Moreover, Calliope_Cal, the intersex protagonist, is the only narrator and major focalizer in the story. Admittedly, Cal is unreliable; nevertheless, his perspective dominates the three generation-spanning family saga and he comments frankly and deliberately on events before his birth and ever since: his voice and his opinion count. In addition, Eugenides adapts not only Classical myth, but employs references to various intersex issues: he quotes historical developments from 19th century Europe to late 20th century US-America, criticizes and ridicules John Money and his diagnostic methods, engages with sex/gender debates, and emphasizes the political significance of ISNA.

As a character, Calliope_Cal is very well contextualized within intersex and hermaphrodite discourses. Thus, the intersex subject that emerges in the fictional realm is not one that represents intersex as a lived reality, but *Middlesex* depicts intersex as a multi-faceted discourse and makes Calliope_Cal an *intertextual subject*.

Yet another kind of intersex memoir is Thea Hillman's *Better Word*. Hillman disapproves of the mythologization of intersex characters in fiction, criticizes the pathologization of intersex in medical discourse, and expresses doubts about the essentialist identity politics of ISNA. *Better Word* is not a memoir that focuses on negatives, on the rejection of fictional, medical, or activist representations of intersex, though. Rather, it projects intersex as a subject position characterized by various alliances and draws not only on hermaphrodite or intersex discourses in a narrow sense, but discusses intersections with race, class, and religion, or negotiates coalitions with sexual abuse survivors, LGBT individuals, people with disabilities and a number of others. This presentation, I argue, needs to be read in the context of 1990s queer political positions. In 1987, ACT UP (AIDS Coalition to Unleash Power) was founded in New York and is often considered the starting point for queer politics, a mode of organization around issues, not identities. Throughout the 1990s this mode of organization was explored, and theorized, and in 1997 gender activist Riki Anne Wilchins famously declared that "identity politics really, really sucks" (*Read My Lips* 79).[6] Yet Hillman is very aware of the questions that some strands of queer theory, performativity, and radical constructivism may pose for corporeal intersex experiences and she insists on the 'realness' of the material body for intersex. Thus, *Better Word* presents as a patchwork of spoken word pieces that mirror the various negotiation processes, the struggles for recognition and temporary and local alliances while maintaining one clear voice. This voice connects the pieces and is the stable signifier, the materi(e)al, in the memoir. The intersex subject that emerges in *Better Word*, I contend, is fully textualized, yet never without a material body, and may be called the *performaterial subject*, a subject position that combines the material and the performative.

---

6 On queer and identity politics, see Warner *Fear* and Jagose *Queer*.

Looking Ahead

The above diachronic review of the five synchronic analyses in *Discursive Intersexions* has shown a variety of modes of representation of hermaphrodite and intersex experiences: ranging from *unique subjects* in memoir via *disowned subjects* in medical case studies to *communal subjects* in testimony, and from *intertextual subjects* in fiction to *performaterial subjects* in spoken word memoir; intersex and hermaphrodite narratives are embedded in local and historical discursivities and intersect with power/knowledge-relations. However, the appearance of one or the other subject formation in a given text at a specific point in time has never blotted out other forms of representation. Rather, in 2017, the various forms of representation exist simultaneously. They have multiplied and the rules of what can be said about and what counts as a valuable contribution to the debate are under constant negotiation. Activists' strategies vary from groups that focus on special issues such as *Advocates for Informed Choice* (AIC legal), who target legal issues or *Inter/Act*, an organization especially for young intersex people, to diagnosis specific groups such as the *Androgen Insensitivity Support Group* (AISSG), and to global umbrella organizations such as *Organization Intersex International* (OII) with its many national subchapters. Simultaneously, medical research on intersex and DSD continues and developments are commented on and targeted by organizations such as ISNA's follow-up organization *Accord Alliance*, which intervenes by using professional commentary on articles recommended in *Faculty of 1000* (F1000 Prime), an American publishing portal for clinical research and life sciences. Furthermore, popular media representations of intersex still vary from sensationalizing stories about Belgian fashion model and intersex activist Hanne Gaby Odiele, to rumors about individuals who may or may not be intersex such as pop singer Lady Gaga or 800m World Champion Caster Semenya to sympathetic pieces or documentaries such as *Too Fast to be a Woman? The Story of Caster Semenya* (2011). Similarly, legal developments range from Malta's *Gender Identity, Gender Expression and Sex Characteristics Act* (2015) that, for the first time in the world, explicitly protects intersex infants' rights to physical integrity and outlaws genital surgery without informed consent, to the so-called bathroom bills that a Republican representative introduced in Texas in 2015 to ban intersex and transgender people from the use of public bathrooms that match their gender identity. All these acts and developments receive applause and critique from different political camps. Underlying all of this, I believe, the debate about the meaning of intersex still remains: is intersex an identity or a condition? Who has the power to define and to name the characteristics that make a person intersex? Yet when it comes to the question of how meaning is produced and what a text means, literary and cultural studies are never far off.

In my introduction to this study, I used the 2009 special issue of *GLQ* on intersex to outline the scope of *Discursive Intersexions* and to emphasize the contribution an analysis of intersex representation from the perspective of literary and cultural studies could make and I now return to this introduction and summarize my contribution to the debate: in 2009, guest editor Iain Morland titled his introduction to the *GLQ* special issue "Lessons from the Octopus." The title alludes to Suzanne Kessler's seminal study *Lessons from the Intersexed* (1998), yet shifts the teaching subject from intersex people to the octopus, in other words, to the conservative intersex model based on the Baltimore Protocols. Morland compares this intersex model to an ideological octopus (cf. Morland "Lessons" 195) due to its multidisciplinarity, and calls for similarly multidisciplinary criticism of the octopus model. The octopus metaphor is borrowed from Justin Lewis' study on television, *The Ideological Octopus* (1991). Lewis described television as "a monster, a creature whose tentacles squirmed into almost every avenue of our cultural life" (*Ideological* 4) due to its "prodigious growth" (4). Even more frightening than the octopus' growth, however, seemed Lewis' conclusion that "hegemonic power [...] depends upon its ability to resonate with different audiences in different ways" (205). TV, it turned out, acted as an octopus, precisely because it did not advance one clear and simple message, one meaning, but because its messages were undetermined, i.e. ambiguous, and were decoded very differently by different people. Moreover, Lewis argued, "an ambiguous TV program can be just as manipulative as an unambiguous one" (205) and TV was therefore deemed not just a vigorously growing monster, but an ideologically possessive monster. Ambiguity in meaning is one of the octopus' weapons; it strengthens and even produces its dominant position. Because TV messages are undetermined, they are hard to catch, to pin down. This is true for the octopus as well: typically, an octopus escapes attacks by issuing a distracting ink cloud; the almost boneless structure of its body fits through any crack. Moreover, the octopus has the ability to adapt to its physical environment; some octopus species can change their colors or shift shapes to mimic a predator. With the octopus, ambiguity, flexibility, and indeterminacy are assets, not bonds. Like TV messages, written texts – fictional, factual or somewhere in between – are also ambiguous, endowed with specific truth claims, yet can never be rid of discursive practices of encoding, decoding, of interpretation and, put simply, of reading. To learn from the octopus, then, is to make use of that ambiguity and indeterminacy. It may be impossible to give intersex or hermaphroditism a single and truly determined meaning, yet, I suggest, plurality, variety, indeterminacy, and even opposition need not be feared but be wielded as weapons – so that the lesson from the octopus may become the lesson the octopus will be taught.

I close this investigation of discursive intersections on intersex and hermaphroditism with three short examples that indicate how intersex representations explore ever new ways of making meaning: the award-winning "auto/biographical documentar[y]" *Orchids: My Intersex Adventure* (2010) by documentary film maker Phoebe Hart (Hart "Orchids" 80) complicates notions of authenticity and memory by making Hart's personal experience as an AIS-woman the object of the documentary. Her movie, Hart explains, is "an invitation for others to 'come along for the intersex ride'" (88) and to experience the "intersex gaze" (85). On the "ride" across Australia's mainland, Hart is shown outing herself randomly to strangers on the way; a strategy she refers to as the "empowered reveal" (87). In addition to the 'reveal,' Hart's explicit embrace of non-intersex audiences carries intersex and the movie literally and metaphorically out into the country and into the world. Yet Hart does not take on the world alone, but meets and interviews other intersex people on the way. Moreover, her sister Bonnie, also a person with AIS, accompanies her on the trip and acts as a camera woman. Thereby, Hart never appears as an isolated figure but is mirrored by her sister and shown within a community, a strategy Jack Halberstam calls "doubling" (*Queer Time* 78). In contrast to Halberstam's example of doubling in the transgender movie *By Hook or by Crook* (2001) that refuses to "acknowledge the existence of a straight world" (94), *Orchids* negotiates intersex as a reality within the world. However, *Orchids* refuses to acknowledge this world as simply 'straight.' Rather, the random strangers in the movie and mainstream audiences are confronted with intersex as a reality of their only seemingly straight world and Hart explains that she attempted "to create a supportive relationship" ("Orchids" 88) between intersex and non-intersex people.

Such a supportive relationship between intersex and non-intersex people is also represented in Kathleen Winter's *Annabel*. The Canadian novel was published in the same year as *Orchids* and follows intersex protagonist Wayne from birth through adulthood. Wayne's parents, especially his trapper father, raise him as a boy and it is his mother's friend Thomasina who secretly nurtures what the novel refers to as his female side, Annabel. Thomasina does not have answers or tells Wayne what to do, but she is honest and talks to him. Her understanding of intersex is different from medical notions and opens a space for possibilities: "'I wouldn't call what you have a disorder. I'd call it a different order. A different order means a whole new way of being'" (*Annabel* 208). The new way of being that Thomasina projects here turns out to be thoroughly embodied: Wayne eventually stops taking masculinizing hormones and explores the possibilities of his body. When he is found to have self-impregnated himself, Winter strays from biologically sanctioned intersex descriptions and confronts the seemingly straight world with queer possibilities. Some reviewers comment that this "subplot strains credulity" (Syms n.p.) and it certainly distances Wayne_Annabel's experience from intersex realities, yet I would suggest that Winter employs the qualities of fiction and metaphor to underline the physical aspect of the experience. In the novel, intersex is not about the gender Wayne_Annabel negotiates, but about the experience of inhabiting a body that is largely uncharted and full of surprises. With *Annabel*, Winter creates a space for intersex experiences that are deemed medically impossible. While many texts in this study present their narratives as true, because they were biologically or medically sanctioned or because they were based on real life experiences, Winter's *Annabel* is fiction and employs fictional elements to tell a story that may be incredible, yet, I contend, not necessarily less true. Similar to Hillman's *Better Word*, both *Orchids* and *Annabel* present intersex as a fully embodied, performaterial subject position. Moreover, the intersex subject is no longer alone, but is shown to have (and muster) allies in the (seemingly) straight world. Thereby, intersex is no longer restricted to mythical, medical, or activist settings or discourses, but is installed as a subject position firmly grounded in the real world, put simply, an *inter-active subject*.

One of the latest examples for the growing plurality of intersex representations in print and film is MTV's teen series *Faking It* (2014). Set in the suburbs of Austin, Texas, *Faking It* opens its second season with the revelation that one of the main characters is intersex. During the production of the show, script writers collaborated with the intersex youth group Inter/Act to portray Lauren, the intersex character, as 'real' as possible. Yet the intersex organization did not only advise the script writers, but is also featured within the show as the character is shown posting in Inter/Act's online forum. While *Faking It* is hardly original in its general setting or plot lines – the show uses an all-American high school façade to negotiate teenage sexuality and identity – it contrasts with current political events in Texas. If the Republican bathroom bills were passed, then *Faking It*'s Lauren would be punishable by up to one year in prison and up to a $4,000 fine every time she used the women's bathroom. It remains to be seen how far the cooperation between activists and producers and their wish to portray Lauren as 'real' carries the AIS poster girl and her Texan high school friends.

Appendix
Bodies beyond the Binary in Books and Movies: An Anglophone Chronology

Year of first publication in English	List of titles
1960	Sturgeon, Theodore. *Venus Plus X*. 1960. Vintage Books, 1999.
1969	LeGuin, Ursula K. *Left Hand of Darkness*. 1969. Berkeley Publishing Group, 2000.
1980 [1874]	Foucault, Michel. *Herculine Barbin (Being the Recently Discovered Memoirs of a Nineteenth Century French Hermaphrodite)*. Pantheon Books, 1980.
1984	Banks, Iain. The Wasp Factory. Macmillan, 1984.
1986	McMaster Bujold, Lois. *The Warrior's Apprentice*. Baen Books, 1986. Vorkosigan Saga.

1987-89	Butler, Octavia E. *Dawn*. Warner Books, 1987. Xenogenesis Trilogy. Print. ---. *Adulthood Rites*. Warner Books, 1988. Xenogenesis Trilogy. Print. ---. *Imago*. Warner Books, 1989. Xenogenesis Trilogy.
1990	Barlowe, Wayne. *Expedition: Being an Account in Words and Artwork of the 2358 A.D. Voyage to Darwin IV*. Workman Publishing Company, 1990.
1991-97	Jones, Gwyneth. *White Queen*. Gollancz, 1991. Aleutian Trilogy. ---. *North Wind*. Gollancz, 1994. Aleutian Trilogy. ---. *Phoenix Café*. Gollancz, 1997. Aleutian Trilogy.
1991	Thomas, Thomas T. *CryGender*. Baen Books, 1991.
1992	Jennings, Gary. *Raptor*. Doubleday, 1992.
1995 [1930]	Delarue-Mardrus, Lucie. *The Angel and the Perverts*. 1930. Trans. Anna Livia. New York UP, 1995.
1995	Scott, Melissa. *Shadow Man*. Tor Books, 1995.
1995	Park, Paul. *Celestis*. Tor Books, 1995.
1997	Flanagan, Mary. *Adèle*. Bloomsbury Publishing, 1997.
1998	Leigh, Stephen. *Dark Water's Embrace*. Phoenix Pick, 1998.
2000	Older, Julia. *Hermaphroditus in America*. Appledore Books, 2000.
2000	Ebershoff, David. *The Danish Girl*. Viking Press, 2000.
2001	Hillman, Thea. *Depending on the Light*. Manic D Press, 2001.
2002	Eugenides, Jeffrey. *Middlesex*. Picador, 2002.
2002	Reese, James. *The Book of Shadows*. Hartorch, 2002.

2003	Reichs, Kathy. *Bare Bones*. Scribner, 2003.
2003	Tracy, P. J. *Monkeewrench*. G.P. Putnam's Sons, 2003.
2004	Howe, Julia Ward. *The Hermaphrodite*. Ed. Gary Williams. U of Nebraska P, 2004. [previously unpublished fragment, written 1846/1847].
2005	*Both*. Dir. Lisset Barcellos. Solaris Films, 2005. Film.
2005	Kwa, Lydia. *The Walking Boy: A Novel*. Key Porter Books, 2005.
2006	Esehagu, Rosemary. *The Looming Fog*. Oge Creations Books, 2006.
2005	Lees, Lisa. *Fool for Love*. Lulu, 2005.
2006	Lees, Lisa. *A Queer Circle of Friends*. Lulu, 2006.
2006 [1907]	Body, N.O. *Memoirs of a Man's Maiden Years*. 1907. Ed. Hermann Simon. Trans. Deborah Simon. U of Pennsylvania P, 2006.
2006	Gentle, Mary. *Ilario: The Lion's Eye*. Gollancz, 2006.
2007	Gentle, Mary. *Ilario: The Stone Golem*. Eos, 2007.
2007	*XXY*. 2007. Dir. Lucía Puenzo. Pyramide Distribution, 2008. Film.
2008	Hillman, Thea. *Intersex (for Lack of a Better Word)*. Manic D Press, 2008.
2008	Curtin, Amanda. *The Sinkings*. U of Western Australia P, 2008.
2009	Muir, r. *Skin*. Create Space, 2009. Digital file.
2009	Ranalli, Gina. *Sky Tongues*. Swallowdown Press, 2009.
2009	*The Last Summer of La Boyita*. Dir. Julia Solomonoff. Travesia Productions, 2009. Film.
2010	Byrd, Michael. *Hermaphrodite: The Contract*. Publish America, 2010.
2010	*Orchids. My Intersex Adventure*. Dir. Phoebe Hart. Hartflicker Moving Pictures, 2010. Film.

2010	Pery, Aaron. *Hermaphrodite Revenge*. Smashwords, 2010.
2010	Winter, Kathleen. *Annabel*. House of Anansi Press, 2010.
2012	Robinson, Kim Stanley. *2312*. Orbit, 2012.
2012	Simon, Lianne. *Confessions of a Teenage Hermaphrodite*. Faie Miss, 2012.
2012	Horner, Andrea Leigh. *Beauty for Ashes. Tales of the Short and Beautiful*. CreateSpace, 2012.
2012	McBride, Belinda. *The Bacchi*. Loose Id, 2012.
2013	Woods, Chavisa. *The Albino Album: A Novel*. Seven Stories Press, 2013.
2013	Brugman, Alyssa. *Alex As Well*. The Text Publishing Company, 2013.
2013	Tarttelin, Abigail. *Golden Boy*. W&N, 2013.
2013	Hoppen, Jane. *In Between*. Bold Strokes Books, 2013.
2013	Eliason, Rachel. *The Case of Nikki Pagan*. Rachel Eliason, 2013.
2013-17	Lam, Laura. *Pantomime*. Strange Chemistry, 2013. Micah Grey series #1. ---. *Shadowplay*. Strange Chemistry, 2014. Micah Grey series #2. ---. *Masquerade*. 2017. Micah Grey series #3.
2014	Birdsall, Bridget. *Double Exposure*. Sky Pony Press, 2014.
2014	Veaux, Alexis de. *Yabo*. Redbone Press, 2014.
2014	Butler, Alec. *Rough Paradise*. Quattro Books, 2014.
2014	Ottoman, E. E. *Song of the Spring Moon Waning*. Less Than Three Press, 2014.
2014	Apps, Aaron. *Dear Herculine*. Ahsahta Press, 2014.
2014-16	*Faking It*. Season 1-3. Created by Dana Min Goodman and Julia Wolov. Executive Producer Carter Covington. MTV, 2014-16.

2015	Headford, Cheryl. *Ari*. Wayward Ink Publishing, 2015.
2015	Gregorio, I. W. *None of the Above*. Balzer & Bray, 2015.
2015	Ware, Libby. *Lum*. She Writes Press, 2015.
2015	Simon, Lianne. *A Proper Young Lady*. Faie Miss, 2015.
2015	Cremm, Delores. *Province*. Smashword, 2015.
2015	Apps, Aaron. *Intersex: A Memoir*. Tarpaulin Sky Press, 2015.
2017	Viloria, Hida. *Born Both: An Intersex Life*. Hachette Books, 2017.

Bibliography

"Accord Alliance - Better Care. Better Outcomes. Better Lives." *Accord Alliance*. Web. 5 Mar. 2015.
Advocates for Informed Choice. *aiclegal*. Web. 8 May 2015.
AISSG Androgen Insensitivity Syndrome Support Group. *Aissg.org*. Web. 5 Mar. 2015.
Ajootian, Aileen. "Hermaphroditos." *Lexicon Iconographicum Mythologicae Classicae*. Zürich: Artemis & Winkler Verlag, 1990. 268–85. Print.
Alaimo, Stacy, and Susan Hekman, eds. *Material Feminisms*. Bloomington: Indiana UP, 2008. Print.
Allgemeines Landrecht für die Preussischen Staaten von 1794. Frankfurt/Main: Alfred Metzer Verlag, 1970. Print.
Amato, Viola. *Intersex Narratives: Shifts in the Representation of Intersex Lives in North American Literature and Popular Culture*. Bielefeld: transcript, 2016. Queer Studies 12. Print.
American Psychiatric Association, ed. *Diagnostic and Statistical Manual of Mental Disorders*. 3rd edition. DSM-III. Washington, D.C.: American Psychiatric Association, 1980. Print.
Anders als die Anderen. Dir. Richard Oswald. 1919. Film.
Annas, George J. "A National Bill of Patients' Rights." *New England Journal of Medicine* 338.10 (1998): 695–699. Print.
Arbeitsgemeinschaft der Wissenschaftlichen Medizinischen Fachgesellschaften (AWMF). "Störungen der Geschlechtsentwicklung. Angemeldetes Leitlinienverfahren (174-001)." N.p., n.d. Web. 9 Jan. 2015.
Assmann, Aleida. "Vier Grundtypen von Zeugenschaft." *Zeugenschaft des Holocaust: Zwischen Trauma, Tradierung und Ermittlung*. Ed. Fritz

Bauer Institut and Gottfried Kößler. Frankfurt/Main; New York: Campus Verlag, 2007. 33–51. Print.

Atkins, Dawn, ed. Looking Queer: Body Image and Identity in Lesbian, Bisexual, Gay, and Transgender Communities. New York: Haworth, 1998. Print.

Attebery, Brian. *Decoding Gender in Science Fiction.* New York: Routledge Chapman & Hall, 2002. Print.

Augustine, Saint. *Confessions.* Trans. R. S. Pine-Coffin. London: Penguin UK, 2003. Print.

Baier, Angelika. "Beyond the Either/or?! : Literatur über Hermaphroditismus am Beispiel von Ulrike Draesners Roman *Mitgift.*" *Aussiger Beiträge* 4 (2010): 79–92. Print.

Bal, Mieke. "Working with Concepts." *European Journal of English Studies* 13.1 (2009): 13–23. Print.

Banks, J. A. "The Woman Question." *The Times Literary Supplement* 9 Oct. 1976: 1117. Print.

Barad, Karen. "Posthumanist Performativity: Toward an Understanding of How Matter Comes to Matter." *Signs* 28.3 (2003): 801–831. JSTOR. Web. 14 May 2015.

Barbin, Herculine. *Herculine Barbin: Being the Recently Discovered Memoirs of a Nineteenth-Century French Hermaphrodite.* Ed. Foucault, Michel. Trans. Richard McDougall. New York: Pantheon Books, 1980. Print.

---. *Herculine Barbin, Dite Alexina B.* Ed. Foucault, Michel. Paris: Gallimard, 1978. Print.

---, and Michel Foucault. *Über Hermaphrodismus.* Ed. Wolfgang Schäffner and Joseph Vogl. Trans. Annette Wunschel. Frankfurt/Main: Suhrkamp Verlag, 1998. Print.

Barchiesi, Alessandro. "Narrative Technique and Narratology in the Metamorphoses." Hardie 180–99.

Barrett, Estelle, and Barbara Bolt, eds. *Carnal Knowledge: Towards a "New Materialism" through the Arts.* London; New York: I. B. Tauris, 2013. Print.

Barthes, Roland. "The Death of the Author." *Image Music Text.* New Ed edition. London: Fontana Press, 1993. 142–148. Print.

---. "Theory of the Text." *Untying the Text: A Post-Structuralist Reader*. Ed. Robert Young. London and Boston: Routledge & Kegan Paul, 1981. 31–47. Print.

Bauer, Robin. *Queer BDSM Intimacies*. Houndmills: Palgrave Macmillan, 2014. Print.

Beck, Max. "Hermaphrodites With Attitude Take to the Streets" Chase and Coventry *Chrysalis* 45–50. Print.

Bergland, Renee, and Gary Williams, eds. *Philosophies of Sex: Critical Essays on* The Hermaphrodite. Columbus: Ohio State UP, 2012. Print.

Bird, R. P. Letter. *The Sciences* (July/August 1993): n.p. Print.

Bloch, Iwan. *Das Sexualleben unserer Zeit in seinen Beziehungen zur Modernen Kultur*. Berlin: L. Marcus, 1919. Internet Archive. Web. 26 Jan. 2015.

Blumenberg, Hans. *Work on Myth*. Trans. Robert M. Wallace. Cambridge: The MIT Press, 1988. Print.

Bodies Like Ours. "Lisset Barcellos' Film Both." *Bodies Like Ours. Intersex Information and Peer Support*. Forum. May-Nov. 2005. Web. 25 Aug. 2014.

Body, N.O. *Aus eines Mannes Mädchenjahren*. 1907. Ed. Hermann Simon. Berlin: Edition Hentrich, 1993. Print.

---. *Memoirs of a Man's Maiden Years*. Ed. Hermann Simon. Trans. Deborah Simon. Philadelphia: U of Pennsylvania P, 2006. Print.

Both. Dir. Lisset Barcellos. Solaris, 2005. Film.

Brenner, David. "Re-Dressing the 'German-Jewish': A Jewish Hermaphrodite and Cross-Dresser in Wilhelmine Germany." *Borders, Exiles, Diasporas*. Ed. Elazar Barkan and Marie-Denise Shelton. Stanford: Stanford UP, 1998. 32–45. Print.

Brisson, Luc. *Sexual Ambivalence: Androgyny and Hermaphroditism in Graeco-Roman Antiquity*. U of California P, 2002. Print.

Brunner, José. "Medikalisierte Zeugenschaft. Trauma, Institution, Nachträglichkeit." *Die Geburt des Zeitzeugen nach 1945*. Göttingen: Wallstein Verlag, 2012. 93–110. Print.

Bullough, Bonnie, Vern L. Bullough, Marilyn A. Fithian, William E. Hartman, and Randy Sue Klein, eds. *How I Got into Sex: Leading Researchers, Sex Therapists, Educators, Prostitutes, Sex Toy Designers, Sex Surrogates, Transsexuals, Criminologists, Clergy, and More...* Amherst: Prometheus Books, 1997. Print.

Butler, Judith. "Doing Justice to Someone: Sex Reassignment and Allegories of Transsexuality." *GLQ: A Journal of Lesbian and Gay Studies* 7.4 (2001): 621–636. Print.

---. *Gender Trouble: Feminism and the Subversion of Identity*. New York: Routledge, 1990. Print.

Butler, Octavia E. *Lilith's Brood*. New York: Grand Central Publishing, 2000. Print.

By Hook or by Crook. Dir. Harriet Dodge, and Silas Howard. Steakhouse Productions, 2001. Film.

Cadden, Joan. *Meanings of Sex Difference in the Middle Ages: Medicine, Science, and Culture*. Cambridge; New York, NY, USA: Cambridge UP, 1993. Print.

Caisou-Rousseau, Inger Littberger. *Therese Andreas Bruce : en Sällsam Historia från 1800-talet Levnadsberättels*. Göteborg; Stockholm: Makadam förlag, 2013. Print.

Carey, Benedict. "John William Money, 84, Sexual Identity Researcher, Dies." *The New York Times* 11 July 2006. NYTimes.com. Web. 8 Aug. 2013.

Carroll, Rachel. "Retrospective Sex: Rewriting Intersexuality in Jeffrey Eugenides's *Middlesex*." *Journal of American Studies* 44.1 (2010): 187–201. Print.

Caruth, Cathy, ed. *Trauma: Explorations in Memory*. Baltimore: Johns Hopkins UP, 1995. Print.

---. *Unclaimed Experience: Trauma, Narrative, and History*. Baltimore: Johns Hopkins UP, 1996. Print.

Catani, Stephanie. "Hybride Körper: Zur Dekonstruktion der Geschlechterbinarität in Ulrike Draesners *Mitgift*." *Familien – Geschlechter – Macht*. Ed. Stephanie Catani and Friedhelm Marx. Göttingen: Wallstein Verlag, 2008. 75–93. Print.

Chase, Cheryl. "Affronting Reason." Atkins 205–19.

---. "Hermaphrodites with Attitude: Mapping the Emergence of Intersex Political Activism." Stryker and Whittle 300–314. Print.

---. Letter. "Intersexual Rights." *The Sciences* (July/August 1993): n.p. Print.

---. "Portrait Cheryl Chase." Feinberg *Warrior* 88-93. Print.

---. "What Is the Agenda of the Intersex Patient Advocacy Movement?" *Endocrinologist* 13.3 (2003): 240–2. Print.

Chase, Cheryl, and Martha Coventry, eds. Intersexuality. Spec. issue of *Chrysalis: The Journal of Transgressive Gender Identities* 2.5 (1997): 1–57. Print.

Châtelet, Noëlle. *La Tête en Bas*. Paris: Seuil, 2003. Print.

---. *Mit dem Kopf Zuerst*. Köln: KiWi-Taschenbuch, 2004. Print.

Chesnet, […]. "The Question of Identity; the Malformation of the External Genital Organs; Hypospadias; an Error About Sex." 1860. Barbin, *Memoirs* 124-128.

Clement, Sarah. "Female Flaneur: Outsider to Flanerie." *The Image of the Outsider in Literature, Media, and Society*. Eds. Will Wright and Steven Kaplan. Pueblo: Society for the Interdisciplinary Study of Social Imagery, University of Southern Colorado, 2002. 289–92. Print.

Colapinto, John. *As Nature Made Him. The Boy Who Was Raised as a Girl*. New York: HarperCollins, 2000. Print.

---. "Gender Gap." *Slate Magazine* 3 June 2004. Web. 8 May 2015.

---. "The True Story of John/Joan." *Rolling Stone* 12 Nov. 1997: 54–97. Print.

Collado-Rodríguez, Francisco. "Of Self and Country: U.S. Politics, Cultural Hybridity, and Ambivalent Identity in Jeffrey Eugenides's *Middlesex*." *International Fiction Review* 33.1-2 (2006): 71–83. Print.

Connolly, William E. "Voices from the Whirlwind." *In the Nature of Things: Language, Politics, and the Environment*. Eds. Jane Bennett and William Chaloupka. Minneapolis: U of Minnesota P, 1993. 197–225. Print.

Consortium on the Management of Disorders of Sex Development. *Clinical Guidelines for the Management of Disorders of Sex Development in Childhood*. Whitehouse Station: Accord Alliance, 2008. Print.

---. *Handbook for Parents*. Whitehouse Station: Accord Alliance, 2006. Print.

Coole, Diana, and Samantha Frost, eds. *New Materialisms: Ontology, Agency, and Politics*. Durham: Duke UP Books, 2010. Print.

Crapanzano, Vincent. "'Self'-Centering Narratives." *The Yale Journal of Criticism: Interpretation in the Humanities* 5.3 (1992): 61–79. Print.

Creighton, Sarah, J. Alderson, S. Brown, and C. L. Minto. "Medical Photography: Ethics, Consent and the Intersex Patient." *BJU International* 89.1 (2002): 67–71. Print.

Creighton, Sarah, Julie Greenberg, Katrina Roen, and Del La Grace Volcano. "Intersex Practice, Theory, and Activism. A Roundtable Discussion." Morland *GLQ* 249–260.

Culler, Jonathan. *Literary Theory: A Very Short Introduction*. Oxford: Oxford UP, 2000. Print.

Curtin, Amanda. *The Sinkings*. Crawley: U of Western Australia P, 2008. Print.

Cvetkovich, Ann. *An Archive of Feelings: Trauma, Sexuality, and Lesbian Public Cultures*. Duke UP, 2003. Print.

Daston, Lorraine, and Katharine Park. "The Hermaphrodite and the Orders of Nature: Sexual Ambiguity in Early Modern France." *GLQ: A Journal of Lesbian and Gay Studies* 1.4 (1995): 419–438. Print.

Delarue-Mardrus, Lucie. *The Angel and the Perverts*. ('L'Ange et les Pervers') 1930. Trans. Anna Livia. New York: New York UP, 1995. Print.

Delcourt, Marie. *Hermaphrodite: Myths and Rites of the Bisexual Figure in Classical Antiquity*. Trans. Jennifer Nicholson. London: Studio Books, 1961. Print.

Deutscher Ethikrat. *Intersexualität: Stellungnahme*. Berlin: Dt. Ethikrat, 2012. Print.

Diamond, Milton. "Sexual Identity, Monozygotic Twins Reared in Discordant Sex Roles and a BBC Follow-Up." *Archives of Sexual Behavior* 11.2 (1982): 181-185. Print.

Diamond, Milton, and H. Keith Sigmundson. "Sex Reassignment at Birth: Long Term Review and Clinical Implications." *Archives of Pediatrics and Adolescent Medicine* 151 (1997): 298–304. Print.

Diderot, Denis, and Jean le Rond d' Alembert, eds. "Hermaphrodite." *Encyclopédie, ou Dictionnaire Raisonné des Sciences, des Arts et des Métiers, etc*. 2013. Web. 8 May 2015.

Dobkin, Marjorie Housepian. *The Smyrna Affair*. New York: Harcourt Brace Jovanovich, 1971. Print.

Dobler, Jens, ed. *Prolegomena zu Magnus Hirschfelds Jahrbuch für Sexuelle Zwischenstufen (1899-1923): Register, Editionsgeschichte, Inhaltsbeschreibungen*. Hamburg: von Bockel, 2004. Print. Schriftenreihe der Magnus-Hirschfeld-Gesellschaft 11.

Dolphijn, Rick, and Iris van der Tuin. *New Materialism: Interviews & Cartographies*. Ann Arbor: MPublishing, University of Michigan Library, 2012. Print.

Donoghue, Emma. "Imagined More Than Women: Lesbians as Hermaphrodites, 1671-1766." *Women's History Review* 2.2 (1993): 199–216. Print.

Downing, Lisa, Morland, Iain, and Sullivan, Nikki. *Fuckology: Critical Essays on John Money's Concepts*. Chicago: U of Chicago P, 2014. Print.

Draesner, Ulrike. Interview by Fridtjof Küchemann. "Über den Körper schreiben." *Frankfurter Allgemeine Zeitung*. 9 May 2002. Web. 15 Aug. 2014.

---. *Mitgift*. München: Luchterhand Verlag, 2002. Print.

Dreger, Alice, ed. Intersexuality. Spec. issue *The Journal of Clinical Ethics* 9.4 (1998). Print.

---. "Doctors Containing Hermaphrodites: The Victorian Legacy." Chase and Coventry 15-22.

---. *Hermaphrodites and the Medical Invention of Sex*. London: Harvard UP, 1998. Print.

---, ed. *Intersex in the Age of Ethics*. Hagerstown: University Publishing Group, 1999. Print.

---. "Shifting the Paradigm of Intersex Treatment" *Intersex Society of North America*. 2003. Web. 25 Mar. 2014.

Dreger, Alice, C. Chase, A. Sousa, P. A. Gruppuso, and J. Frader. "Changing the Nomenclature/Taxonomy for Intersex: A Scientific and Clinical Rationale." *Journal of Pediatric Endocrinology and Metabolism* 18 (2005): 729–33. Print.

Dreger, Alice, and April M. Herndon. "Progress and Politics in the Intersex Rights Movement: Feminist Theory in Action." Morland *GLQ* 199–224.

Eckert, Lena [Christina Annalena]. *Intervening in Intersexualization: The Clinic and the Colony*. Diss. Utrecht University, 2010. dspace.library.uu.nl. Web. 15 Sept. 2014.

Ellis, Havelock. *Studies in the Psychology of Sex*. Vol I - VI. 1897-1928. Project Gutenberg. Web. 13 May 2015.

Epstein, Julia. *Altered Conditions: Disease, Medicine, and Storytelling*. New York: Routledge, 1995. Print.

---. "Either/Or—Neither/Both: Sexual Ambiguity and the Ideology of Gender." *Genders* 7 (1990): 99–142. Print.

Eugenides, Jeffrey. Interview. "A Conversation With Jeffrey Eugenides." *Oprah* 6 May 2007. Web. 27 Aug. 2014.

---. Interview by Bram van Moorhem. "The Novel as a Mental Picture of Its Era." *3 A.M. Magazine*, 2003. Web. 11 May 2015.

---. Interview by Geraldine Bedell. "He's Not like Other Girls." *The Guardian* 6 Oct. 2002. Web. 26 Aug. 2014.

---. Interview by Jonathan Safran Foer. *Bomb Magazine* 81.Fall (2002): 75–80. Print.

---. Interview by Laura Miller. "Interview with Jeffrey Eugenides." *Salon* 16 Oct. 2002. Web. 20 Aug. 2014.

---. Interview. "Q&A With Jeffrey Eugenides." *Oprah* 6 May 2007. Web. 27 Aug. 2014.

---. *Middlesex*. London: Bloomsbury, 2003. Print.

---. *The Virgin Suicides*. London: Bloomsbury, 1993. Print.

Faden, Ruth, and Tom Beauchamp. *A History and Theory of Informed Consent*. New York: Oxford UP, 1986. Print.

Faderman, Lillian. *Surpassing the Love of Men: Romantic Friendship & Love Between Women from the Renaissance to the Present*. New York: Harper, 2001. Print.

Faderman, Lillian, and Brigitte Eriksson, eds. *Lesbian-Feminism in Turn-of-the-Century Germany (Stories and Autobiographies)*. Weatherby Lake: Naiad Press, 1980. Print.

---. *Lesbians in Germany: 1890's-1920's*. Tallahassee: Naiad Press, 1990. Print.

Faking It. Dir. Carter Covington. MTV, 2014. Television series.

Fausto-Sterling, Anne. "How Many Sexes Are There?" *The New York Times* 3 Dec. 1993: n.p. Web.

---. *Myths of Gender: Biological Theories about Women and Men*. New York: Basic Books, 1985. Print.

---. Reply to letters of readers. *The Sciences* (July/August 1993): n.p. Print.

---. *Sexing the Body: Gender Politics and the Construction of Sexuality*. New York: Basic Books, 2000. Print.

---. "The Five Sexes, Revisited." *The Sciences* 40.4 (July/August 2000): 18–23. Print.

---. "The Five Sexes: Why Male and Female Are Not Enough." *The Sciences* (March/April 1993): n.p. Print.

Feder, Ellen K. "Imperatives of Normality: From 'Intersex' to 'Disorders of Sex Development.'" Morland *GLQ* 225–247.

Federal Prohibition of Female Genital Mutilation Act of 1995. Congress.gov, 1995-6. Web. 10 May 2015.

Feinberg, Leslie. *Transgender Warriors: Making History from Joan of Arc to Dennis Rodman*. Boston: Beacon Press: 1996. Print.

---. *Trans Liberation: Beyond Pink or Blue*. Boston: Beacon Press, 1999. Print.

Feldherr, Andrew. "Metamorphosis in the Metamorphosis." Hardie 163–79.

Felman, Shoshana. "Education and Crisis, or the Vicissitudes of Teaching." *Testimony: Crises of Witnessing in Literature, Psychoanalysis, and History*. Shoshana Felman and Dori Laub. New York: Routledge, 1992. 1–56. Print.

Flanagan, Mary. *Adèle*. New York: W.W. Norton, 1997. Print.

---. *Das Begehren der Anderen*. Berlin: Ullstein, 1998. Print.

Foucault, Michel. *Abnormal: Lectures at the Collège de France 1974-1975*. Ed. Arnold I. Davidson. Trans. Graham Burchell. London: Verso, 2003. Print.

---. *Discipline and Punish: The Birth of the Prison*. Trans. Alan Sheridan. New York: Vintage Books, 1995. Print.

---. Introduction. Barbin *Memoirs* vii-xvii.

---. "The Discourse on Language." *The Archaeology of Knowledge and the Discourse on Language*. Trans. Alan Mark Sheridan-Smith. New York: Pantheon Books, 1972. 215–237. Print.

---. *The History of Sexuality, Vol I: The Will to Knowledge*. New York: Vintage, 1990. Print.

---. "The Subject and Power." *Michel Foucault: Beyond Structuralism and Hermeneutics*. Ed. Hubert L. Dreyfus, and Paul Rabinow. Chicago: U of Chicago P, 1983. 208–26. Print.

---. "Truth and Power." *Power/Knowledge: Selected Interviews and Other Writings, 1972-1977*. Ed. Colin Gordon. New York: Pantheon Books, 1980. 109–133. Print.

---. "Two Lectures." *Power/Knowledge: Selected Interviews and Other Writings, 1972-1977*. Ed. Colin Gordon. New York: Pantheon Books, 1980. 78–108. Print.

---. "What Is an Author?" *The Foucault Reader: An Introduction to Foucault's Thought*. Ed. Paul Rabinow. London: Penguin Books, 1991. 101–120. Print.

Freud, Sigmund. *Beyond the Pleasure Principle*. Trans. James Strachey. Seattle: Pacific Publishing Studio, 2010. Print.

Freud, Sigmund, and Josef Breuer. *Studien über Hysterie*. Frankfurt/Main: Fischer TB, 2011. Print.

Garber, Eric, and Lyn Paleo. *Uranian Worlds: A Guide to Alternative Sexuality in Science Fiction, Fantasy, and Horror*. Boston: G. K. Hall, 1990. Print.

Genette, Gérard. *Palimpsests: Literature in the Second Degree*. Trans. Channa Newman and Claude Doubinsky. Lincoln: U of Nebraska P, 1997. Print.

Gender Identity, Gender Expression and Sex Characteristics Act. Act XI of 2015. Chapter 540, 1-7. Malta, 1 April 2015. Socialdialogue.gov.mt. Web. 13 May 2015.

Ghattas, Dan Christian. *Human Rights between the Sexes: A Preliminary Study on the Life Situations of Inter*individuals*. Trans. Adrian de Silva. Berlin: Heinrich-Böll-Stiftung, 2013. Print. Heinrich Böll Foundation. Publication Series on Democracy 34.

Gilbert, Ruth. *Early Modern Hermaphrodites: Sex and Other Stories*. New York: Palgrave, 2002. Print.

Giles, Jacob. *Tractus de Hermaphrodites; Or, A Treatise of Hermaphrodites*. London: E. Curll, 1718. Project Gutenberg. Web. 8 May 2015.

Gilman, Sander L. Preface. "Whose Body Is It Anyway? Hermaphrodites, Gays, and Jews in N.O. Body's Germany." Body *Maiden Years* vii-xxiv.

Goldie, Terrie. *The Man Who Invented Gender: Engaging the Ideas of John Money*. Vancouver: U of British Columbia P, 2014. Print. Sexuality Studies Series.

Goujon, E. "A Study of Incomplete Hermaphroditism in a Man." 1869. Barbin *Memoirs* 128-144

Graf, Fritz. "Myth in Ovid." Hardie 108–21.

Graham, Allen, *Intertextuality*. New York: Routledge, 2011. Print. The New Critical Idiom.

Green, Annie. "My Beautiful Clitoris." Chase and Coventry 12.

Gregor, Anja. *Constructing Intersex: Intergeschlechtlichkeit als Soziale Kategorie*. Bielefeld: transcript, 2015. Print. Soma Studies 2.

Groneberg, Michael. "Mythen und Wissen zur Intersexualität - Eine Analyse Relevanter Begriffe, Vorstellungen und Diskurse." *Zwitter beim Namen Nennen: Intersexualität zwischen Pathologie, Selbstbestimmung und Leiblicher Erfahrung*. Eds. Kathrin Zehnder, and Michael Groneberg. Bielefeld: transcript, 2010. 83–144. Print. Gender Studies.

Groveman, S. A. "The Hanukkah Bush: Ethical Implications in the Clinical Management of Intersex." Dreger *Clinical Ethics* 356–359.

Gur, Batya. *So habe ich es mir nicht vorgestellt*. ('Lo Kach Tearti Li'). München: Goldmann, 1998. Print.

Haeberle, Erwin. "Justitias Zweischneidiges Schwert - Magnus Hirschfeld als Gutachter in der Eulenburg-Affäre." *Sexualität zwischen Medizin und Recht*. Ed. Klaus Beier. Stuttgart: Gustav Fischer, 1991. 5–20. Archiv für Sexualwissenschaft. Web. 8 May 2015.

Hahn, Barbara. *Unter Falschem Namen: Von der Schwierigen Autorschaft der Frauen*. Frankfurt/Main: Suhrkamp Verlag, 1991. Print.

Halberstam, J. Jack. *Female Masculinity*. Durham: Duke UP, 1998. Print.

---. *In a Queer Time and Place: Transgender Bodies, Subcultural Lives*. New York: New York UP, 2005. Print.

Halperin, David M. "Achilles and Patroclus." *The Oxford Classical Dictionary*. Ed. Simon Hornblower, and Antony Spawforth. 1999. Print.

Hampson, Joan. "Hermaphroditic Genital Appearance, Rearing and Eroticism in Hyperadrenocorticism." *Bulletin of the Johns Hopkins Hospital* 96.6 (1955): 265–273. Print.

Hampson, John, Joan Hampson, and John Money. "The Syndrome of Gonadal Agenesis (Ovarian Agenesis) and Male Chromosomal Pattern in Girls and Women: Psychologic Studies." *Bulletin of the Johns Hopkins Hospital* 97.3 (1955): 207–226. Print.

Haraway, Donna. "A Manifesto for Cyborgs: Science, Technology, and Socialist Feminism in the 1980s." *The Haraway Reader*. New York: Routledge, 2004. 7–45. Print.

Hardie, Philip R. Introduction. Hardie 1–12.

---, ed. *The Cambridge Companion to Ovid*. Cambridge: Cambridge UP, 2006. Print.

Hard, Robin. *The Routledge Handbook of Greek Mythology: Based on H. J. Rose's Handbook of Greek Mythology*. New York: Routledge, 2008. Print.

Harper, Catherine. *Intersex*. Oxford: Berg, 2007. Print.

Harrison, Stephen. "Ovid and Genre: Evolutions of an Elegist." Hardie 79–94.

Hartmann, Andreas. "Im Falschen Geschlecht. Männliche Scheinzwitter um 1900." *Der Falsche Körper. Beiträge zu einer Geschichte der Monstrositäten*. Ed. Michael Hagner. Göttingen: Wallstein, 1995. 187–220. Print.

Hart, Phoebe. "Orchids, Intersex and the Auto/Biographical Project." *Studies in Documentary Film* 7.1 (2013): 79–91. Print.

---, dir. *Orchids: My Intersex Adventure*. Hartflicker Moving Pictures, 2010. Film.

Hassan, Ihab. "Toward a Concept of Postmodernism." *The Postmodern Turn: Essays in Postmodern Theory and Culture*. Columbus: Ohio State UP, 1987. 84–96. Print.

Hausen, Karin. "Family and Role-Division. The Polarization of Sexual Stereotypes in the Nineteenth Century. An Aspect of Dissociation of Work and Family Life." *Social History of the Family in Nineteenth and Twentieth Centuries Germany*. Ed. Richard Evans and W. R. Lee. London: Croom Helm, 1981. 51–83. Print.

Hausman, Bernice L. *Changing Sex: Transsexualism, Technology, and the Idea of Gender*. Durham: Duke UP Books, 1995. Print.

---. "Do Boys Have to Be Boys? Gender, Narrativity, and the John/Joan Case." *NWSA Journal* 12.3 (2000): 114–138. Print.

Hedwig and the Angry Inch. Dir. John Cameron Mitchell. Killer Films, and New Line Cinema, 2001. DVD.

"Hermaphroditus." *The Encyclopædia Britannica: A Dictionary of Arts, Sciences, Literature and General Information*. 11th ed. 1911. Wikisource. Web. 14 Aug. 2014.

Herbert, Marilyn. *Bookclub-In-A-Box Discusses Middlesex, a Novel by Jeffrey Eugenides. The Complete Guide for Readers and Leaders*. S.l.: Bookclub in a Box, 2005. Print.

Hermaphrodites Speak! Dir. Cheryl Chase, and Intersex Society of North America. N.p., 1995. Film.

Hermaphrodites with Attitude. Newsletter by the Intersex Society of North America. Winter 1995–Winter 2005. *Isna.org*. Web. 13 May 2015.

Herrn, Rainer. "Magnus Hirschfeld, sein Institut für Sexualwissenschaft und die Bücherverbrennung." *Mitteilungen der Magnus-Hirschfeld-Gesellschaft* 39-40 (2008): 18–22. Print.

Herzer, Manfred. *Magnus Hirschfeld Leben und Werk eines Jüdischen, Schwulen und Sozialistischen Sexologen*. Frankfurt/Main: Campus, 1992. Print.

Hester, J. David. "Intersex and the Rhetorics of Healing." Sytsma 47–71.

---. "Rhetoric of the Medical Management of Intersexed Children. New Insights into 'Disease', 'Curing', 'Illness' and 'Healing.'" *Genders OnLine Journal* 38 (2003): n.p. Web. 8 May 2015.

Hillman, Thea. *Depending on the Light*. San Francisco: Manic D Press, 2001. Print.

---. *Intersex (for Lack of a Better Word)*. San Francisco: Manic D Press, 2008. Print.

---. Interview. "Thea Hillman: The Inner Sanctum of Intersex." 11 Dec. 2008, *Jewcy*. Web. 11 May 2015.

Hirschfeld, Magnus. "Die Intersexuelle Konstitution." *Jahrbuch für Sexuelle Zwischenstufen, Band I. Auswahl aus den Jahrgängen 1899 - 1923*. Ed. Wolfgang Johann Schmidt. Frankfurt/Main: Qumran-Verlag, 1984. 9–26. Print.

---. "Die Objektive Diagnose der Homosexualität." *Jahrbuch für Sexuelle Zwischenstufen unter besonderer Berücksichtigung der Homosexualität* 1.1. Ed. Wissenschaftlich-humanitäres Comitée. Leipzig: Max Spohr, 1899. 4–35. Print.

---. "Drei Fälle von Irrtümlicher Geschlechtsbestimmung." *Medizinische Reform. Wochenzeitschrift für Soziale Medizin, Hygiene und Medizinalstatistik* 14.51 (1906): 614–17. Print.

---. Epilogue. Body *Maiden Years* 109-11.

---. *Sappho und Sokrates: Wie Erklärt sich die Liebe der Männer und Frauen zu Personen des Eigenen Geschlechts?* Leipzig: Spohr, 1922. Print.

---. *Von Einst bis Jetzt. Geschichte einer Homosexuellen Bewegung, 1897-1922*. Eds. Manfred Herzer, and James Steakley. Berlin: Verlag Rosa Winkel, 1986. Print.

Hochstetter, Gustav (H. O. Chstetter). "Aus Eines Mannes Dienstmädchenjahren." *Lustige Blätter: Schönstes Buntes Witzblatt Deutschlands* 22.28 (1907): n.p. Print.
Hoenes, Josch and Michael_a Koch. Einleitung. Trans*fer und* Inter*aktion*. Hoenes/Koch (eds.). 7-22.
Hoenes, Josch and Michael_a Koch (eds.). Trans*fer und* Inter*aktion: Wissenschaft und Aktivismus an den Grenzen heteronormativer Zweigeschlechtlichkeit*. Oldenburg: BIS Verlag, 2017. Oldenburger Beiträge zur Geschlechterforschung 15. Print.
Hofmann, Michael. *After Ovid: New Metamorphoses*. New York: Farrar, Straus and Giroux, 1996. Print.
Holmes, Morgan, ed. *Critical Intersex*. Farnham: Ashgate, 2009.
---. *Intersex: A Perilous Difference*. Cranbury: Associated UP, 2008. Print.
---. "In(to) Visibility: Intersexuality in the Field of Queer." Atkins 221–6.
---. "Is Growing up in Silence Better Than Growing up Different?" Chase and Coventry 7–9.
---. "Portrait." Feinberg *Warrior* 139.
Holmqvist, Sam M.. "Könsväxlingar: Nedslag. Svensk Translitteraturhistoria 1800-1900." Thesis. Uppsala Universitet, 2014. Web.
Hornblower, Simon, Antony Spawforth, and Esther Eidinow. *The Oxford Classical Dictionary*. Oxford: Oxford UP, 2012. Print.
Howe, Julia Ward. *The Hermaphrodite*. Ed. Gary Williams. Lincoln: U of Nebraska P, 2009. Print.
Hsu, Stephanie. "Ethnicity and the Biopolitics of Intersex in Jeffrey Eugenides's *Middlesex*." *MELUS: The Journal of the Society for the Study of the Multi-Ethnic Literature of the United States* 36.3 (2011): 87–110. Print.
Hutcheon, Linda. *A Poetics of Postmodernism: History, Theory, Fiction*. New York: Routledge, 1988. Print.
---. *The Politics of Postmodernism*. New York: Routledge, 2002. Print.
Hutcheon, Linda, and Joseph Natoli, eds. *A Postmodern Reader*. Albany: State U of New York P, 1993. Print.
Imperato-McGinley, Julianne, R. E. Peterson, T. Gautier, and E. Sturla. "Androgens and the Evolution of Male-Gender Identity among Male Pseudohermaphrodites with 5α-Reductase Deficiency." *New England Journal of Medicine* 300.22 (1979): 1233–7. Print.

Internationale Vereinigung Intergeschlechtlicher Menschen. "IVIM - OII-Deutschland." *OII-Deutschland (IVIM)*. Web. 6 Jan. 2015.

Intersex Society of North America. "DSD Symposium 2006 (Proceedings)." *ISNA*. Web. 5 Mar. 2015.

---. "What Does ISNA Do?" *ISNA*. Web. 5 Mar. 2015.

---. "Why Is ISNA Using 'DSD'?." *ISNA*. 24 May 2006. Web. 5 Mar. 2015.

Isau, Ralf. *Die Galerie der Lügen*. Bergisch Gladbach: Bastei Lübbe, 2007. Print.

Jagose, Annamarie. *Queer Theory: An Introduction*. New York: New York UP, 1997. Print.

James, Edward. *The Cambridge Companion to Science Fiction*. Cambridge: Cambridge UP, 2003. Print.

Judd, Catherine. "Male Pseudonyms and Female Authority in Victorian England." *Literature in the Marketplace: Nineteenth-Century British Publishing and Reading Practices*. Eds. John O. Jordan and Robert L. Patten. Cambridge: Cambridge UP, 1995. 250–68. Print.

Jungblut, Peter. *Famose Kerle: Eulenburg - eine Wilhelminische Affäre*. Hamburg: MännerschwarmSkript, 2003. Print.

Kaldera, Raven. "Agdistis' Children: Living Bi-Gendered in a Single-Gendered World." Atkins 227–32.

Kampmann, Renate. *Fremdkörper: Ein Leonie-Simon-Roman*. Reinbek: rororo, 2007. Print.

Kaplan, Marion A. *The Making of the Jewish Middle Class: Women, Family, and Identity in Imperial Germany*. New York: Oxford UP, 1991. Print.

Karkazis, Katrina Alicia. *Fixing Sex: Intersex, Medical Authority, and Lived Experience*. Durham: Duke UP, 2008. Print.

Katz, Jonathan Ned. *Gay/Lesbian Almanac: A New Documentary*. New York: Harper & Row, 1983. Print.

---. *The Invention of Heterosexuality*. Chicago: U of Chicago P, 2007. Print.

Keilson-Lauritz, Marita. "Zur 'Inneren' Geschichte des Jahrbuchs für Sexuelle Zwischenstufen." Dobler 9–32.

Kempendorff, P. "Aus Eines Mannes Mädchenjahren." Review. *Der Türmer. Monatsschrift für Gemüt und Geist*. 9 (1907): 495–99. Print.

Kennedy, Hubert. *Karl Heinrich Ulrichs: Leben und Werk*. Hamburg: MännerschwarmSkript, 2001. Print.

---. *Ulrichs: The Life and Works of Karl Heinrich Ulrichs, Pioneer of the Modern Gay Movement*. Boston: Alyson Publications Inc, 1988. Print.
Kenney, E. J. Introduction. Ovid xiii–xxix.
Kessler, Suzanne J. *Lessons from the Intersexed*. New Jersey: Rutgers UP, 1998. Print.
---. Letter. *The Sciences* (July/August 1993): n.p. Print.
---. "The Medical Construction of Gender: Case Management of Intersexed Infants." *Signs* 16.1 (1990): 3–26. Print.
Kessler, Suzanne J., and Wendy McKenna. *Gender: An Ethnomethodological Approach*. Chicago: U of Chicago P, 1978. Print.
Kilian, Eveline. *GeschlechtSverkehrt: Theoretische und Literarische Perspektiven des Gender-bending*. Königstein/Taunus: Ulrike Helmer, 2004. Print.
Kinsey, Alfred C., Wardell B. Pomeroy, Clyde E. Martin, and Paul H. Gebhard. *Sexual Behavior in the Human Female*. 1953. Bloomington: Indiana UP, 1998. Print.
Kinsey, Alfred C., Wardell B. Pomeroy, and Clyde E. Martin. *Sexual Behavior in the Human Male*. 1948. Bloomington: Indiana UP, 1998. Print.
Kirchhofer, Anton. "The Foucault Complex: A Review of Foucauldian Approaches in Literary Studies." *Zeitschrift für Anglistik und Amerikanistik* 45.4 (1997): 277–299. Print.
Klöppel, Ulrike. "Zur Aktualität Kosmetischer Operationen 'uneindeutiger' Genitalien im Kindesalter." *Bulletin Zentrum für Transdisziplinäre Geschlechterstudien* 42 (2016): n. pag. Web.
---. "Die Experimentelle Formierung von Gender zwischen Erziehung und Biologie. Der John/Joan-Fall." *Sexualität als Experiment. Identität, Lust und Reproduktion zwischen Science und Fiction*. Eds. Nicolas Pethes, and Silke Schicktanz. Frankfurt: Campus, 2008. 71–90. Print.
---. *XX0XY Ungelöst: Hermaphroditismus, Sex und Gender in der Deutschen Medizin; eine Historische Studie zur Intersexualität*. Bielefeld: transcript, 2010. Print.
Koch, Michaela. "Niemand will's gewesen sein: Strategien autobiographischen Schreibens und literaturwissenschaftlicher Forschung zu Intergeschlechtlichkeit am Beispiel von N.O. Bodys *Aus eines Mannes Mädchenjahren*." *Transfer und Interaktion*. Hoenes/Koch (eds.), 291-304.

---. "Das geständige Geschlecht. Selbst- und Fremdpositionierungen im 'Fall' Herculine Barbin." *Inter*geschlechtliche Körperlichkeiten – Diskurs/Begegnungen im Erzähltext*. Eds. Angelika Baier, and Susanne Hochreither. Wien: zaglossus verlag, 2014. 193-214. Print.

Koch-Rein, A. Anson. "Intersexuality-In the 'I' of the Norm? Queer Field Notes from Eugenides' *Middlesex*." *Quer durch die Geisteswissenschaften: Perspektiven der Queer Theory*. Eds. Elahe Haschemi Yekani, and Beatrice Michaelis. Berlin: Querverlag, 2005. 238–52.

Koyama, Emi. "Intersex Initiative: DSD Controversy FAQ." *Intersex Initiative*. 29 June 2008. Web. 5 Mar. 2015.

Krafft-Ebing, Richard von. *Psychopathia Sexualis: The Case Histories*. 1886. Chicago: Solar Books, 2011. Print.

Krämer, Fabian. "'Under so viel wunderbarlichen und seltsamen Sachen ist mir nichts wunderbarlichers und seltsamers fürkommen.' Vom 'Auftauchen' des Hermaphroditen in der Frühen Neuzeit." *1-0-1 [one 'o one] intersex. Das Zwei-Geschlechter-System als Menschenrechtsverletzung*. Eds. Neue Gesellschaft für Bildende Kunst e.V., and AG 1-0-1 intersex. Berlin: NGBK Neue Gesellschaft für Bildende Kunst, 2005. 150–157. Print.

Kristeva, Julia. "Word, Dialogue, and Novel." *Desire in Language: A Semiotic Approach to Literature and Art*. Eds. Leon S. Roudiez, and Alice Jardine. Trans. Thomas Gora. New York: Columbia UP, 1980. 64–90. Print.

Kwa, Lydia. *The Walking Boy*. Toronto: Key Porter, 2005. Print.

Lakshmanan, Joseph L. Letter. *The Sciences* (July/August 1993): n.p. Print.

Lambda Literary Awards. "Overview of LLF Awards." *Lambda Literary*. Web. 18 Aug. 2014.

Lanser, Susan Sniader. *Fictions of Authority: Women Writers and Narrative Voice*. Ithaca: Cornell UP, 1992. Print.

Laqueur, Thomas. *Making Sex: Body and Gender from the Greeks to Freud*. Cambridge: Harvard UP, 1992. Print.

Larbalestier, Justine. *The Battle of the Sexes in Science Fiction*. Middletown: Wesleyan UP, 2002. Print. The Wesleyan Early Classics of Science Fiction Series.

Laub, Dori. "Bearing Witness, or the Vicissitudes of Listening." *Testimony: Crises of Witnessing in Literature, Psychoanalysis and History*.

Shoshana Felman and Dori Laub. New York: Routledge, 1992. 57–74. Print.

Lee, Peter, Christopher Houk, Faisal Ahmed, and Ieuan Hughes. "Consensus Statement on Management of Intersex Disorders." *Pediatrics* 118.2 (2006): e488–e500. Print.

Le Guin, Ursula K. *The Left Hand of Darkness*. New York: Ace Books, 1987. Print.

Lejeune, Philippe. *On Autobiography*. Ed. Paul John Eakin. Minneapolis: U of Minnesota P, 1995. Print. Theory and History of Literature 52.

Lewis, Justin. *The Ideological Octopus: Exploration of Television and Its Audience*. New York: Routledge, 1991. Print.

Leys, Ruth. *Trauma: A Genealogy*. Chicago: U of Chicago P, 2000. Print.

Lyotard, Jean-François. *The Postmodern Condition: A Report on Knowledge*. Minneapolis: University of Minnesota Press, 1984. Print. Theory and History of Literature v. 10.

Mak, Geertje. "'So We Must Go behind Even What the Microscope Can Reveal': The Hermaphrodite's 'Self' in Medical Discourse at the Start of the Twentieth Century." *GLQ: A Journal of Lesbian and Gay Studies* 11.1 (2005): 65–94. Print.

Mann, Franziska. "Aus Eines Mannes Mädchenjahren." Review. *Frauen-Rundschau* 8 (1907): 493–4. Print.

Mann, Jenny C. "How to Look at a Hermaphrodite in Early Modern England." *SEL Studies in English Literature 1500-1900* 46.1 (2006): 67–91. Print.

Mehlmann, Sabine. *Unzuverlässige Körper: Zur Diskursgeschichte des Konzepts Geschlechtlicher Identität*. Königstein/Taunus: Ulrike Helmer Verlag, 2006. Print.

Melzer, Patricia. *Alien Constructions: Science Fiction and Feminist Thought*. Austin: U of Texas P, 2006. Print.

Mendelsohn, Daniel. "Mighty Hermaphrodite." Review of *Middlesex* by Jeffrey Eugenides. *The New York Review of Books* 7 Nov. 2002. Web. 26 Aug. 2014.

Méndez, Juan E. "Report of the Special Rapporteur on Torture and Other Cruel, Inhuman or Degrading Treatment or Punishment. (A/HRC/22/53)." Ed. UN Human Rights Council. 1 Feb. 2013. Web. 9 Jan. 2015.

Merzbach, Georg. "Bücherbesprechungen: Aus Eines Mannes Mädchenjahren." Review. *Monatsschrift für Harnkrankheiten, Psychopathia Sexualis und Sexuelle Hygiene* (1908): 101–2. Print.
Mildenberger, Florian. "Diskursive Deckungsgleichheit – Hermaphroditismus und Homosexualität im Medizinischen Diskurs (1850-1960)." *Medizin, Geschichte und Geschlecht: Körperhistorische Rekonstruktionen von Identitäten und Differenzen*. Eds. Frank Stahnisch, and Florian Steger. Stuttgart: Franz Steiner, 2005. 259–84. Print. Geschichte und Philosophie der Medizin.
Money, John. "Ablatio Penis: Normal Male Infant Sex-Reassigned as a Girl." *Archives of Sexual Behavior* 4.1 (1975): 65–71. Print.
---. *A First Person History of Pediatric Psychoendocrinology*. New York: Kluwer Academic/Plenum Pub., 2002. Print.
---. *Gendermaps: Social Constructionism, Feminism, and Sexosophical History*. New York: Continuum, 1995. Print.
---. "Hermaphroditism, Gender and Precocity in Hyperadrenocorticism: Psychologic Findings." *Bulletin of the Johns Hopkins Hospital* 96.6 (1955): 253–264. Print.
---. Letter.*The Sciences* (July/August 1993): n.p. Print.
---. *Principles of Developmental Sexology*. New York: Continuum, 1997. Print.
---. *Reinterpreting the Unspeakable: Human Sexuality 2000: The Complete Interviewer and Clinical Biographer, Exigency Theory, and Sexology for the Third Millennium*. New York: Continuum, 1994. Print.
---. "Serendipities on the Sexological Pathway to Research in Gender Identity and Sex Reassignment." *Journal of Psychology & Human Sexuality* 4.1 (1991): 101–113. Print.
---. *Sin, Science, and the Sex Police: Essays on Sexology & Sexosophy*. Amherst: Prometheus Books, 1998. Print.
---. *The Impresario. A Novel*. London: Bodley Head, 1959. Print.
---. *The Lovemap Guidebook: A Definitive Statement*. New York: Continuum, 1999. Print.
---. *Venuses Penuses: Sexology, Sexosophy, and Exigency Theory*. Buffalo: Prometheus Books, 1986. Print.
Money, John, and Anke A. Ehrhardt. *Man & Woman, Boy & Girl: Gender Identity from Conception to Maturity*. Baltimore: Johns Hopkins UP, 1972. Print.

Money, John, and Patricia Tucker. *Sexual Signatures: On Being a Man or a Woman*. Boston: Little Brown & Co, 1975. Print.

Money, John, Joan Hampson, and John Hampson. "An Examination of Some Basic Sexual Concepts: The Evidence of Human Hermaphroditism." *Bulletin of the Johns Hopkins Hospital* 97.4 (1955): 301–319. Print.

---. "Hermaphroditism: Recommendations Concerning Assignment of Sex, Change of Sex and Psychologic Management." *Bulletin of the Johns Hopkins Hospital* 97.4 (1955): 284–300. Print.

---. "Sexual Incongruities and Psychopathology: The Evidence of Human Hermaphroditism." *Bulletin of the Johns Hopkins Hospital* 98.1 (1956): 43–57. Print.

Moreno, Angela. "In America They Call Us Hermaphrodites." Chase and Coventry 11-12.

Morland, Iain. "Between Critique and Reform: Ways of Reading the Intersex Controversy." Holmes *Critical* 191–213.

---, ed. *Intersex and After*. Spec. issue of *GLQ: A Journal of Lesbian and Gay Studies* 15.2 (2009). 191–356. Print.

---. "Intersex Treatment and the Promise of Trauma." *Gender and the Science of Difference: Cultural Politics of Contemporary Science and Medicine*. Ed. Jill A. Fisher. New Brunswick: Rutgers UP, 2011. 147–163. Print. Studies in Modern Science, Technology, and the Environment.

---. "Intimate Violations: Intersex and the Ethics of Bodily Integrity." *Feminism and Psychology* 18.3 (2008): 425–30. Print.

---. "Introduction: Lessons from the Octopus." Morland *GLQ* 191–197.

---. "Plastic Man: Intersex, Humanism and the Reimer Case." *Subject Matters: A Journal of Communications and the Self* 3/4.2/1 (2007): 81–98. Print.

---. "Postmodern Intersex." Sytsma 319–32.

---. "The Injustice of Intersex: Feminist Science Studies and the Writing of a Wrong." *Toward a Critique of Guilt: Perspectives from Law and the Humanities*. Ed. Matthew Anderson. New York: JAI Elsevier, 2005. 53–75. Print.

---. "What Can Queer Theory Do for Intersex?" Morland *GLQ* 285–312.

---. "Why Five Sexes Are Not Enough." *The Ashgate Research Companion to Queer Theory*. Ed. Noreen Giffney and Michael O'Rourke. Farnham: Ashgate Publications, 2009. 33–48. Print.

muir, r. *Skin*. CreateSpace, 2009. Digital file.

Müller, Klaus. *Aber in Meinem Herzen Sprach eine Stimme so Laut: Homosexuelle Autobiographien und Medizinische Pathographien im Neunzehnten Jahrhundert*. Berlin: Männerschwarm Verlag, 1991. Print.

Nahman, Michal Rachel. "Embodied Stories, Pragmatic Lives: Intersex Body Narratives on the Net." MA Thesis. York University Toronto, 2000. Web.

Nancy, Jean-Luc, and Magali Le Mens. *L'hermaphrodite de Nadar*. Foto edition. Grâne: Creaphis Edition, 2009. Print.

Nandi, Jacinta. "Germany Got It Right by Offering a Third Gender Option on Birth Certificates." *The Guardian* 10 Nov. 2013. Web. 9 Jan. 2015.

Neugebauer, Franz Ludwig von. "Interessante Beobachtungen aus dem Gebiete des Scheinzwittertums." *Jahrbuch für sexuelle Zwischenstufen unter besonderer Berücksichtigung der Homosexualität* (1902): 31–40. Print.

---. *Hermaphroditismus beim Menschen*. Leipzig: Dr. Werner Klinkhardt, 1908. Print.

Neuhaus, Mareike. "Inventions of Sexuality in Kathleen Winter's *Annabel*." *Studies in Canadian Literature/Etudes en Littérature Canadienne* 37.1 (2012): 123–140. Print.

Neuman, Shirley, ed. *Autobiography and Questions of Gender*. London: Frank Cass Publishers, 1991. Print.

---. "Autobiography, Bodies, Manhood." Neuman *Autobiography* 137–65.

Nugent, Georgia. "This Sex Which Is Not One: De-Constructing Ovid's Hermaphrodite." *Differences: A Journal of Feminist Cultural Studies* 2.1 (1990): 160–85. Print.

Organization Intersex International – OII. *OII Intersex Network*. n.d. Web. 6 Jan. 2015.

Oudshoorn, Nelly. *Beyond the Natural Body: An Archaeology of Sex Hormones*. New York: Routledge, 1994. Print.

Ovid. *Metamorphoses*. Trans. A. D Melville. Oxford: Oxford UP, 2008. Print.

Pagonis, Pidgeon. "I Really Have to Go." *Advocates for Informed Choice Blog*, 24 Mar. 2015. Web. 18 Apr. 2015.

Paramaguru, Kharunya. "Germans Get a New Third Gender Option at Birth." *Time* 1 Nov. 2013. Web. 9 Jan. 2015.

Pare, Ambroise. *On Monsters and Marvels*. U of Chicago P, 1995. Print.

Parens, Erik, ed. *Surgically Shaping Children: Technology, Ethics, and the Pursuit of Normality*. Baltimore: Johns Hopkins UP, 2008. Print.

Peters, Kathrin. *Rätselbilder des Geschlechts: Körperwissen und Medialität um 1900*. Zürich: Diaphanes, 2010. Print.

Pinkus, Karen. "'Hermaphrodite Poetics.'" *Arcadia – International Journal for Literary Studies* 41.1 (2006): 91–111. Print.

Plato. *Symposium*. Trans. Robin Waterfield. Oxford: Oxford World's Classics, 2008. Print.

Porter, Roger J. "Figuration and Disfigurement: Herculine Barbin and the Autobiography of the Body." Neuman *Autobiography* 122–36.

Preves, Sharon E. *Intersex and Identity: The Contested Self*. New Brunswick, N.J: Rutgers University Press, 2003. Print.

Prosser, Jay. *Second Skins: The Body Narratives of Transsexuality*. New York: Columbia UP, 1998. Print.

Pryce-Jones, David. "Suburban Sympathies." Review of *The Impresario* by John Money. *The Times Literary Supplement* 13 Nov. 1959: 664. Print.

Ranalli, Gina. *Sky Tongues*. Portland: Swallowdown Press, 2009. Print.

Redick, Alison. "What Happened at Hopkins: The Creation of the Intersex Management Protocols." *Cardozo Journal of Law and Gender* 12.1 (2005): 289–96. Print.

Reese, James. *The Book of Shadows*. New York: Hartorch, 2002. Print.

---. "The Book of Shadows Q and A." jamesreesebooks.com, n.d. Web. 21 Aug. 2014.

Reichs, Kathy. *Bare Bones: A Novel*. New York: Scribner, 2003. Print.

Reis, Elizabeth. *Bodies in Doubt: An American History of Intersex*. Baltimore: Johns Hopkins UP, 2009. Print.

---. "Divergence or Disorder?: The Politics of Naming Intersex." *Perspectives in Biology and Medicine* 50.4 (2007): 535–543. *Project MUSE*. Web. 5 Mar. 2015.

Roen, Katrina. "Clinical Intervention and Embodied Subjectivity: Atypically Sexed Children and Their Parents." Holmes *Critical* 15–40.

Rolker, Christof. "Der Hermaphrodit und Seine Frau. Körper, Sexualität und Geschlecht im Spätmittelalter." *Historische Zeitschrift* 297.3 (2013): 593–620. Print.

Romano, Allen J. "The Invention of Marriage: Hermaphroditus and Salmacis at Halicarnassus and in Ovid." *The Classical Quarterly* 59.02 (2009): 543–561. Print.

Römer, Lucien Sophie Albert Marie von. "Vorläufige Mitteilungen über die Darstellung eines Schemas der Geschlechtsdifferenzierungen." *Jahrbuch für Sexuelle Zwischenstufen unter Besonderer Berücksichtigung der Homosexualität* 6 (1904): 327–356. Print.

Rosario, Vernon A. "Quantum Sex: Intersex and the Molecular Deconstruction of Sex." Morland *GLQ* 267–284.

Roscher, Wilhelm H. *Ausführliches Lexikon der Griechischen und Römischen Mythologie* 1.2. Leipzig: B.G. Teubner, 1884-6. Web. 10 May 2015.

Rousseau, Jean-Jacques. *Confessions*. Ed. Patrick Coleman. Trans. Angela Scholar. Oxford: Oxford UP, 2000. Print.

Rubin, David A. "'An Unnamed Blank That Craved a Name': A Genealogy of Intersex as Gender." *Signs* 37.4 (2012): 883–908. Web. 10 May 2015.

Runte, Annette. *Biographische Operationen. Diskurse der Transsexualität*. München: Wilhelm Fink Verlag, 1996. Print.

Saglimbeni, Fabio. "Cal(lie): The Hermaphrodite as an Outsider in *Middlesex* by Jeffrey Eugenides." *American Solitudes: Individual, National, Transnational*. Ed. Donatella Izzo, Giorgio Mariani, and Paola Zaccaria. Rome: Carocci, 2007. 176–83. Print.

Schneider, Robert. *Die Luftgängerin: Roman*. München: K. Blessing, 1998. Print.

---. *Schlafes Bruder*. 1992. Leipzig: Reclam, 2007. Print.

Schochow, Maximilian. "Aus 'Monstern' Bürger Machen. Chirurgische Interventionen an Hermaphroditischen Körpern." *Von Monstern und Menschen. Begegnungen der Anderen Art in Kulturwissenschaftlicher Perspektive*. Eds. Gunter Gebhard, Oliver Geisler, and Steffen Schröter. Bielefeld: transcript, 2009. 89–116. Print.

---. *Die Ordnung der Hermaphroditen-Geschlechter: Eine Genealogie des Geschlechtsbegriffs*. Berlin: Oldenbourg Akademieverlag, 2009. Print.

Schulz, Christian. *Paragraph 175 (Abgewickelt): Homosexualität und Strafrecht im Nachkriegsdeutschland*. Hamburg: Männerschwarm Verlag, 1994. Print.

Scott, Melissa. *Shadow Man*. Maple Shade: Lethe Press, 2009. Print.

Sedgwick, Eve Kosofsky. *Touching Feeling: Affect, Pedagogy, Performativity*. Durham: Duke UP, 2003. Print.
Sedgwick, Eve Kosofsky, and Adam Frank, eds. *Shame and Its Sisters: A Silvan Tomkins Reader*. Durham: Duke UP, 1995. Print.
Seer, Ursula. "'Dann Bist Du Wieder ein Ganz Normales Mädchen' Embodiment und Subjektivität in Intersexgeschichten." *Gender_queer Ethnografisch. Ausschnitte einer Schnittmenge*. Eds. Katrin Amelang, Beate Binder, Anika Keinz, and Sebastian Mohr. Berlin: Panama Verlag, 2010. 133–43. Print. Berliner Blätter. Ethnographische und Ethnologische Beiträge 54.
Senelick, Laurence. "Enlightened by Morphodites: Narratives of the Fairground Half-and-Half." *Amerikastudien/American Studies* 44.3 (1999): 357–78. Print.
Seyffert, Oskar. *Dictionary of Classical Antiquities*. London: S. Sonnenschein and Co., 1894. Web. 14 Aug. 2014.
Shostak, Debra. "'Theory Uncompromised by Practicality': Hybridity in Jeffrey Eugenides' *Middlesex*." *Contemporary Literature* 49.3 (2008): 383–412. Print.
Sifuentes, Zachary. "Strange Anatomy, Strange Sexuality: The Queer Body in Jeffrey Eugenides' *Middlesex*." *Straight Writ Queer: Non-Normative Expressions of Heterosexuality in Literature*. Eds. Richard Fantina, and Calvin Thomas. Jefferson: McFarland, 2006. 145–57. Print.
Sigusch, Volkmar. *Geschichte der Sexualwissenschaft*. Frankfurt: Campus, 2009. Print.
Silberman, Lauren. "Mythographic Transformations of Ovid's Hermaphrodite." *The Sixteenth Century Journal* 19.4 (1988): 643–652. Print.
Simon, Hermann. "In Search of Karl Baer." Body *Maiden Years* 113-136.
---. "N. O. Body und Kein Ende." *Jüdische Welten: Juden in Deutschland vom 18. Jahrhundert bis in die Gegenwart*. Eds. Marion Kaplan, and Beate Meyer. Göttingen: Wallstein, 2005. 225–30. Print.
---. "Wer War N. O. Body?" Body *Mädchenjahre* 167–246.
Smith, Sidonie, and Julia Watson. *Reading Autobiography: A Guide for Interpreting Life Narratives*. Minneapolis: U of Minnesota P, 2010. Print.
Smith, William. *Dictionary of Greek and Roman Biography and Mythology*. London: J. Murray, 1880. Web. 14 Aug. 2014.

Sophocles. *Oedipus*. London: Theatre Communications Gr, 2001. Print.
Spivak, Gayatri Chakravorty. "Subaltern Studies: Deconstructing Historiography." *Selected Subaltern Studies*. Eds. Ranajit Guha, and Gayatri Chakravorty Spivak. New York: Oxford UP, 1988. 3–33. Print.
Spörri, Myriam. "N. O. Body, Magnus Hirschfeld und die Diagnose des Geschlechts: Hermaphroditismus um 1900." *L'Homme* 14.2 (2003): 244–261. Print.
Spurgas, Alyson K. "(Un)Queering Identity: The Biosocial Production of Intersex/DSD." Holmes *Critical* 97–122.
Steakley, James. "Iconography of a Scandal: Political Cartoons and the Eulenburg Affair in Wilhelmine Germany." *Hidden from History: Reclaiming the Gay and Lesbian Past*. Eds. Martin Duberman, Martha Vicinus, and George Chauncey. New York: Plume, 1990. 233–63. Print.
---. *The Homosexual Emancipation Movement in Germany*. New York: Arno/Ayer, 1975. Print.
Steinachs Forschungen/Der Steinach-Film. Prod. Nicholas Kaufmann. Universum Film-AG, 1922/23. Film.
Stoller, Robert J. *Sex & Gender: On the Development of Masculinity & Femininity*. London: Karnac Books, 1994. Print.
Stone, James. "The Mirror of Hermaphroditus." *Style* 36.1 (2002): 169-96. Print.
Streuli, Jürg, Effy Vayena, Yvonne Cavicchia-Balmer, and Johannes Huber. "Shaping Parents: Impact of Contrasting Professional Counseling on Parents' Decision Making for Children with Disorders of Sex Development." *The Journal of Sexual Medicine* 10.8 (2013): 1953–1960. Print.
Stryker, Susan, and Aren Aizura. *The Transgender Studies Reader 2*. New York: Routledge Chapman & Hall, 2013. Print.
Stryker, Susan, and Stephen Whittle. *The Transgender Studies Reader*. New York: Routledge, 2006. Print.
Sturgeon, Theodore. *Venus Plus X*. New York: Vintage Books, 1999. Print.
Syms, Shawn. "*Annabel* by Kathleen Winter." Review. *Quill and Quire* July 2010. Web. 17 Apr. 2015.
Sytsma, Sharon, ed. *Ethics and Intersex*. Dordrecht: Springer, 2006. Print.

Tali, Kal. *Worlds of Hurt: Reading the Literatures of Trauma*. Cambridge: Cambridge UP, 1996. Print. Cambridge Studies in American Literature and Culture 95.

Tardieu, Ambroise. *Question médico-légale de l'identité dans ses rapports avec les vices de conformation des organes sexuels : contenant les souvenirs et impressions d'un individu dont le sexe avait été méconnu (2e édition) / par Ambroise Tardieu,...* J.-B. Baillière et fils (Paris), 1874. *Gallica*. Web. 30 May 2014.

The Last Summer of La Boyita. Dir. Julia Solomonoff. Travesia Productions, 2009. Film.

"The Sexes: Biological Imperatives." *Time Magazine*, 8 Jan. 1973, n.p. Web. 1 Nov. 2013.

Too Fast to Be a Woman?: The Story of Caster Semenya. Dir. Maxx Ginnane. Rise Films, 2011. Film.

Tracy, P. J. *Monkeewrench*. New York: Signet, 2003. Print.

TransInterQueer e.V. *transinterqueer.org*. n.d. Web. 13 May 2015.

Trans_Inter_Queer-Projekt "Antidiskriminierungsarbeit & Empowerment für Inter*" in cooperation with IVIM / OII (eds.). *Inter* & Sprache - Von "Angeboren" bis "Zwitter."* 2015. Web.

Turner, Stephanie S. "Intersex Identities: Locating New Intersections of Sex and Gender." *Gender and Society* 13.4 (1999): 457–479. *JSTOR*. Web. 8 Aug. 2013.

Turrentine, Jeff. "She's Come Undone." Review of *Middlesex* by Jeffrey Eugenides. *Los Angeles Times*, 1 Sept. 2002. Web. 18 Aug. 2014.

U. (anonymous). "Body, N. O., *Aus Eines Mannes Mädchenjahren*." Review. *Zeitschrift für Kinderforschung mit besonderer Berücksichtigung der pädagogischen Pathologie* 12 (1907): 320. Print.

Ulrichs, Karl Heinrich. *Inclusa: anthropologische Studien über mannmännliche Geschlechtsliebe*. Selbstverlag des Verfassers, in Commission bei Heinrich Matthes, 1864. Web. 11 May 2015.

---. *Memnon, Teil 1. Die Geschlechtsnatur des mannliebenden Urnings*. Schleiz, Germany: C. Hübscher'sche Buchhandlung, 1868. Web. 11 May 2015.

---. *Memnon, Teil 2 Die Geschlechtsnatur des mannliebenden Urnings*. Schleiz, Germany: C. Hübscher'sche Buchhandlung, 1868. Web. 11 May 2015.

---. *Vindex Social-juristische Studien über mannmännliche Geschlechtsliebe.* 2. Auflage. Leipzig, Germany: Max Spohr, 1898. Web. 11 May 2015.

Van Heesch, Margriet. "Do I Have XY Chromosomes?" Holmes *Critical* 123–46.

Vermeil, Francois Michel. *Mémoire pour Anne Grandjean, connu sous le nom de Jean-Baptiste Grandjean, accusé & appellant: contre Monsieur le Procureur Général, accusateur & intimé.* Paris: Louis Cellot, 1765. Web. 11 May 2015.

Volcano, Del LaGrace. *The Herm Portfolio.* Morland *GLQ* 261-5.

Völling, Christiane. *Ich war Mann und Frau. Mein Leben als Intersexuelle.* Köln: Fackelträger, 2010. Print.

Voß, Heinz-Jürgen. *Making Sex Revisited: Dekonstruktion des Geschlechts aus Biologisch-medizinischer Perspektive.* Bielefeld: transcript, 2010. Print.

Wacke, Andreas. "Vom Hermaphroditen zum Transsexuellen. Zur Stellung von Zwittern in der Rechtsgeschichte." *Festschrift für Kurt Rebmann zum 65. Geburtstag.* Ed. Kurt Rebmann. München: C.H.Beck, 1996. 861–903. Print.

Warner, Michael. *Fear Of A Queer Planet: Queer Politics and Social Theory.* Minneapolis: U of Minnesota P, 1993. Print.

Webb, Jessica. "Herculine Barbin: Human Error, Criminality and the Case of the Monstrous Hermaphrodite." *Hosting the Monster.* Eds. Holly Lynn Baumgartner, and Roger Davis. Amsterdam: Rodopi, 2008. 153–162. Print.

Weich, David. "Jeffrey Eugenides Has It Both Ways." Review of *Middlesex* by Jeffrey Eugenides. *Powell's Books*, 10 Oct. 2006. Web. 11 May 2015.

Welter, Barbara. "The Cult of True Womanhood: 1820-1860." *American Quarterly* 18.2 (1966): 151–174. JSTOR. Web. 5 Mar. 2015.

Westphal, Carl. "Die Konträre Sexualempfindung: Symptom eines Neuropathologischen (Psychopathischen) Zustandes." *Archiv für Psychiatrie und Nervenkrankheiten* 2 (1869): 73–108. Web. 14 May 2015.

Wilchins, Riki Anne. *Read My Lips: Sexual Subversion and the End of Gender.* Ithaca: Firebrand Books, 1997. Print.

Williams, P., and M. Smith. "Open Secret: The First Question." Science Series. BBC, 1980. Television.

Wing, Nathanial. "How Herculine's/Abel's Story Is Simplified: Bringing Truth to Sexuality in Herculine Barbin." *Between Genders: Narrating Difference in Early French Modernism*. Newark: U of Delaware P, 2004. 103–30. Print.

Winter, Kathleen. *Annabel*. London: Vintage, 2012. Print.

Woodbridge, Linda. *Women and the English Renaissance: Literature and the Nature of Womankind, 1540 - 1620*. Brighton: Harvester Press, 1984. Print.

World Health Organization. *Eliminating Forced, Coercive and Otherwise Involuntary Sterilization. An Interagency Statement HCHR, UN Women, UNAIDS, UNDP, UNFPA, UNICEF and WHO*. Geneva: WHO Press, 2014. Web. 10 May 2015.

XXY. Dir. Lucía Puenzo. Pyramide Distribution, 2008. Film.

Young, Allan. *The Harmony of Illusions: Inventing Post-Traumatic Stress Disorder*. Princeton: Princeton UP, 1997. Print.

Zajko, Vanda. "'Listening With' Ovid: Intersexuality, Queer Theory, and the Myth of Hermaphroditus and Salmacis." *Helios* 36.2 (2009): 175–202. Print.

Zehnder, Kathrin. *Zwitter beim Namen nennen: Intersexualität zwischen Pathologie, Selbstbestimmung und leiblicher Erfahrung*. Bielefeld: transcript, 2010. Print.

Zwischengeschlecht.org. Blog. Web. 6 Jan. 2015.

Cultural Studies

Marc Wagenbach, Pina Bausch Foundation (eds.)
Inheriting Dance
An Invitation from Pina

2014, 192 p., 29,99 € (DE),
ISBN 978-3-8376-2785-5
E-Book: 26,99 € (DE), ISBN 978-3-8394-2785-9

Gundolf S. Freyermuth
Games | Game Design | Game Studies
An Introduction
(With Contributions by André Czauderna,
Nathalie Pozzi and Eric Zimmerman)

2015, 296 p., 19,99 € (DE),
ISBN 978-3-8376-2983-5
E-Book: 17,99 € (DE), ISBN 978-3-8394-2983-9

Heike Paul
The Myths That Made America
An Introduction to American Studies

2014, 456 p.,
24,99 € (DE), ISBN 978-3-8376-1485-5
available as free open access publication
E-Book: ISBN 978-3-8394-1485-9

**All print, e-book and open access versions of the titels in our entire list
are available in our online shop www.transcript-verlag.de/en!**

Cultural Studies

*geheimagentur, Martin Jörg Schäfer,
Vassilis S. Tsianos (eds.)*
The Art of Being Many
Towards a New Theory and Practice of Gathering

2016, 288 p., 34,99 € (DE),
ISBN 978-3-8376-3313-9
E-Book: 34,99 € (DE), ISBN 978-3-8394-3313-3

*Pablo Abend, Mathias Fuchs, Ramón Reichert,
Annika Richterich, Karin Wenz (eds.)*
Digital Culture & Society
Vol. 2, Issue 1/2016 –
Quantified Selves and Statistical Bodies

2016, 196 p., 29,99 € (DE),
ISBN 978-3-8376-3210-1
E-Book: 29,99 € (DE), ISBN 978-3-8394-3210-5

**All print, e-book and open access versions of the titels in our entire list
are available in our online shop www.transcript-verlag.de/en!**